The Song of the Blessed One

A Contemporary Translation of

The Bhagavad Gita

with Commentaries

by Swami Anand Nisarg

Dragon Publishing

ISBN 978-0-9782393-1-2

http://www.mystery-school.net

Contents

Section II – Commentaries on the Gita

Section III – The Godsong

"Agni, Fire of Love"
Ma Leela Prem - 2007

Introduction

This is a book consisting, in fact, of three books. The first is the Bhagavad Gita itself, the most significant holy book to have come out of the Indian tradition. The Gita is a sacred text of a unique quality that explains within it the entire process of mysticism, and does so in a way that continues to be particularly relevant in today's world. This is because it frames all of its teachings in the context of a world of struggle and warfare; this is very much the world in which we find ourselves today. Whether or not it is a physical war, the society we exist in is one where there is struggle and conflict all around us. It is a text that is not designed to teach mysticism to mendicants or hermits who isolate and separate themselves from human society and life, it does not create a contemplative utopia of peaceful inner development; instead it is very much a 'field guide' to the battlefield of everyday life, and how to live up to the challenges that life gives us at every step of that battle.

The second book is the book of commentaries on the verses of the Gita. These commentaries are necessary because of the cultural gap caused by thousands of years and the differences between Indian and western society. The society of Krishna's India does not exist anymore, not even in India, much less in the west. A living person with awareness can understand and see through the spaces where the Gita's verses presume understanding based on relative cultural understanding; but if you lack access to someone with that awareness, these commentaries will help to clarify the application of the Gita's verses.

The final book is the Godsong: a modern and esoteric set of teachings that are also a sort of commentary to the Gita, but not a literal commentary. They are a mystical commentary providing further teaching on the mystic path, and like the Gita, the Godsong is a living book where your understanding of each reading of it will grow as you grow in your practice as a meditator and a mystic.

If you wish to study this book as part of your practice as a mystic, it would be recommended that you read the Gita itself first, without the commentaries. In this way you will process it, some of it intellectually and some of it externally. When you have done so you can go on to read the Gita again with commentaries, which should clarify some aspects of the text.

Furthermore, the Godsong and the Gita should continue to be read as you continue to practice meditation, and you will find that your practical and real experience of meditation will continue to clarify more of the layers of symbolism of these books, and in turn these books will provide you with new impulses that will strengthen your meditation.

Finally, it is important to note that merely reading the Gita, if you do not go on to act on its teachings by practicing meditation, awareness, and devotion in your every day life, will be of little use to you.

Mysticism is not an intellectual study. It is a practice. You must practice it yourself, no set of words will give you understanding, only living out the instructions of the Gita on your own will allow you to gain true understanding.

~ *Swami Anand Nisarg*

You are welcome to visit Swami Anand Nisarg's Mystery School website at http://www.mystery-school.net.

"Master's Embrace"
Ma Leela Prem - 2007

The Bhagavad Gita

A Modern Translation

Why Study the Gita?

The Bhagavad Gita is one of the most ancient of holy scriptures. It is a teaching presented to us by Krishna, one of the greatest of all the Masters, one who became a living embodiment of the Mystery.

Who was Krishna, historically? This much is known: today he is worshiped by Hindus as a god. Indeed, no living entity is more deserving of that title of 'God,' but we cannot overlook the fact that he was an incarnate entity.

Krishna lived approximately five thousand years ago. He was a king, and his kingdom was in the subcontinent of India. He was born into incredible wealth, and unlike later Masters never rejected this wealth or his title.

Krishna was clearly recognized in his own time as a great Master, even from a very young age. It is clear that at this time, the average person was not yet under the false notion that to be spiritual one has to be old, or poor, or reject the world. Far from rejecting the world, Krishna totally involved himself in it. He embraced music, love, beauty, and even war.

The key to understanding Krishna's way, which is indeed the way of all Masters, is to understand that one must not reject matter, but attachment to matter. One must not reject action, but attachment to action. By renouncing attachment, one embraces the moment, accepts whatever is happening and whatever one must do at any moment, and one can thus be total in one's consciousness. Krishna's greatness as a Master and a man is that he was the fullest embodiment of a human being; he was able to be total in everything he was and did.

Krishna lived in a time of conflict. His closest friend and student, Arjuna, was a prince of the most powerful dynasty of kings in India at that time, the Kurus. He and his brothers were the rightful rulers of that dynasty, but their positions were usurped by their cousins, the sons of King Dhirtarashtra. The resulting civil war in India, the Mahabharata ('great war'), was the most devastating war that had ever befallen the earth to that point.

Krishna fought in the final and most devastating battle of that war, the battle of Kurukshetra, where he served as charioteer to his friend Arjuna. It was in this battle that Krishna is said to have recited the Bhagavad Gita to Arjuna. The Gita was a summary of Krishna's entire teaching, phrased as an argument to convince a reluctant Arjuna that he had to go through with the battle.

What is the relevance of Krishna and the Gita for the modern world? The themes of the Gita address the fundamental causes of human suffering, our delusions, and Krishna's own method of transformation. I have taught in the past that all teachers have a Mystery School, which is less a term for a specific institution and more so a term describing a particular process of transformation advocated by a given teacher for the people of his own time and place. Although this would seem to make the relevance of Krishna's Mystery School very far removed from our own time and place, there are in fact many elements to his teaching that would make his Mystery School particularly relevant to us.

Krishna's India was a very different place from the India of today. It was a land of spectacular wealth, as opposed to poverty. Krishna was teaching to people who, by the standards of societies of that age, were living extremely opulent lifestyles, lives of comfort and material riches. In that sense, Krishna's methods are very appropriate to our own society, and particularly to those of the educated and comfortable western world.

But even more significant is the fact that Krishna's society was being menaced by the forces of materialism. Much like our own culture, Krishna lived in a world where a large portion of the 'establishment' had become consumed with a materialistic philosophy. They had rejected the notion of a deeper dimension to life, and they saw material success as the be all and end all of existence.

This is the most significant connection to our own era. People have become so divorced from the mystical that they have lost a sense of peace in themselves, and have attempted to substitute it, as they did in Krishna's time, with the pursuit of wealth and comfort.

It was due to this situation that the Mahabharata war had to be fought. Arjuna's enemies, the sons of Dhirtarashtra, were the main advocates of this philosophy and way of living. Thus, whether the full Gita was recited by Krishna at the battle of Kurukshetra, or whether it was simply a collection and summary of Krishna's way, its recitation at the battle is of symbolic significance. The battle was a real event, just as one must really act in one's life to oppose unconsciousness, but it was also a symbolic conflict. It symbolized the battle between consciousness and unconsciousness, between a merely materialistic animal existence, or an essential and conscious way of being and living.

Read the Gita as a message for today. Connect to Krishna's essence, and be transformed.

How to Study the Gita

1. *Was Krishna a divine being?*

Yes.

2. *Are we divine beings?*

Yes.

3. *Are we different from Krishna?*

In the sense that we are under the veil of Maya, illusion, yes. But in the sense of the essential, we are non-different from Krishna-Brahma. Krishna is completely part of the Mystery, and we are as well, in the sense that anything about us that is real is part of the Mystery.

4. *Is Krishna to be worshiped?*

Krishna is to be shown devotion and veneration in his form as a Master; he is to be glorified in his form as the eternal Brahma. This does not mean being worshiped religiously. It means being mindful of Krishna's significance as an archetype.

5. How does someone in this day and age benefit from the Bhagavad Gita? How do we use it in our lives?

The Gita itself holds the keys to these questions. The first step is to read the Gita, in its entirety.

After that, the Gita will work for people at different levels depending on where they are in their lives. It would be a very good idea for anyone to read a little of the Gita every day. Many great individuals, from Thoreau to William James, to Aldous Huxley, to Gandhi read the Gita daily. For some, this can be simply as inspiration, or intellectual stimulation; something you can do at the start of your day to put you on the right mental footing for the whole day. For others, reading the Gita is itself an act of devotion, particularly if it is the Gita as written by your own teacher.

But the other important step is to practice what the Gita teaches. There are three essential practices present in the Gita. The first is non-attachment to actions. This is where you focus, meditatively, on staying in the moment, on acting without 'lust of result.' Do things for their own sake, not because you want a particular result, or do nothing without desiring to necessarily avoid action. The second essential practice is the dedication of all action to the Divine. Offer all your actions to the Divine, to Brahma, to Krishna, and in that way lose your attachment to their ends. You are only a vessel for the Divine. One particular aspect of this is the dedication of food to the Divine. Food is always a karmic product; the food you eat is the result of the death of an animal or plant being. By consciously and simply dedicating your food to the Divine before you eat, you will be able to free yourself of the Karma that would be brought about by eating it unconsciously. You give consciousness to your act of eating, and in that way purify your action and honour the life that you had to take in order to survive. The last essential is devotional practices. There are many described in the Gita, from intense yogic practices to the chanting of holy names. Regardless of which of Krishna's methods you feel you can follow, the key is to practice meditational methods every day. While at first it is a good idea to try several different methods, when you find one that works for you it is best to stick to it, so that you can explore it in depth. This does not mean you are forbidden to experiment with other techniques after that, just that you should keep doing the one you have chosen consistently.

Note: Of all of the methods advocated by Krishna, the method of mantra chanting is perhaps the most attractive, and one of the simplest to incorporate into your life. The ideal mantras are the OM, or the 'Hare Krishna' mantra ("Hare Krishna Hare Krishna Krishna Krishna Hare Hare Hare Rama Hare Rama Rama Rama Hare Hare"). The former mantra is good for slow repetition, and the latter is especially good for rapid repetition matched with motion or ecstatic dancing. However, I will attach a very important warning to the practice of mantras in general: be aware! Mantra practice is beyond useless, it is actually detrimental, if it is not done with extreme care. The key is that you must recite your mantras with total awareness. If you cannot be paying complete attention to your chanting, you will actually be using the mantra as a distraction, meant to help lull you into deeper sleep, rather than wake you up. Be sure that every word you chant is lucid, clear to your ears, well pronounced, and being given your total attention. With that being considered, allow yourself to open, chant, and become a vessel for the bliss of the Divine.

'The Gita's Terms Explained

There are certain words in the teachings of Krishna that simply cannot be translated into any equivalent English forms, or if they were translated, the translation would leave much to be desired. It is difficult enough to try to express the inexpressible language of the Mystery in words. But it is harder still to take these words and transfer them easily from one tongue to the next.

Even the particulars of the English language make this task more daunting. Sanskrit is a holy language, with what seems like an intentional design, made to facilitate the transmission of spiritual concepts as much as possible. Not so, English. Our language is filled with words that have multiple connotations, like 'love' and 'truth.' These words can mean more than one thing, or sometimes will mean something different to virtually everyone. In addition, our culture's lack of a rich mystical influence means that there are certain mystical concepts that English simply does not have a word for.

Due to this, I have been forced in certain cases to retain the original Sanskrit words and introduce them to the reader. I hope most of these words will be explanatory in the Gita itself, but I will also endeavour to explain them here.

First off, there are obviously the place and proper names. These are all being kept as they are. The battle where the Gita is being recited is called the battle of Kurukshetra. Krishna and Arjuna are hopefully self-explanatory. Sanjaya and King Dhirtarashtra are the two characters recounting this conversation. Technically it is thus Sanjaya who is 'telling the story' of the Gita.

It is the King's sons, Arjuna's enemies the Kurus, who Arjuna must kill. There are many other characters named in the first chapter, including Bhisma, Drona, Bhima and others. These are all legendary figures who fought in the Mahabharata.

The more significant Sanskrit terms represent spiritual or philosophical ideas. One of these terms is the word 'Karma,' which is a familiar word to many today but the meaning of which is often still unclear. Karma does not refer to some kind of divine punishment or reward system. Many people think that Karma means in essence that if you do something 'good' you will be rewarded by the Divine, and if you do something 'evil' you would be punished. In reality, Karma has nothing to do with this. Karma is the consequences of unconsciousness. When you are attached to certain results, you will commit actions that are unconscious of what is truly real in the present. These actions will have consequences, sometimes pleasant and sometimes not. But ultimately, all unconscious or attached behaviour will lead to suffering because inevitably you find that you will either fail in your ambitions, or you will be unable to hold on to what you have, or you will be unsatisfied with what you desired. All things change, and when you are acting out of a resistance to change or the idea that you can control change, a desire for things to be a certain way or become a certain way, you will end up suffering. This is Karma.

Another important set of Sanskrit terms is the 'gunas.' The gunas are best translated as 'three elements of material being.' In Vedic teachings there are three basic states that, in combination, can describe any aspect of human condition. The first is Tamas, heaviness. It is the state of deep ignorance or animal-like behaviour. It is the condition of caring only for survival, the baser instincts.

The second is Rajas, the fiery state. It is passion, being energetic and active. It is lust, being consumed with wants and obsessed with the senses. It is the state of intellectual desires.

The third is Sattvas. It is lightness, or the state of truth. It is peacefulness, relaxation, higher aspirations, compassion and higher thinking.

All people, and things, have a combination of these three elements within them. In people, it could be said that most will have one element more in prominence than others. Attila the Hun may have had more of Tamas, Vincent Van Gogh of Rajas, and Albert Einstein of Sattvas. But they all have a little of each, and you may see that you have days when you act more like Albert Einstein, and other days when you act more like Attila the Hun.

The old Vedic religious systems taught that you should try to achieve the state of Sattvas; but Krishna teaches that all three of these states are different kinds of attachments. One is attachment to gross needs (mostly of the body), another is attachment to lusts of the emotions, and the third to more complex concepts of the mind and heart. It is Krishna's teaching that you should transcend all attachments.

'Yoga' is another term from the Gita. This word is meant to describe techniques and practices, methods to be used to attain awareness. The types of Yogas that Krishna describes are what are known as Dhyana Yoga, the Yoga of awareness, and Karma or Bhakti Yoga, the Yoga of devotional acts.

The literal meaning of Yoga is also very important. Yoga means 'union.' To achieve the state of Yoga is to achieve a united inner self, and to be united with the existence that is all around you. This force of existence is the 'Brahman,' the divine consciousness, the soul of all life. Likewise, 'Nirvana' is a term describing this state of unitedness. It is when you have become awake to your connection to the supreme soul, the Brahman.

The last two terms that should be explained here are 'Sannyasin' and 'Guru.' The term 'Sannyasin' means 'one who renounces,' and it refers to an initiate or practitioner of Krishna's Mystery School. A Sannyasin renounces his attachments, and is dedicated to awareness and devotion. Typically, a Sannyasin will be an initiate of a 'Guru,' a spiritual Master. This is someone who has obtained this condition of awareness, of Nirvana, and who is now in a condition to assist others in their efforts to reach the same in themselves.

Chapter 1

(Introductory note: The first chapter of the Gita sets the scene of the battle of Kurukshetra. Here King Dhirtarashtra, back in his castle, has made a request of his sage Sanjaya to use Sanjaya's visionary powers to detail the events of the battle. At the Battlefield, Arjuna and his brothers the Pandavas are with Krishna, ready to fight King Dhirtarashtra's sons. The chapter provides details about specific individuals involved in the battle on both sides, and culminates with Arjuna's decision not to fight.)

1. *King Dhirtarashtra said:*

In the place of pilgrimage, the place called Kurukshetra, there has assembled desiring to do battle my army, and the army of the sons of Pandu. What did they do O Sanjaya?

2. *Sanjaya said:*

After studying the deployment of the soldiers of the Pandavas, King Duryodhana [son of Dhirtarashtra] was approached at that time by his holy teacher, Bhisma. The King addressed him.

3. Look upon the armies of the sons of Pandu, holy teacher, great spirit. They have been arranged by the son of Drupada [Dhirstadyumna], your own best student.

4. Here in the army are great warriors, mighty bowmen like Bhima and Arjuna, who are equal in prowess to Yuyudhanah, Virata or Drupada, also great fighters.

5. There are also very strong heroes like Dhirstaketu, Cekitana, KasiRajas, Purujit, Kuntibhojah and Saibya. They are legends among our people.

6. Yudhamanyu and mighty Tamaujah, and the very mighty son of Subhadra; as well as the sons of Draupadi are all certainly great charioteers.

7. Take note of those in our forces now, Best of the Teachers, and tell me which among the captains of my armies are particularly powerful.

8. Your good self, Bhisma, and also Karna and Kirpa have never lost in battle. Ashvatthama, Vikarna and the son of Somadatta are certainly great warriors as well.

9. Others also, many heroes are prepared to risk their lives for my sake. They are equipped with a variety of terrible weapons, and all of them are experienced strategists.

10. Our strength is beyond accounting, totally defended by you, Bhisma, while the forces of the Pandavas are only well defended by Bhima.

11. In the key fronts of the battle, also everywhere, all of us must give our respect and support to you, and assure our victory.

12. Thus to bring joy to his army, Bhisma, grandsire of the Kuru dynasty blew his conch shell. It vibrated loudly, like the roar of a lion.

13. In response, the Kurus rang out with conch shells and large drums, small drums and kettledrums, as well as horns. These were suddenly sounded all at once, and that combined sound became deafening.

14. On the opposing side, on a great chariot with white horses were Krishna and Arjuna. In response, they sounded their divine conch shells.

15. Krishna blew the conch shell named Pancajanya, and Arjuna blew the conch named Devadatta. Also, Bhima, famous for feats of strength and a voracious appetite, blew the conch named Pundra.

16. The conch named Anantavijaya was blown by the son of Kunti, King Yuhdhisthirah. Nakula and Sahadeva blew the conch hells named Sughosa and Manipuspaka.

17. Also the King of Kasi and great archer Sikhandi, and the great warriors Dhirstadyumna, Virata and Satyaki, who had never been defeated in combat.

18. Drupada, the son of Draupadi as well, my king, and the son of Subhadra the great-armed. Each and all blew their conch shells separately.

19. That vibration shattered the hearts of the sons of Dhirtarashtra and the sky and the earth were all resounding tumultuously.

20. At that time, positioned as to be looking upon the sons of Dhirtarashtra, was he whose flag was marked with Hanuman the monkey-god, Arjuna the son of Pandu. He was preparing to fire his arrows, taking up his bow, when he suddenly spoke these words to Krishna, my king:

21. *Arjuna said:*

Most accurate one, please keep my chariot in between both of the armies, so that I might look upon all whom are ready to do battle in this place.

22. All those with whom I will have to try to oppose in this terrible battle.

23. Let me see those who will be fighting, those gathered here, wishing to aid the dark minded son of Dhirtarashtra.

24. *Sanjaya said:*

O Son of Kings, thus addressed by Arjuna, Krishna placed the great chariot right between both of the armies.

25. In front of Bhisma, Drona, and all the Kings of the land, he said: behold all of them, the gathered Kurus.

26. There Arjuna saw standing his fathers and grandfathers, teachers and uncles, brothers and sons and grandsons. Friends too, and in-laws and past allies. All of these were gathered in both sides, both armies.

27. After seeing them all, the different relatives of the son of Kunti, moved by a higher compassion and overwhelmed by grief, Arjuna spoke:

28. He said: after seeing all these, my people, all ready for battle, it makes my limbs shake and my mouth go dry, Krishna.

29. My body trembles and my hair stands on end, my bow slips from my hand, and my skin feels as if it's aflame.

30. Also, I cannot continue, I cannot just forget what is on my mind. Krishna, I see only disasters.

31. Nor do I see any good in killing my own people in combat. Nor do I desire victory, Krishna, or the joy of ruling a kingdom.

32. What use to us is the kingdom, Krishna? What enjoyment from living either? What happiness is there in doing this for the sake of ruling a kingdom?

33. All of them, those here on the field of battle, would be losing their riches and lives: my teachers, fathers, grandfathers, uncles and great-grandfathers.

34. Uncles, fathers-in-law, grandsons, brothers-in-law – all these relatives I would never wish to kill. I would have to kill them, Krishna.

35. Even if I could exchange their deaths for the Three Worlds, never mind this kingdom of the earth, what joy would there be for me, Krishna, if I must kill the sons of Dhirtarashtra?

36. Certainly I would be in the wrong if I killed all of these opponents. I have no right to slay the sons of Dhirtarashtra, as well as my own friends and relatives. How could I ever be happy after doing such a thing, Krishna?

37. Even if they do not see, overpowered by greed in their hearts, that killing a relative or attacking a friend are wrong acts.

38. Why should we not know that these are wrong acts? Would not the destruction of a dynasty be a criminal act if done by those who can see the evil of it, Krishna?

39. The destruction of a dynasty destroys the way of that society, it disrupts the eternal religion, and all the families are warped by unlawful activities and decadence.

40. When decadence has taken place, Krishna, do not families become unhealthy? Women of the families become polluted and produce unwanted children.

41. These unwanted children create a lawless society, destroy families. And if the family falls apart, then offerings of food and water to the ancestors stop being performed.

42. Such flawed people, the destroyers of society and unwanted children which they create will devastate social laws and family laws forever.

43. Krishna, I have heard from the priests that men who ruin the family ways will reside forever in hell.

44. I regret our strange choice to commit such terrible acts; we were driven by greed, by my desire to become a king. This has led us to try to kill our relatives.

45. Even if I did not resist, unarmed, as the sons of Dhirtarashtra killed me on the field, it would be a better thing.

46. *Sanjaya said:*

Thus having spoken, Arjuna sat down again on the chariot, on the battlefield, putting aside his bow and arrows. He was distressed by grief in his heart.

Chapter 2

1. *Sanjaya said:*

Thus he was overwhelmed with compassion, his eyes full of tears and regret. Krishna spoke to him these words:

2. *The Blessed One said:*

From where has this dirtiness of regret come upon you, at this very critical hour? This is practiced by those who don't know the true essence. This line of thought doesn't lead to a higher dimension; it will only lead you to disgrace, Arjuna!

3. Do not take to helplessness, you who are the son of Partha. This behaviour does not suit you. It is a petty weakness of sentimentality, give it up! Get up, you who are the punisher of your enemies!

4. *Arjuna said:*

How can I attack with arrows men like Bhisma and Drona, who are worthy of my veneration, o Krishna?

5. They are my superiors. Certainly I should not kill such great beings. It would be better to live as a beggar in this very life, than to desire to gain by killing my superiors in society! It would be too difficult to enjoy any such pleasures if they are tainted with blood.

6. Nor do we even know what would be better; we can't know if we shall conquer or they will. But I know that by killing those before me, the sons of Dhirtarashtra, I would not wish to live.

7. I am afflicted now by hesitation and weakness. I ask you to help me – my spirit is confused in my heart. Tell me what would be

right. I am your disciple; I surrender unto you. Tell me what can be known.

8. I do not see how I can be free of that which fills me with grief and clouds my senses. Even if I were to gain a Kingdom in this world as great as the heavenly kingdoms, and power as great as the Gods', it would not free me from this.

9. *Sanjaya said:*

Saying this to Krishna, Arjuna the punisher of his enemies declared: "Krishna, I shall not fight." Then he fell silent.

10. O my King, descendant of Bharata, Krishna then smiled and spoke to the grieving Arjuna, right in the midst of the two great armies.

11. *The Blessed One said:*

You are grieving for that which is not worthy of grief. Speaking from wisdom you would say that no life is lost, now or ever. You would not grieve over death.

12. There has never existed a time when I was not, or you were not, or these were not, any of these kings. Nor shall there ever be a time when we will not be.

13. Any who lives a mortal life in a body will experience childhood, youth, and old age. Likewise, they will achieve other forms of life beyond this one. One who is focused will not be blind to this.

14. Son of Queen Kunti, it is only the senses that see the winter and summer of suffering and joy. They come and go, but are in no way permanent. One must accept them all, Scion of Bharata.

15. Finest of Men, one who isn't disturbed by these things, who is the same in happiness and suffering, he has discovered patience. For one like this, the nectar of liberation is obtainable.

16. There is nothing in this world that lasts forever as it is. The only thing that is unchanging is the eternal. These two forces, the essential and the nonessential, have been studied by the seekers of truth.

17. Know the essential to be indestructible, and to be found throughout your entire body. No person or thing can harm it.

18. Our physical bodies are easily destroyed, but the essence within them is said to be eternal. It is beyond all measure, and indestructible. Therefore, you may fight, Scion of Bharata!

19. One who thinks himself the slayer, or one who thinks himself slain, is in delusion. The essential cannot destroy nor be destroyed.

20. Nor is it ever born, nor does it ever die. It has never been created, nor will it ever be created, nor is it being created. It is unborn, eternal, permanent. That which is eternally ancient is not killed, even if its body is being killed

21. If you know this essence to be unborn, unchangeable, indestructible, and always existing, then how can you believe that you can cause harm or death to anything essential, Son of Partha?

22. Just as one gives up old worn out clothes, and accepts and wears new clothes, in the same way does the embodied essence give up old or worn bodies, and take on new ones.

23. This essence can never be cut with a blade or burned by fire, nor will water make it wet, nor will wind dry it.

24. This essence cannot be broken, burned, dissolved, or desiccated. It is certainly immortal, omnipresent, immutable, unchangeable, and eternally as it is.

25. It is invisible, and beyond the understanding of the mind. This essence cannot be altered. Thus, if you are aware of this, you should not feel regret.

26. But even if you think that this essence is one that is always being reborn and dying, there is still no reason to grieve.

27. For anyone who is born is sure to die. This is known for certain. Thus there is no reason to grieve for that which was bound to occur.

28. That which in the beginning has no form, gains form in the middle, and then is destroyed and once again becomes formless. All things are such, Scion of Bharata, so why grieve?

29. Some will see this essence as awe-inspiring. They will describe it as a Mystery. It is likewise awe-inspiring to one who hears of this Mystery. For to any who hear of it, it will be beyond all comprehension.

30. The essential self is eternal and cannot be killed. It is the Mystery. It is within all beings, Scion of Bharata. Thus you need not grieve for any living things.

31. One's own spiritual nature must also be considered. You should never hesitate, for to your spiritual nature, there is nothing that suits you better than being a warrior. It is your destiny to be a warrior. You have no other choice.

32. When it naturally occurs, conflict such as this can open the doors to higher consciousness. For those who are kings, this is a very fortuitous event.

33. Thus, if you see this as a spiritual duty, to avoid fighting now will go against your nature and lead to the loss of your prestige. You will gain only further disturbance in this way.

34. You will be shamed before all the people, and they will speak ill of you forever as one who was not true to his nature. For a man of insight, such a fate is much worse than death.

35. If you quit the battle out of fear, your fellow warriors who currently honour you will judge you as unworthy of any respect.

36. Your enemies will be able to speak terrible slanders against you. This will be more terrible to you than anything else.

37. If you die here, you will gain a higher state of consciousness. If on the other hand you are victorious, you will have the world. Thus arise, Son of Kunti, be secure in the determination to fight.

38. Joy and sorrow are equal in gain and loss, as are victory and death. Thus if you approach any of these without attachment, you will never incur distress.

39. I have described all of this to you intellectually, but you must understand this from the perspective of enlightened consciousness, beyond the limits of intellectual thought. If you can enter into enlightened thought, you will be free of the restrictions of karmic consequences.

40. Even in attempting this form of understanding you cannot go wrong. Even if you can reach a limited form of enlightened understanding, it will help to decrease your distress.

41. If you are determined to be conscious, to be enlightened, you will achieve greater unity to reality, my beloved friend. There are various paths by which you can reach this enlightenment, and thus be free from internal division.

42. All of these flowery words have been said before by those who had not actually achieved this enlightenment, by those who claim to be religious. But there is no substitute for the actual experience.

43. Being filled with desires, including the desire for consciousness itself, but also for material comforts, these false religionists engage in elaborate ceremonies in the hope of gaining material goals.

44. Those who are attached to such things are actually deluded. They cannot focus their consciousness on enlightenment; they will never transcend their minds.

45. The old scriptures mostly relate to the states of material being, the gunas. But you should attempt to transcend these gunas altogether, Arjuna. Go beyond duality, in a pure state of existence, free from notions of desire, centred in your soul.

46. That which can be found in a drop of water can also be found in the vast ocean. Likewise, all that can be known in studying religion can be understood in a true way by a man who has become aware of the Brahman, the supreme consciousness.

47. It is certainly right of you to follow your duties in society, but do it without lust of result. You should not perform actions for the sake of some desired result, nor should you seek to avoid action for the sake of some desire.

48. Act according to your true nature, in a balanced state. Give up your attachments to desires of success, or fear of failure, Arjuna. Being balanced, taking all things equally, this is Yoga. This is being united.

49. Leave all of your harmful Karma far behind, by becoming united to Enlightenment. This is called Buddha-Yoga, Conqueror of the World. Try to surrender to this consciousness. Do not try to hold on to false desires for that which is unreal.

50. One who is in consciousness can be freed, even in this very life, from concern about all good or bad results. Thus, for the sake of being united, follow this art of Yoga in all you do.

51. Great mystics can give up all Karma and its consequences by entering this state of consciousness. They are freed from the restrictions of birth and death, and reach a state that is beyond any suffering.

52. When your consciousness takes you beyond the dark forest of illusion, then you will no longer need to rely on seeking knowledge or on what you already think you know.

53. When your interest in religion is no longer motivated by your desires, you will achieve absolute transcendental enlightenment. Then you have achieved union.

54. *Arjuna said:*

How do you recognize someone who is in this state, Krishna? How does one in this state speak? How does he sit? How does he walk?

55. *The Blessed One said:*

One such as this is free of any kind of investments, Son of Partha, and free of mental notions. Purely centred in his soul, fulfilled. One who obtains this is said to have achieved awareness.

56. One who is surrounded by miseries without himself being distressed, one who is surrounded by happiness without himself being invested, free from desire, fear or anger. He whose awareness is steady, he is called a mystic.

57. One who avoids sentimentality, regardless of the situation, takes good or bad results without pride or envy, he is in a state of awareness.

58. When he can draw inside himself, like the turtle draws its limbs into its shell, separating the senses from the sensed, he is in a state of awareness.

59. Some abstain from the material sources of pleasure for the sake of appearing religious, but will secretly keep lusting for these things. But one who actually gives up the lust for these things, he will experience a vastly greater pleasure.

60. Son of Kunti, even while trying to be a man of consciousness, the senses can become agitated and the mind can throw you off track.

61. Keep all these senses under control. They should all be focused upon me. One who can thus dedicate all his senses to a single focus is in a state of awareness.

62. One who is undisciplined in the senses will develop attachment. Attachment leads to desire. Desire leads to anger.

63. Anger leads to deludedness. Deludedness leads to false perceptions. And one who perceives the unreal cannot be aware. Such a person will fall.

64. One who has become free of desire and repulsion, who does not allow his senses to be wildly led by outer lusts, he has come under the control of his own soul, and has attained freedom of the soul. He has obtained a divine blessing.

65. Achieving this blessing leads to the end of all misery. For one who is in such bliss, enlightenment will soon follow.

66. Enlightenment cannot happen if you are not unified. Nor can bliss. Nor peace. And how can there be joy without peace?

67. If one is being led by the senses, constantly distracted by one's mind, one's awareness is lost. One becomes like a boat on a windswept ocean.

68. Thus, Great Warrior, one who can make the distinction between the senses and the sensed, he is in awareness.

69. When others are in the dark of the night, such a person is awake and in control. And what others consider being awake, the mystic knows to be nothing but the dark of night.

70. As the oceans are constantly being filled by water flowing into them, so is one constantly being filled with desires. One who is trying to fulfill all his desires will never be at peace.

71. But in giving up desires, living free of lust or a sense of material possessiveness, you lose the ego. You attain peace.

72. Son of Partha, one who is unaware of the real can never gain this spiritual state. But if you can obtain this state, even at the very end of life, you will reach the divine Nirvana.

Chapter 3

1. *Arjuna said:*

If you think that awareness is better than actions born of desire, Krishna, why are you trying to cause me to commit such horrid acts?

2. Your words are clear yet they confuse me. So please tell me now directly, what must I do that will benefit me?

3. *The Blessed One said:*

As I have already told you, my faultless friend, there are two paths to follow in this world. There is the Yoga of awareness followed by the spiritual philosophers, and the Yoga of devotional acts followed by the mystics.

4. You cannot become free of Karma by avoiding actions. Nor can you gain success by mere renunciation.

5. For there is not even a single moment in this life when you are free from some kind of action. You are forced to be in constant activity of some kind, merely by virtue of being alive. This is the reality of the gunas.

6. Even if you control all the five senses through mental willpower, you are still constantly engaged in thoughts and desires. Anyone who believes he can truly do nothing is a foolish soul, a false religionist.

7. One who starts to control the senses with the mind, Arjuna, by focusing the senses upon uniting, will reduce attachment and be by far the better.

8. Take whatever action is required. To take action is better than to avoid it. You cannot even maintain your body without taking action.

9. Actions done for spiritual purposes are better than any other form of actions. Son of Kunti, action to this end will serve excellently to free you from attachments.

10. In the ancient times, having performed the spiritual rituals, the god Brahma said, "By these rituals you shall be increasingly prosperous. Let the spirit bring to you all good things."

11. The divine spirits are pleased by ritual sacrifices. These spirits will reward you in return. By this mutual service, you will obtain the greatest of blessings.

12. The spirits will provide you with all of the necessities of life, being in turn given what they need by your rituals performed in gratitude. But one who receives what is given in life by the spirits, without in turn giving thankful ritual, is certainly a thief.

13. Devotees who eat food that has been purified by the ritual of devotional gratitude are relieved of any guilt associated with that food. But those who eat gluttonously and without gratitude or awareness are committing terrible deeds.

14. Our bodies grow from food. Our food grows from the rain. The rain is thanks to the spirits. We must act to honour them.

15. You should know that all actions come from Brahma, they are a direct manifestation of the Divine. So Brahma is everywhere, and will always be present in our rituals.

16. Therefore one who does not follow the way of ritual in this life, one who lives shamefully only for the pursuit of desires, is wasting his life, Son of Partha.

17. However, anyone who finds bliss in his soul will enlighten his soul. A man who is satisfied with his own being will not have to perform any outer spiritual actions.

18. Certainly the performance of his duties would have no purpose, but also there is no purpose for him to avoid the performance of his duties. For in all of this world he need not seek any purpose whatsoever.

19. Thus, always without attachment, do whatever duties you will. By doing all work without attachment, a man achieves the highest.

20. By doing such work it is known that King Janaka and other lords achieved their great spiritual powers. And you must also consider that the lesser people will be observing how you act; you must consider them.

21. Whatever a man in a position of respect does, certainly the common people will see it as an example. Whatever he does, all the world will follow.

22. Son of Partha, there is no duty in all the Three Worlds that I must perform. There is nothing that I want, nothing I could gain. But clearly I too take action.

23. If ever I did not take action, or perform actions carelessly, all men would follow my example in every respect, Son of Partha.

24. All of these worlds would be put into ruin if I did not set an example. I would be the cause of undesirable births, and all life would have to be destroyed.

25. The ignorant are greatly attached to taking karmic action. Scion of Bharata, the wise must do the same. In this way, they can slowly lead the common people to detachment.

26. They must strive not to lead the foolish away from awareness; they should not give the foolish cause to avoid working. Instead, the wise must give them some work that will lead them in the right direction.

27. In the material world, the gunas cause all kinds of activities to occur. Deluded by the ego, the soul believes that he is the one who is acting.

28. But the one who knows truth, Great Warrior, he understands the gunas and Karma, and the difference between the senses and that which is sensed. With this perspective he will avoid attachment.

29. These elements of reality (gunas) will delude people, and they become attached to actions and desires in the material world. These people are either lacking in wisdom, or they are lazy. One who is wise should not try to disturb them.

30. Surrender all actions unto me by being conscious, aware of the self. Be without lusting for any result, be without possessiveness, and free from reluctance, fight.

31. Those who follow my instructions regularly are human beings performing divine acts. With devotion and without desire, they all become free from the bondage of Karma.

32. However, those who out of jealous desire do not follow my instructions regularly, they are foolish in every way. Know this well, they are all ruined without consciousness.

33. Even an intelligent man, though he may try otherwise, is still controlled by the elements of the material world. All living beings are subject to this, so what good will self-restriction do?

34. Of the senses and the sensed, of what you desire and also what you wish to avoid, you should put all of these under some control. You should never be controlled by them, or else these things will distract you from being conscious.

35. It is better to follow your own discipline, even badly, than it would be to follow someone else's discipline even if you did it perfectly. Even if your own path leads you to death, it is better. For following the path of others is more dangerous than death.

36. *Arjuna said:*

Then what is it that motivates a man toward false action? Even if they do not wish to, it seems that men are drawn to it by force, Scion of Virshni.

37. *The Blessed One said:*

This is desire and anger, born out of the Raja guna (the element of all-consuming passion) that leads men to great error. Know that in this world, it is the great enemy.

38. Just as fire is concealed within smoke, or a mirror concealed by dust, or as an embryo is concealed in the womb, so does reality become concealed in desires.

39. By this is consciousness hidden from the self. It is the eternal enemy. Also, Son of Kunti, one is never fulfilled in the fire of lust.

40. The senses, perceptions, and the mind are called the thrones of desire. Lust deludes all of these, hiding the true awareness of the embodied being.

41. Thus you must begin by disciplining the senses, Lord of the Bharatas. You must curb this great symbol of falsehood, which destroys both awareness and knowledge of the self.

42. The senses are said to be superb, but the mind is said to be greater still, and awareness is even greater than the mind. But the centre is even greater than awareness.

43. Thus awareness leads to centred consciousness, by focusing and steadying the mind. Great Warrior, you will conquer the greatest enemy if you conquer desire.

Chapter 4

1. *The Blessed One said:*

I taught this Yoga to the Sun, Vivasvan, and he taught Manu, the father of humanity. Manu then taught it to King Ikshvaku.

2. Thus, one after the other received this teaching, understood by Kings. But in time this knowledge of the great Yoga became scattered, Defeater of your Enemies.

3. This very same ancientmost Yoga I am speaking to you today. You are my devotee, you are my friend also, thus this Mystery is transcendental.

4. *Arjuna said:*

You were born much later than the Sun, so how am I to understand that in the beginning of time you had taught him?

5. *The Blessed One said:*

I have had many births, and you as well Arjuna. I know them all, but you do not remember them, Defeater of your Enemies.

6. Though I was unborn, my undiluted soul existed as the transcendental form of myself within the great Lord. Being in this state, it is my choice when I incarnate my soul into this world.

7. Whenever and wherever true spirituality has become deteriorated, Scion of Bharata, and there is a predominance of false religion, I will appear at that time.

8. I will help the true students, and I will cause strife to the wrongdoers. I will remind people of the true way. I will appear age after age.

9. Anyone who realizes the reality of my transcendental birth and actions will never take birth again in this form. Instead he too will connect to me, Arjuna.

10. Free of attachment, fear, and anger, fully connected to me, in me, by awareness purified of many wrongdoings, he will obtain spiritual love with me.

11. All who surrender unto me, them I surely reward. All men follow my path, Son of Partha, in every respect.

12. Desiring great power and success in their material actions, men make sacrifices to the spirits. Those who do so are certainly rewarded in their limited material ambitions.

13. The four divisions of human society were created by me, so that any man would do the work best suited to his dominant element. Although you may realize me to be the father of this, you must also realize that I am the eternal, which is free of action.

14. I am never affected by any actions, nor do I have any ambitions. Thus any who realizes me will never become attached to the Karma of actions.

15. Thus, knowing that actions were done by past masters who indeed attained awakening, take action now, as the ancient ones did.

16. Even the intelligent are deluded as to what is action and what is inaction. I will explain action to you, so that in being aware of this you will be free from misfortune.

17. You must understand which action is right and which is wrong. You must understand when not to act, and when to enter action.

18. When you can see non-doing in doing, and doing in non-doing, then you have gained awareness in the world. You will be in unity, even if you take all kinds of actions.

19. One whose efforts are free of lust of result, who gives his actions as sacrifice to the Divine, he will be called wise by the awakened ones.

20. Having given up the lust of result, being satisfied without any false security, such a person will be in non-doing, even though he takes many actions.

21. Focusing the mind and the soul, without lust of result, giving up all sense of possession, only working for what is needed to maintain the body and soul, one doing so will never go wrong.

22. Fulfilled by the good things that come of their own accord, beyond duality, free of jealousy, equally steady in success or failure, one doing so may take action and remain free from reaction.

23. One who is detached from the elements, who is free, whose wisdom is in awareness, who acts for the sake of gratitude, his work is entirely unified.

24. Brahma is found in the sacrifice, and Brahma is found in the fire (where the sacrifice is performed). And Brahma is found in the one who makes the sacrifice. Brahma is certainly attainable to any whose actions are united with Brahma.

25. Some worship the spirits through ritual, but mystics worship perfectly through the fire of Brahma, thus making sacrifice of sacrifice.

26. Others practice restraint of the senses, offering their senses, like hearing, to the fire. But others offer the sound that is heard by the senses to the fire.

27. Also, others control the actions of the senses, and the breath. But others practice the focusing of their soul to union; they offer their urge for awareness in the fire of sacrifice.

28. Others sacrifice their possessions, their comforts, in the vows of the eightfold discipline. Others take the strict vow of sacrifice in wisdom, in the advancement of awareness.

29. Others offer the ingoing and outgoing breath, or stopping the movement of the ingoing to the outgoing breath. Others are drawn to the trance of stopping all breath, or giving up food and offering the ingoing breath as sacrifice to the outgoing.

30. All of these methods of sacrifice and what are understood as purification rituals may appear different. But those who gain some success in any of these do come closer to the eternal space of Brahma.

31. For those who follow no practices there is nothing on this world or the other, Best of the Kurus.

32. Thus various kinds of practices have been spread by word of mouth from the priests. Learn of all of them, because awareness of one will lead to freedom.

33. But greater than the sacrificing of material possessions is the offering of being aware, punisher of your enemies. Son of Partha, all actions reach their end in totality.

34. Try to understand these things by approaching one who is wise, by humbly asking him, and providing service to him. He can initiate you into awareness, because he is aware and can see what is real.

35. Son of Pandu, you shall gain freedom from ever being deluded again. You will see the great soul (Atman) that is in all things, or in other words that is in me.

36. Even if you are the greatest sinner of all sinners, with the boat of awareness you will be able to go beyond all such sins and completely cross the ocean of suffering.

37. Just as firewood in a blazing fire turns to ashes, Arjuna, in the fire of awareness all material Karma similarly turns to ashes.

38. There is nothing that exists in this world that can be compared in holiness to awareness. He who gains experience in Yoga over time will enjoy the bliss of the soul.

39. A dedicated man will gain awareness. He will be very drawn to it, and focus his senses in it. Having gained awareness in his senses, he very soon gains a deeper spiritual peace.

40. For a fool who rebukes this path, with no dedication, or one who is filled with doubts and cannot trust, it will be very difficult for him to find happiness in this world or the other.

41. One who renounces lust of result through Yoga will cut down his doubts with the sword of awareness. When you are centred in your soul your actions will never bind you, o Conqueror.

42. Thus cut off your doubts with the weapon of the soul. They are born of ignorance, and cover your heart. Centred in Yoga, Scion of Bharata, stand and fight!

Chapter 5

1. *Arjuna said:*

Krishna, first you are giving praise to the renunciation of activities, then you give praise to Yoga. Please tell me definitively which one is more beneficial.

2. *The Blessed One said:*

Renunciation of work or the work of Yoga, both of them lead to the way of openness. But of the two, the work of Yoga is better than the renunciation of all work.

3. He should be understood always as the renouncer, who neither rejects nor desires. Free of duality, Great Warrior, he is always happily liberated from bondage.

4. The ill-informed say that Yoga is different from witnessing. When you are involved in one, you are completely enjoying the results of both.

5. Whatever achievement is gained by witnessing, one can also attain through Yoga. You can attain unity through either method, if you have eyes to see.

6. But simply renouncing all things without taking up Yoga, Great Warrior, can afflict you with misery. One who practices Yoga will be engaged. He can attain Brahma easily that way.

7. A pure soul practicing Yoga is centred in his soul, having conquered the senses. He will have compassion to all living beings, and though he acts he will never become attached.

8. One who knows reality will think: 'I am never involved in doing, even though I am seeing, hearing, feeling, smelling, eating, defecating, dreaming and breathing.'

9. Let one always consider thusly, although they may be talking, giving, taking, opening and closing, and generally involving the senses in activities.

10. Dedicate all works to Brahma. One who takes actions, but without attachment, is always free of wrongdoing, like a lotus leaf is not touched by the water upon which it rests.

11. Purified of body, mind, awareness and the senses, practitioners of Yoga perform all actions while giving up attachment. This purifies the soul.

12. One thus practicing, giving up the lust of result, achieves unswerving peace. One who does not practice this, acting with desired results in mind, will always become attached.

13. Renouncing all activities of the mind, one who is so focused will always be blissful. In the city of nine gates (the body), one must be embodied in such a way that you desire no action nor any result.

14. The master of this city will claim no possession of it, nor cause its people (parts) to take actions. Nor will he be connected to the results of any activities, but only act naturally.

15. Likewise the greater king of all the cities (Brahma) will not accept any saintliness or sin. It is only individual beings who are deluded to believe so, their awareness clouded by ignorance.

16. However, when ignorance is destroyed by awareness, the awareness of a living being becomes like a golden dawn, revealing the highest.

17. One whose consciousness is always thus focused, one whose soul is always thus focused, one whose trust is always thus focused, one whose total comfort is only in this, he achieves unity. By awareness all doubts are swept away.

18. Well armed with true wisdom and gentleness, the learned will see no difference in the priest, the cow, the elephant, the dog, or the outcast.

19. Those whose mind is focused on seeing the unity will certainly conquer birth and death, even in this lifetime. As Brahma is perfectly united, so shall the united be in Brahma.

20. One who is completely aware of Brahma is in Brahma. He will neither rejoice when good things happen nor will he become unhappy when bad things happen.

21. One whose soul is not clouded by nonessential pleasures will enjoy the bliss of the soul. By uniting to Brahma you unite to your soul, and enjoy unlimited bliss.

22. The senses are certainly the source of pleasures, and also of suffering. All of these things shall come and all things shall pass. Son of Kunti, the enlightened never revel in such things.

23. One who is able to tolerate desire and anger born of lusts, in this very body before it dies – he who can accept it all will find happiness in his humanity.

24. One who has inner happiness, focusing inwardly and enjoying the inner world, he is certainly a mystic. Being aware of the reality of Brahma, he obtains enlightenment in Brahma.

25. Those who are inwardly active achieve enlightenment in Brahma. They are free of any wrongdoing. They have destroyed duality, are focused on the soul, and are doing a service to all living things.

26. Those who are free of desire and anger, the saintly ones who have control of consciousness, the ones who have become aware of the soul, they are assured to gain enlightenment in Brahma.

27. Suspend nonessential sensory forces, like sound and eyesight, in the space between the eyes. Keep the incoming and outgoing breath in the nostrils.

28. In this way controlling the senses, awareness, and the mind, the seeker will be destined for liberation. He will discard desires, fear and anger. He will certainly be forever free.

29. The receiver of offerings and sacrifices, the great lord of all the worlds and their rulers, the benefactor of all living beings, one who knows me as this will achieve peace.

Chapter 6

1. *The Blessed One said:*

He who acts according to what must be done, without being drawn into lust of result, he is a Sannyasin and a mystic. Not so, he who does no work and thus no devotion either.

2. What they call Sannyas (renunciation), you must know as uniting (Yoga), Son of Pandu. Certainly, no mystic can become anything without giving up the divided desires of the self.

3. For the beginner at Yoga, practicing a discipline is said to be the means. For one who has attained in Yoga, the cessation of all such activities is said to be the means.

4. When one does not involve himself in the senses or in activities, renouncing all desires, at that time one is said to have reached the height of Yoga.

5. One must free the soul from the mind, never allowing the soul to be clouded. The mind can be the great friend of the soul, but the great enemy as well.

6. For the soul that is in control of the mind, the mind is certainly the friend. But for the soul who has failed to be in control of the mind, due to dividedness, the mind is the greatest enemy.

7. One who has triumphed over the mind has obtained peace. He has completely entered the supersoul. He will be the same in heat, cold, happiness, sadness, honour, and dishonour.

8. By awareness and experience, a soul is focused in his senses, centred, and fulfilled. It is said such a mystic is greatly advanced.

He will see that pebbles, great stones, and pure gold are all the same.

9. One who is highly advanced will be able to see enlightenment in allies, patrons, enemies, neutral parties, messengers, those who envy him, his relatives, those said to be saintly, and those said to be sinners.

10. A mystic must constantly be meditative, his entire soul in a place of aloneness. Alone, always watching the mind, not drawn toward anything, free of possessiveness.

11. On holy ground, his soul seated firmly. Neither too high nor too low, on sacred grass covered with soft cloth and deerskin.

12. Thus, with the mind focused on a single point, regulating the mind, senses and activities, sitting in a fixed position, one should practice Yoga techniques to clear the soul.

13. Keep the head, neck and body straight and unmoving, still. Looking only at the tip of your own nose and not in other directions.

14. The soul will be at peace, free of fear, innocent. Totally overcoming the mind, focusing it on me, the practitioner being situated in me is the ultimate goal.

15. Constantly practicing with the entire soul in this way, the mystic will attain peace, the great Nirvana, the endless sky.

16. One who eats too much is not united, neither is one who fasts too much. Nor one who sleeps too much, nor one who stays awake, Arjuna.

17. Practice the work of balanced eating, playing, and working to maintain yourself. The one who is balanced in sleep and wakefulness through Yoga will see less and less suffering.

18. When the mind is particularly focused, it certainly becomes centred in the soul. Freed of the desire for all kinds of things, at that time it is said to be united.

19. Just as a lamp does not flicker when there is no wind, so does a mystic whose mind is focused remain constant in the unity of the soul.

20. In that state where mental activities cease, being distinguished from the essential through Yoga, a pure soul aware of the soul becomes fulfilled by the soul.

21. The supreme bliss that can be attained by transcendent enlightenment is such that one in it will never again move from it.

22. What is gained by this attainment is nothing more than that state, whereby even the greatest misery will not move you from it.

23. You must know this: all of the suffering of the world can be overcome by the trance of Yoga.

24. The practice of Yoga must be done firmly, without deviation. You must completely give up all the turmoils of the mind, born of desires. Focusing the mind and all the senses, all the time.

25. Gradually, step by step, one should concentrate the mind by awareness and with determination. When you are centred in the soul, thoughts will no longer trouble you.

26. All kinds of things can disturb the mind, making it flicker from one thing to another with no centre. One must release attention from all of these distractions, returning into the centeredness of the soul.

27. The mystic whose mind is in great peace will attain the highest bliss. His passions made peaceful, liberated by Brahma, he is beyond all his past errors.

28. Thus engaged in his eternal soul, the mystic is beyond all impurities. In bliss, constantly connected to Brahma, he obtains the greatest joy.

29. The soul that exists in all beings is also in your soul. One who has united the self by Yoga will see everything with the same eyes.

30. Whoever sees me in all things and all things in me is not far from me, nor am I far from him.

31. He who is devoted to me is in the oneness that is in the heart of all beings. He is entirely in that oneness, in spite of himself; the mystic remains in me.

32. He who sees that his soul is everywhere and the same, Arjuna, whether in happiness or misery, such a man is considered a perfect mystic.

33. *Arjuna said:*

This system you have broadly described, Great Warrior, seems impossible for me. I know I am too restless and unsteady.

34. Krishna, the mind is an unstable thing, constantly in strong turmoil and uncontrollable. I think that to focus it would be as difficult as trying to catch the wind.

35. *The Blessed One said:*

Great Warrior, there is no doubt that the mind is unstable, and difficult to focus. But through practice, Son of Kunti, and detachment, it can be focused.

36. In my opinion, unity is extremely difficult to obtain without disciplining the mind. But a centred soul is a realistic goal that can be achieved, if you know the right means.

37. *Arjuna said:*

What of one who had the trust, but could not achieve unity due to a troubled mind, and thus fails in mysticism? Krishna, what is the fate of such a person, who has failed to reach the highest?

38. Krishna, mighty warrior, being thus unsuccessful in both material and spiritual ambitions, such a person could belong to neither realm. Lost from the path of the Divine, will he not perish like a scattered cloud?

39. This is my doubt, Krishna. I ask you to satisfy my doubts. Other than you, I am sure no one else could do this.

40. *The Blessed One said:*

Son of Partha, nothing is destroyed in this world or the other. Thus no one is truly lost who had started on this path.

41. One who has done this work but not completed it will reach higher realms, and after dwelling there for many years will again take birth in a wealthy or spiritual household.

42. He might take birth in a family of mystics, who are wise. But this type of birth is very rare.

43. He will be able to regain the level of enlightenment that he had in his previous form, and after that may continue on the way of perfection, Son of Kuru.

44. Due to his past work, he will be drawn automatically to this practice. He will be curious about Yoga, and will see past the dogmas of ritualistic religion.

45. Working in discipline, such a mystic is cleansed of wrongdoing. After many births, having achieved the great power, he attains the highest.

46. The mystic is greater than the ascetic, and also greater than the wise. He is considered greater than those who succeed in the material world. Thus, Arjuna, simply become a mystic.

47. And of all the mystics, those who are within me, within themselves, in total trust, giving devotional service, they are considered by me to be the finest.

Chapter 7

1. *The Blessed One said:*

With your mind directed to me, Scion of Partha, practicing Yoga in awareness of me, try to hear how you can become completely aware, and free of doubt.

2. I shall fully explain to you this awareness and this knowledge, which once known, there will remain nothing further in this world to know.

3. Out of thousands of men, one will struggle for the higher power. And of those thousands struggling, only one will know me in reality.

4. Earth, water, fire, air, the ether, the mind, awareness and the false ego; all of these are my own eightfold energies in division.

5. These are inferior forms. But besides these there is another form. Endeavour to understand this superior form of me. This superior form is life, the living beings, Great Warrior, who make use of these elements of matter.

6. In this way, know that there are these two forms whose intermingling produced all things. I encompass all creation and destruction in existence.

7. Conqueror, beyond me there is no greater thing. Everything that you see, all that is, is in me; like pearls strung on a thread.

8. Son of Kunti, I am the flavour in water, I am the light of the sun and moon, I am the sound OM that is in all mantras, I am the vibration in the ether, I am the genius in man.

9. I am also the original fragrances of the earth, I am the heat in fire. I am the life of all things. I am the austerity of the ascetics.

10. Mine is the seed of all living beings. Son of Partha, try to understand that which is eternal. I am the awareness of the aware. I am the skill of the skilful.

11. I am the strength of the strong, free of lust or attachment. I am the natural sexuality of all beings, Lord of the Bharatas.

12. And all of the elements of beings: Sattvas (truth), Rajas (passion), and Tamas (heaviness), all of them come from me. Do not try to know me in their light. You must instead understand them in my light.

13. There are three gunas (elements of being), and by these is the whole universe in delusion. It cannot see me above these, greater and never-ending.

14. It is very difficult to transcend this maya (illusion) of the gunas, but it is actually my own energy. Thus those who surrender unto me will go beyond this illusion.

15. The foolish, the lowest of men who do not surrender unto me, have had their understanding stolen by this illusion. They have accepted being in darkness.

16. There are four kinds of people who will trust and render service unto me, Arjuna. They are those who are in distress, those who are curious, those who desire material gain, and those who understand the real, Greatest of the Bharatas.

17. Of them only those who understand the real, and the devotees, are special. I am very close to those who understand deeply. And they are very close to me.

18. All of these are certainly great, but it is my opinion that one who understands the real has the same soul as me. He is certainly in the state of the united soul, in me, which is certainly the highest goal.

19. After many births and deaths, one who is aware surrenders unto me. Thus everything becomes the divine consciousness, and this supersoul is the most rare of experiences.

20. One who is lacking full awareness will surrender to other spirits, and will follow the corresponding disciplines according to their natures.

21. Whichever and whatever form of spirit a devotee wishes to be devoted to with trust, I will certainly grant him the opportunity.

22. Being inspired by his trust in the devotion to that spirit he is drawn to, he will obtain what he desires from it. This is in fact arranged by me.

23. But these results are only transitory, appropriate to those of limited knowing who go to the spirits. But those who are directly my devotees will reach me.

24. Those who have limited consciousness believe me to be an impersonal force. They do not know me as the great work, the force of life, never-ending and most sublime.

25. Nor do I make myself visible to everyone. Those persons who are foolish, clouded by their connection to illusion, cannot understand me as the unborn and never-ending.

26. I am completely informed of the past, present and future, Arjuna. I also know all living beings, but none of them know me.

27. Scion of Bharata, the duality of desire and hate is born of illusion. All living beings fall into this delusion upon taking birth, Conqueror of your Enemies.

28. But those persons who have by trust erased all their past wrongdoings, they have become freed from duality, and thus delusion. They will devote themselves to me with great will.

29. All of those who seek to take shelter in me, for escape from the cycles of birth and death, such persons are actually Brahma. They know all that are transcendental acts.

30. Those who know the laws of life, that govern all spirits, know me. Even at the time of death they know me, and their minds unite to me.

Chapter 8

1. *Arjuna said:*

What is Brahman? What is the self? What is Karma, greatest of beings? What is it to be alive? And what are the beings called the spirits?

2. Who is the Lord of Devotion and how is he here, in this very body, Great Warrior? And how can you be known at the time of death by those who are not unfocused?

3. *The Blessed One said:*

The highest infinite is called Brahma. It is the eternal self. It is the source of all life, and its creations are called Karma.

4. Its physical form has an ever-changing nature. It is the universe, and all the spirits. I am certainly part of this supersoul, incarnated in this body, great one.

5. At the end of this life, he who leaves his body remembering me will go into my being. Of this achievement there is no doubt.

6. At the end of your life, whatever you are remembering, that will be the state of being you achieve, Son of Kunti.

7. Thus, at all times, remember me. Fight for me. Surrender your mind and awareness unto me, and you will attain with no doubt.

8. By the practice of Yoga, without distracting the mind, through constantly thinking of it the supreme and divine individuality will be attained.

9. Always focus on the all knowing, the most ancient, the master of all, smaller than an atom, the maintainer of all things, beyond intellectual understanding, whose form is brighter than the sun and overcomes all darkness.

10. At the time of death, without being distracted by the mind, in full devotion, practicing the mystic Yoga, focusing all life-energy on the space between the eyebrows, one will achieve the transcendent individuality in the Divine.

11. That which the priests call the OM, entered into by the great sages, the hermits; that which is practiced by those who desire innocence, that which they struggle for in their lives, I will explain to you now very simply.

12. Controlling all the doors of the body, securing the mind inside one's heart, fixing the life-energy of your soul on the top of your head, this is how to practice Yoga.

13. Thus this one word, OM, becomes Brahma. Anyone who leaves their body while remembering me and vibrating this word will achieve the great goal.

14. Without distracting the mind, anyone who regularly remembers me will very easily reach my state, Scion of Partha, by regularly practicing Yoga.

15. Achieving me, being reborn, the great souls will not return to this plane of the temporary, this place of miseries. They have achieved the great power.

16. They are raised up to the world of Brahma-being. Arjuna, they return to me, they arrive, but will never take birth again.

17. They know that one day of Brahma is like a thousand ages. Those who understand know also that at the end of one thousand ages of night, there comes the day.

18. All living beings are born from the unborn, at the beginning of the day. At the coming of the night, all is once more absorbed into that which is called unborn.

19. This is the sum of all living beings, being born and born again and also inevitably destroyed at the coming of the night, Son of Partha, being born once more at the arriving of the dawn.

20. But in that great nature, there is the uncreated behind all that is created. It is eternal. As all that is created is destroyed, that which is uncreated is never destroyed.

21. That which is said to be the uncreated and perfect is known as the ultimate goal, which, once gained, one never returns from. This is my supreme home.

22. It is the greatest individuality, Son of Partha, which can be achieved by absolute devotion. For it is located within this very life that surrounds all that we see.

23. Different kinds of mystics return and do not return at different times, depending on the time that they have left. I shall explain this to you, Greatest of the Bharatas.

24. Fire, the light of day, under the waxing moon, during the six months that the sun is in the north; in these times, those who leave the body will go to Brahma, if they know Brahma.

25. In smoke, at night, under the waning moon, during the six months that the sun is in the south; in these conditions the mystic will achieve the light of the moon, and will return.

26. There are certainly these two ways of passing, in light and darkness; such is the opinion written in the scriptures of the world. Going by the one, you will never return, but going by the other you will come back again.

27. Son of Partha, even if he is not aware of these things, the true mystic is never confused. Thus, just be constantly focused on Yoga, Arjuna.

28. Studying the scriptures, performing rituals, practicing self-denial, giving charity, and performing other works that show your faith; all of these things are surpassed by the learned yogi, who just naturally achieves the highest resting place.

Chapter 9

1. *The Blessed One said:*

I am singing this great secret unto you. For you are not jealous. And so this taught knowledge will become true understanding. Knowing which, you will be freed from this limited world of suffering.

2. This is the King of Knowledge, the King of Secrets, the Purest, Transcendental. It is understood only by directly experiencing. It is the way. It brings great bliss in its practice, and lasts for all time.

3. Such people as are without trust in this way, mighty fighter, without attaining me they will continue coming back from death to the paths on the wheel of suffering (Samsara) the world of illusion.

4. The entire world is filled with me in an impersonal form. Although not all living beings are in me, I am in all of them.

5. Although not all beings can see that they are in me, if you witness you will find the union in my divinity. I am the force that maintains all life, though I am not myself part of life, for I am the source behind it.

6. Just as wherever the wind blows it is part of the great sky, so are all living things part of me. Try to understand this.

7. Son of Kunti, all living things enter my nature at the end of time. And again, at the beginning of time I create them anew.

8. Entering into my nature, I will create again and again all of these things that live. By my will, life automatically springs.

9. I am not bound by any of these actions, Conqueror. I am neutral to all of these actions, not attached.

10. Through me, through my attention, all life emanates, both the animate and inanimate. Son of Kunti, it is for this reason that the world exists.

11. Foolish men reject me when I take on a body. They do not know my higher life. I am the great deity of all that is.

12. They are fools in their hopes, fools in their actions, fools in their lack of understanding. They are deluded, demonic and wicked, and the things they seek comfort in are nothing but illusions.

13. But the great souls, Scion of Partha, have taken shelter in my divine nature. Without being distracted by their minds, they perform service, being aware that the source of existence is never-ending.

14. They are always singing devotionally of me, working with determination, offering signs of respect (namaste), and always practicing devotional ritual to me.

15. Others, by cultivating awareness, practice rituals to me as the dual, the non-dual, the infinitely diverse, or the single universal form.

16. I am the ritual of the priests. I am the performing of sacrifices. I am the offering. I am the healing herb. I am the mantra. I am the ritual fuel, I am the ritual fire, and I am the ritual itself.

17. I am the father of this universe. I am the mother, the friend, the grandfather. I am what can be known, and what purifies. I am the OM. I am all of the great scriptures.

18. I am the goal, the caregiver, the Lord, the watcher, the home, the safe place, the best friend, creation and destruction, the earth, the place of rest, the undying seed.

19. I give warmth and cold. I give rain, and drought. And I am immortality, death, spirit, and matter, Arjuna.

20. It is my will also that some will know the threefold teaching. Those who drink the soma juice, or purify themselves of wrongdoing by prayerful worship to gain passage to the realm of the god Indra, they enjoy the celestial divine pleasures of the gods.

21. When the vast pleasures of these heavens are exhausted, these holy beings fall back down to the world of mortals. Thus those who follow the threefold teaching to seek the pleasures of heaven will ultimately only gain repeated birth and death.

22. Those who have no such goal, but only focus their mind on me, they are practicing properly. Those who are always focused in this way will be united, protected, and supported by me.

23. Those who are devotees of other gods, who are trusting in their worship, they too worship me though they may not know it, Son of Kunti.

24. I am surely the one who enjoys all rituals. I am the Lord. Those who do not know the reality of me will fall down.

25. Those who worship the Gods will go to the Gods; those who worship the ancestors will go to the ancestors. Those who worship ghosts will go to the ghosts. Those who are my devotees will go to me.

26. A leaf, a flower, fruit, or simple water. Anyone who offers these in devotion unto me, I will accept them, so long as they are offered with pure spirit.

27. Whatever you do, whatever you eat, whatever you offer, whatever you give, whatever disciplines you practice, Son of Kunti, do so as an offering to me.

28. In this way, you will be free of the Karma of being bound to good or bad results. Having your soul firmly focused on the Yoga of renunciation (Sannyas), you will attain my freedom.

29. I am equal to all living beings. I hate no one, nor do I hold any dearer than others. But those who practice service with devotion unto me are in me, and I am certainly in them.

30. Even if one commits the most abominable acts, but is practicing service unto me without fail, he is certainly to be treated as a saint, because he is certainly determined in his intentions.

31. Very soon he becomes natural in his soul, and gains a lasting peace, Son of Kunti. I declare that no devotee of mine will ever perish.

32. Scion of Partha, those who specifically seek shelter in me, whether they are from a low background, or women, or merchants, or untouchables, even they will go to the highest place.

33. How much more certainly will the priests, the righteous, the devotees, the honourable kings! So while you are in this transient world, full of suffering, gain the gift of service unto me.

34. Become my devotee, always thinking of me. Worship me; give motions of respect (namaste) to me. You will come completely to me; your soul will unite with me totally through devotion.

Chapter 10

1. *The Blessed One said:*

Mighty warrior, just hear me once more, in this great teaching which I will give you for your benefit, because you are my friend.

2. The spirit beings will never know my majesty; the great sages will never know. For I am the source of everything that makes up the spirit beings and the great sages.

3. Anyone who knows me as uncreated, without beginning, he knows me as the great divinity. He is without delusion. Among all those destined to die, only he will be freed from wrongdoing.

4. Enlightenment, awareness, freedom from doubt, forgiveness, truthfulness, disciplined senses, disciplined mind, joy, suffering, birth and death, fear and courage.

5. Non-violence, balance, fulfillment, guilt, giving, fame, infamy; all of these different natures of living beings are arranged by me.

6. The seven great sages, and the four originators of humanity, were all born of me. They were created by my mind, as were all of the people of this existence.

7. Anyone who knows this reality as miracles of Yoga will be able to practice Yoga without fail. Of this there is no doubt.

8. I am the source of all creation. From me come all things. Knowing this, the enlightened become devoted to me with great fervour.

9. Their minds focused on me, their lives dedicated to me, they share this enlightenment with one another. They will constantly talk about me, finding joy in divine bliss.

10. They are always practicing service from their devotion. They are filled with the ecstasy of love. I give to them that unity of enlightenment by which they come unto me.

11. To them I give a particular grace. Any ignorance caused by darkness within their hearts, I can destroy with the bright lamp of awareness.

12. *Arjuna said:*

The Great Brahma, the Great Force, the Pure Greatest Being. The First Individuality, Transcendent, the Lord of the Spirits, Uncreated and Most Miraculous.

13. The sages all say these things of you. Even the divine sage Narada, and Asita, Devala, and Vyasa all say this. Now you are yourself explaining this to me.

14. I accept all of these claims that you are making, Krishna. No one can know you in your fullness, Blessed One, not even the divine or demonic spirits.

15. You know, personally, your soul through your soul, Greatest One. Creator of Everything, Lord of Everything, Spirit of Spirits, Father of the World.

16. Tell me in detail of how you have earned this divine and miraculous soul, the miracle by which you can remain within all dimensions at once.

17. Great Yogi, how shall I know you and think of you always? In which various natures are you to be thought of by me, Blessed One?

18. Describe again to my satisfaction the miraculous uniting of the soul, Destroyer of Doubt. Although I have been hearing you, I have not yet attained the nectar.

19. *The Blessed One said:*

Yes, I will speak unto you of the divine miracle of the soul. I will explain the main points, Best of the Kurus, for there is no limit to how far I could expand on this.

20. Arjuna, I am the soul. I am within the heart of all living beings. I am the beginning, the middle and the end of all life.

21. Of the Gods I am Vishnu. Of all lights I am the glowing Sun. Of all the winds I am the solar wind. Of all the planetary bodies I am the moon.

22. Of all the scriptures (Vedas) I am the Samveda (the first). Of all the divine spirits I am the king of heaven. Of all the senses I am the mind. And of all living beings I am the living force of consciousness.

23. Of all the demigods I am Shiva. And of all the lesser demigods I am the Lord of the Treasures. Of the elementals I am fire, and of all mountains I am Mt. Meru, the holy mountain.

24. Son of Partha, know me to be the prince of the priests, the hierophant. Of all the commanders I am the General. Of all the sources of water, I am the ocean.

25. Of all the great sages I am Bhirgu (the son of God). Of all the vibrations I am the voice in the silence. Of all rituals I am chanting. Of all immobile objects I am the Himalayas.

26. Of all the trees the Banyan, of all the divine sages Narada, of the divine choir Citraratha, of the magicians the wise Kapila.

27. Among horses know me as Uccaihishrava who was made from the tempestuous ocean. Of the noble elephants Airavata, and among human beings the King of Kings.

28. Of all weapons I am the thunderbolt. Of cows, I am Kamadhuk. Of the causes for begetting children I am true love. Of serpents I am Vasuki.

29. I am also Ananta of the hydras. Of all mermen I am the demigod Varuna. Of the ancestors I am Aryama. And of all the judges I am Yama, the lord of death (who judges the time of your death).

30. Of the demons I am Prahlada. Of all the conquering forces I am time. And I am the lion of all the animals, and the divine Garuda, of all the birds.

31. Of all the purifying forces I am the wind. Of all warriors I am Rama. Of all fish I am the shark. And of all rivers I am the Ganges.

32. Of all creation I am the beginning, the middle, and the end, Arjuna. Of all forms of knowledge I am the experiential knowledge of the soul. Of all forms of argument I am logic.

33. Of letters I am the letter A. Of compounds I am the dual compound. I am the eternal aeons, I am the fourfold creator.

34. I am the death of all that is, and the source of all that will be. Of the virtues of women I am fame, beauty, fine words, memory, intelligence, firmness, and patience.

35. Of the songs in the Samveda I am the Brihatsama. Of all poems I am the Gayatri. Of the months of the year I am harvest month. Of all the seasons I am spring.

36. Of all forms of vice I am gambling. I am the splendour of everything splendid. I am victory. I am risk. I am the might of the mighty.

37. Of the descendents of Vrishni I am Vasudeva. Of the Pandavas I am Arjuna. Of the wise I am Vyasa. Of the philosophers I am the philosopher Usana.

38. Of all the legal structures I am just punishment. I am the righteousness of those who seek noble goals. Of all the secrets I am silence. I am the awareness of the aware.

39. Whatever there may be of all living things, I am the seed, Arjuna. Without me, there is nothing that can exist, no living being, animate or inanimate.

40. Nor is there any limit to my divine miracles, Conqueror of Enemies. All of these are only some examples I have spoken out of a vast expanse.

41. Whatever miracles are real, most beautiful and glorious, you must realize that they are only born of a part of my splendour.

42. What could you possibly gain by understanding these things one at a time, Arjuna? I pervade this entire world, while being within one part.

Chapter 11

1. *Arjuna said:*

Just out of your friendship you have spoken to me these great secrets of the soul. Your words have removed my illusions.

2. I have heard from you in detail about the creation and destruction of all living things, Lotus-Eyed One. And I have experienced infinite wonders.

3. Thus what you have spoken is of the real spirit, greatest of divine Masters. Now I wish to see your real divine form, Finest of Individuals.

4. If you think it is possible for me to see this, my Lord, Divine Master of Yoga, show me your eternal soul.

5. *The Blessed One said:*

Scion of Partha, just see my forms; hundreds of thousands of combinations and countless colours.

6. Best of the Bharatas, see the twelve sons of Aditi, the eight Vasus, the eleven forms of Rudra, the two Ashvinis, the forty-nine Maruts, and many other awe-inspiring forms that you have never seen before.

7. In this one place you can see the entire world completely and immediately. Both the mobile and immobile are here in this body, Arjuna, and everything you could wish to see.

8. But you cannot see me with your own eyes. I will give you divine eyes to see my divine mastery of Yoga.

9. *Sanjaya said:*

Thus, after saying this my King, the greatest Divine Master of Yoga, the Praised One, showed unto Arjuna the greatest divine form.

10. Many mouths, many eyes, many awe-inspiring sights, many divine ornaments, and many divine weapons wielded.

11. Divine necklaces (malas), wearing divine dresses, covered in divine perfumes, all awe-inspiring, godly, infinite and present all at once.

12. There were many thousands of suns in the sky all at once, as if their light was the very radiance of the supersoul.

13. Arjuna could see the entire world all in once place, divided into many. This was the God of gods, manifest in that very moment as the universe.

14. Thus Arjuna was overwhelmed with awe, his hair standing on end. He bowed his head in respect, with folded hands toward the Divine, and began to speak.

15. *Arjuna said:*

I can see all the Divine in your divine body. And all the living beings gathered. Lord Brahma and Lord Shiva sitting upon a lotus flower, and all the great sages and the divine serpents.

16. I can see many arms, torsos, mouths and eyes. I can see you in every direction, with no beginning, middle or end, Divine Master of All. I see you as the all.

17. I can see helms, maces, spheres, and radiance, glowing in every direction. I see you, but it is difficult to bear, like blazing flames everywhere or the light of the sun, beyond measure.

18. You must be realized as the absolute, the greatest foundation of the all. You are the infinite upholder of the way. In my opinion you are the eternal supreme individuality.

19. Without beginning, middle or end. Infinite glories, infinite arms, eyes like the sun and moon. I see you with blazing fire burning from your mouth, giving warmth to all existence.

20. From the reaches of space to this earth and filling all in between, are you alone, in all directions. By the sight of your awe-inspiring and terrifying form, the Three Worlds themselves tremble, great soul.

21. You are within the entire school of spirits. Some of them are folding their hands from fear, offering supplication. The great sages proclaim peace, the school of magicians sing their incantations unto you with invocations from the ancient rituals.

22. All of the forms of Shiva, the Adityas, the Vasus and the Sadhyas, the Vishvedevas, the Ashvinu, Maruts, and the ancestors, schools of divine choirs (Gandharvas), Yakshas, demons and mages are all looking upon you in awe.

23. The great form of you has many faces and eyes, Great Warrior. Many arms, waists and legs, many torsos, and many fangs; and upon seeing them all the worlds tremble. As do I.

24. There are many glowing colours reaching to the heavens, open mouths, great glowing eyes. Seeing you I am shaken within my soul. I have lost all balance and my mind is troubled, Vishnu.

25. Seeing your terrible teeth and faces, which are like the fires of death, I have lost all sense of direction. I plead for grace, divine Master, Comforter of Worlds.

26. All of these sons of Dhirtarashtra, and these warrior kings, Bhisma, Drona, Karna, as well as the generals of our armies, they are all within your jaws, mightiest warrior.

27. They are entering, rushing into your terrible fangs. I see some of them, devoured by you, their heads crushed in your teeth.

28. As the rivers flow into the oceans, so do all these kings of the world flow into your mouths, and burn.

29. As moths are drawn into a blazing fire to their destruction, so are all people drawn with great swiftness into your mouths.

30. You are devouring all the people from all directions with your burning mouths glowing. You are covering all the world with your radiance, your terrible rays scouring all, Vishnu.

31. Please show me grace, Lord of the Gods, and explain to me your fierce form. I wish to know you as you really are, for I do not understand your purpose.

32. *The Blessed One said:*

I am Time, the destroyer of worlds. I am that which destroys all who are in the world. And all who are on this battlefield today are doomed to die, except for you.

33. Thus, rise up! Gain fame in conquering your foes. Enjoy the prosperous Kingdom you will gain. For all those here have already been destined to be destroyed by me. You will just be the vessel for this, Arjuna.

34. Drona, and Bhisma, and Jayadratha, and Karna, and all the other great warriors have already been killed by my will. You must destroy them, so be not troubled. Only fight and conquer your enemies.

35. *Sanjaya said:*

Thus hearing Krishna's words, with folded hands, trembling Arjuna offered respectful motions (namaste) many times over. Then he spoke fearfully to Krishna, his voice wavering.

36. *Arjuna said:*

Divine Master of the senses, by your glory the world is rightfully yours. It rejoices in union with you, and the demons are running fearfully in all directions. The whole school of mages is motioning respectfully as well (namaste).

37. Why should they not offer respect unto you, great soul? You are the Superior Brahma, the Divine Creator. Infinite, God of the Gods, Comfort of the World. You are never-ending, and thus beyond the real and unreal.

38. You are the God of gods, the oldest of individuals. You are the great comfort of this existence, you are the knower and the known, and the greater fulfillment. This entire existence is filled by you, infinite form.

39. You control the air, fire, water, the moon. You are the father, the great-grandfather, and I offer honours upon honours unto you.

Let it be so a thousand times over, again and again I offer my respect unto you!

40. Before you and behind you I offer respect. I offer my respect unto you from all directions, because you are all things, limitless strength and limitless force. You envelop all things, thus you are all things.

41. Having assumed you to merely be my friend, Krishna, my dear friend, whatever I may have said was out of foolishness or out of love, without knowing your true greatness.

42. Whenever I may have joked about you or dishonoured you, relaxing and sitting with you while dining together. Or when I was alone or with other friends, ideal one, I ask your forgiveness for all these unthinkable acts.

43. You are the father of all the dimensions, mobile and immobile. You are worthy of worship, the glorious Guru. There is none equal to you. How could there possibly be any who is greater in all the Three Worlds, most powerful lord?

44. Thus I offer up my whole body in respect for you. I beg unto you for mercy, the Divine who is worthy of worship. Like a father unto a son, like a friend unto a friend, like a lover unto his beloved, so I ask you to treat me, divine one.

45. I am filled with joy at seeing this which I had never seen before. But my mind is also shaken with fear. So please grace me once more with your divine form, Master of Gods, Comfort of the World.

46. With your helm, club, and wheel-like weapon (chakra) in your hand, that is how I wish to see you. Thousand-armed one, I wish to see you in your four-armed form, representative of all that is.

47. *The Blessed One said:*

Arjuna, I will gladly show you this great form, through the union of the soul. It completely radiates upon the entire universe, infinitely. It is my most real form, which no one has ever seen prior to you.

48. Never through the priestly rituals, nor by study, nor by charity, nor by any saintly acts, nor strict ascetic acts, has anyone else in this world of matter seen this form before you, greatest warrior of the Kurus.

49. Let it neither trouble nor confuse you to see this horrible form of mine. Free from fear, contented of mind, again simply witness this, my form.

50. *Sanjaya said:*

Thus, speaking in this way to Arjuna, Krishna once again showed him his true form. This brought much fear to him, so once again the great soul returned to his more beautiful form.

51. *Arjuna said:*

Looking once more upon your beautiful human form, Punisher of Enemies, I am now relaxed in my mind, I am once again composed.

52. *The Blessed One said:*

This form of mine that you have seen is very difficult to bear seeing. Even the divine spirits constantly long to gaze upon it.

53. I have never made it possible, either by the study of scripture, or ascetic acts, or charity, or worship, to see me as you have seen me.

54. But through the direct experience of devotion, Arjuna, I have made it possible to see and be aware. In fact, in this way you can enter the real, Great Warrior.

55. Doing my work, see me as the great individual. Being devoted to me, free from intellectual attempts at knowing, one who is without enemies among all living beings will come into me, Son of Pandu.

Chapter 12

1. *Arjuna said:*

Then who are the most true in union: those who are always engaged in devotion, properly venerating you, or those who have moved beyond the senses into the impersonal mystery?

2. *The Blessed One said:*

Those who focus the mind upon me are always practicing veneration to me. They are granted a greater trust by me, they are considered to be most involved in practicing the real.

3. But there are those who are completely engaged in venerating the impersonal, formless mystery that is beyond all the senses, and is also ineffable, omnipresent, unchanging, and immovably fixed in the now.

4. Focusing all of the senses, they are equally open to all things. They achieve me by practicing out of compassion for all living beings.

5. There is much trouble for those who are attached to the impersonal with their minds. Certainly for those who are in a personality, progressing into the impersonal can be achieved, but with much difficulty.

6. But those who renounce all activities to me, who attach to me, without deviating from such Yoga, they can meditate upon me.

7. And I will deliver them from the ocean of constant death and rebirth. Very soon, those whose consciousness is focused on me, I will become them, Scion of Partha.

8. Fix the mind upon me. Apply your awareness to me. You will live in me thereafter – do not doubt it.

9. If you are not able to focus your consciousness on me steadfastly, then by practicing Yoga you will in time develop the will to reach me, great champion.

10. If you are even unable to practice, become dedicated to doing service for me. Even work done for my sake will let you achieve great powers.

11. If you are unable to do this either, then perform the Yoga of Refuge in me. That is, give up the results of all actions, and become in that way centred in your soul.

12. Awareness is certainly better than formal practice. Meditation is even better than mere awareness. But renunciation of the results of actions is better still. By such renunciation you will gain peace.

13. Be without jealousy toward any living being, friendly and kind, with no ego or sense of possession, equal in happiness or sorrow, forgiving.

14. Such a yogi is always fulfilled. Determined, focused on the soul. With the mind and awareness focused on me, such a devotee of mine is very dear to me.

15. People who are never disturbed, and who do not disturb others, and who are free from happiness, distress, fear and worry, such people are also very dear to me.

16. Anyone who is neutral, pure, mastered, carefree, free of misery, the renouncer of all efforts; such a devotee is very dear to me.

17. One who neither takes pleasure nor grieves, does not complain or desire, and renounces the fortunate or unfortunate; such a devotee is very dear to me.

18. One who is equal toward friends or enemies, and who is also so toward honour and dishonour, in cold and heat, happiness and misery, who is balanced and free from attachment.

19. Who is equal in fame or infamy, silent, fulfilled by any situation, who has no home, who is focused in determination; such a devotee is a true human being. And he is very dear to me.

20. Those who completely involve themselves in this, what is called the nectar of the way, with trust, knowing me as the greater; such devotees are very very dear to me.

Chapter 13

1. *Arjuna said:*

Life and the one who experiences life; the battlefield, and he who is aware of the battlefield. I want to understand all of this, and I want to understand awareness and the object of awareness, Krishna.

2. *The Blessed One said:*

Son of Kunti, this body is the battlefield; so is it said by one who knows. Thus, those who know this are called 'aware of the battlefield.'

3. And certainly know me as the one who is aware of the battlefield; of all fields, Scion of Bharata. The field and he who is watching the field; to realize the difference is true awareness, in my opinion.

4. I will explain that field, as it is, and what kind of changes it undergoes and how, and what influence it can have, in brief.

5. It is in many ways described by the sages, by the various chants in various ways, by the sayings of the scriptures (Brahma-Sutras), as having very certain causes and effects.

6. The great elements, ego, enlightenment, the impersonal, the eleven sensations, the five sources of sensation.

7. Desire, hatred, happiness, sorrow, the school, the proof of life, determination; all of these are just some parts of the field, and examples of its interactions.

8. Humility, lack of pride, non-violence, tolerance, simplicity, service toward a saintly teacher, cleanliness, steadiness, focus on the soul.

9. The renouncing of the senses, egolessness, and witnessing the causes of birth, death, age, disease, and sorrow.

10. Being free of attachment, free of associating yourself as a father, husband, homeowner, and so on. And also having obtained constant balance, neither drawn to the desirable nor away from the undesirable.

11. Also by dedicated Yoga, and devotion unto me, without pausing, going into the quiet places, being unattached toward people in general.

12. Constant in awareness of the soul, for the sake of awakening the vision of awareness of the real. All of these things I declare to be awareness. All else is ignorance.

13. I will explain the possible subjects of awareness. And when one tastes the infinite nectar of this awareness, one will know my greater form, Brahma. Then one will be beyond all causes and effects.

14. It has hands and legs everywhere. Eyes, heads, and faces, with ears everywhere, filling all that exists in the world.

15. It is the original source of all the elements (gunas) of the senses, although it is itself without senses. Without being attached, it is the maintainer of all life. And without any physical form, it is the controller of all the physical elements as well.

16. Inside and outside of all living beings, mobile and immobile at once. Indefinable due to its multitude of definitions. Far away, and also near at once.

17. Indivisible, though apparently divided into all living beings. The maintainer of all living beings, that must be understood as the devourer as well as the creator of all.

18. It is in all radiant things, and it is also the source of all radiance. It is said to be beyond all darkness. It is awareness, it is

the source of awareness, it is the longing in everyone's heart to be aware.

19. Thus the battlefield, and awareness, and the possible subjects of awareness have now been explained in brief by me. Any devotee of mine who understands all of this will attain to my nature.

20. You must know the world of matter and the living beings in it as being eternal. Their transformations through the gunas are the result of the interactions of matter.

21. The interaction of matter is said to be the instrument that creates causes and effects. The interactions of living beings are likewise the instruments of the creation of joy and sorrow.

22. Living beings that exist in matter certainly have experiences of matter. These experiences are caused by the gunas. The guna that a living being identifies most closely to will determine his good and bad experiences in his lives.

23. The overseer who allows all of this, the master and true owner is the great divine master, the supersoul. And indeed it is said that the true experiencer within the body is this greater experiencer.

24. Thus, anyone who knows about the living beings, the material world, and the gunas, whatever his present state, he will never again be forced to take birth.

25. By meditating on the soul, some will see the supersoul in the soul. Others will see it through self-inquiry, Yoga, or the works of union.

26. But others still, without any special training, by merely hearing of this from others, will begin to practice. They will also transcend the path of death, for these ones are predisposed to hearing the truth.

27. Whatever comes into existence of any kind, mobile or immobile, know that it is only a great combination of the observer and the subject observed, Best of the Bharatas.

28. Anyone who sees that the great divine master is equally present in all living things; that it is in all mortal things but is itself immortal, that one has true vision.

29. Seeing the divine master equally everywhere, one will find no limit to the soul within the soul. Then one will reach the greater goal.

30. Anyone who sees that regardless of which activities are done in the material realm, one's soul remains free of activity, that one has true vision.

31. When one endeavours to see the separate personalities of living beings as being in fact oneness, then one will attain expansion into Brahma.

32. This soul is eternal, transcendent of matter, infinite. Son of Kunti, though it is in the body, it never acts nor can action be taken upon it.

33. It is the astral force (akasha). It is within all things but can never be affected. Likewise, the soul is everywhere in the body but can never be affected.

34. As the sun gives light to the whole world, this subject gives light to the whole body, Scion of Bharata.

35. Thus with the vision of awareness one can see the difference between the body and the one who witnesses the body. Those living beings who know this will gain liberation from material bondage, and will approach the greater.

Chapter 14

1. *The Blessed One said:*

Again I shall speak of the greatest of all understandings, the supreme understanding. Knowing which, all of the great sages of this realm attained power.

2. Taking shelter in this awareness, having attained the same nature as my own, they are not born even in the time of creation, nor are they destroyed in the time of annihilation.

3. The womb of my material existence is Brahma. Into that womb I seed the possibility of all things, which is the source of all living beings, Scion of Bharata.

4. Son of Kunti, all species of life, all forms that can exist appear. Brahma is the source of all their births, and I am the seed-giving father of them all.

5. Truth (Sattvas), passion (Rajas), and ignorance (Tamas) are the three elements (gunas) born of matter. They condition all eternal living beings who occupy temporary bodies, Great Warrior.

6. There is the element of Sattvas, purest in this existence, that provides illumination and avoids wrongdoing. It conditions one toward happiness and awareness, Sinless One.

7. Know the element Rajas to create desire in the soul. It conditions one to feel longing, which binds you to performing actions that produce Karma, Son of Kunti.

8. But know that the element Tamas is born of a lack of understanding of the real. It is the delusion of all living beings,

producing madness, laziness, and tiredness, that binds one to an animal existence, Scion of Bharata.

9. The element Sattvas attaches you to pleasure, the element Rajas binds you to lust of result, which conceals awareness of the real, Scion of Bharata. But the element Tamas is said to attach you to animal madness.

10. Sometimes Sattvas is in greater proportion than Rajas or Tamas, Scion of Bharata. Other times, Rajas is most prominent, or Tamas.

11. When the element Sattvas is most prominent, all the gates of the body develop illumination and awareness. Thus is it said.

12. When there is an excess of the element Rajas, greed and the uncontrollable longing to act out of desires will develop, Best of the Bharatas.

13. When Tamas is most developed, then darkness, sloth, madness and illusions are certainly manifest, Son of Kuru.

14. But when Sattvas is most developed at the time of death, the embodied being then attains to the pure dimension of the great scholars.

15. One who dies in the element Rajas, he will take birth in the company of those who live in this world of activities. Likewise, one who dies in the element Tamas will take birth among the animals.

16. Activities taken in the element Sattvas are said to be saintly, and result in purification. But actions done in the element Rajas result in sorrow, and actions in the element Tamas result in delusion.

17. From Sattvas is awareness developed. From Rajas is greed developed. And certainly also from Tamas is madness and animalistic delusion likewise developed.

18. Those in Sattvas will move upward. Those in Rajas linger in the middle, and those whose actions are in Tamas fall downward to the abominable.

19. When one sees properly that only the gunas are responsible for action, and knows that there is a force greater than all the gunas, he will ascend to my state of being.

20. When one transcends all three gunas that are produced by one's physical existence, he will gain freedom from the miseries of birth, death and old age.

21. *Arjuna said:*

Which qualities will be present in one who has transcended all three gunas, my Lord? What is the behaviour of one such as this, and how does he succeed in transcending the gunas?

22. *The Blessed One said:*

Son of Pandu, one who neither hates illumination, attachment or delusion even in their presence; nor does he desire them in their absence.

23. One who holds no position is never disturbed by the gunas, and thus witnesses their action. Such a one remains steady and does not waver.

24. One who acts equally when suffering and joy are present in him, who is equally disposed to a lump of earth, a lump of stone, and a lump of gold. One who is equally disposed to the desirable and undesirable, and equally steady when his soul is being praised or defamed by others.

25. Equal in honour and dishonour, equal to groups of friends and enemies, renouncing all efforts, he is said to be risen above the gunas.

26. Also, a person who practices service and the Yoga of Devotion unto me, he will transcend all of the gunas, and become raised to Brahma.

27. I am the foundation of Brahma, of the nectar of immortality, of the infinite and eternal. And of the way of ultimate joy.

Chapter 15

1. *The Blessed One said:*

It is said that there is an eternal banyan tree with its roots above, and its branches below. The leaves are the scriptures. And anyone who knows this tree is a knower of the scriptures.

2. Its branches extend downwards and upwards. They develop from the gunas. Its twigs are the objects of the senses. The tree's roots extend downward, where they are entangled by action in the world.

3. The form of this tree is not visible in this dimension. Never does it end and never does it begin, and never does it have a foundation. This banyan tree with its strong roots must be cut down with the weapon of detachment. This takes great strength.

4. After cutting it one must be watchful to find that place where, once you go, you will never return. One must surrender to the original individuality, from whom all things have come in the beginning, aeons ago.

5. Without false pride and illusion, having conquered faulty associations, eternally in the meditation of the soul, detached from lust, liberated from the duality of joy and sorrow, those who are like this gain eternal clarity.

6. My great abode is not lit by the sun or the moon, nor by any other energy. Those who go there never come back.

7. The part of me that is in the world as a living being is eternal as well. But it must struggle with the mind, and the rest of the senses, that work in the material.

8. As the body acquires various things, the body loses its inner Mastery. In taking all these things one moves away from Mastery, just as the scents will be carried away from a flower by the air.

9. Hearing, seeing, touching, tasting and smelling, and the mind. These are all the senses that one will experience.

10. Foolish people cannot see that anyone who is in a body will lose their body, eventually. They are too busy existing under the spell of the gunas. But those who have the eyes of awareness can see this.

11. Those who work in Yoga can also see this, if they are centred in their soul. But those who have not yet realized the soul will not see this yet, as their consciousness is not yet developed.

12. The sunshine, that by its splendour illuminates the entire world, and the splendour of the moon, and fire; understand that all of this comes from me.

13. Entering the planets and all the living beings, I sustain them by my energy. I nourish the vegetables and all drugs, becoming the juices that make these nourishing.

14. I become the ability to eat in all beings. And the inward and outward breath, which together with the digestion of the four kinds of food keeps the body in balance.

15. I am in the heart of all living beings. From me come memory, awareness, and forgetfulness. And I am the writer of all the known scriptures, and the knower of their teachings.

16. There are two classes of beings in this world: the restricted and the unrestricted. It is said that all living beings in themselves are restricted, but in the oneness they are unrestricted.

17. But it is said that there is also a third class, the greatest individual, the supersoul. He who is inside the threefold worlds, maintains them, and is himself the infinite Master.

18. I am transcendent to both the restricted and the unrestricted, the greatest. Thus I am praised in the world and in the scriptures as the greatest individual.

19. Anyone who views me as such, without doubt, as the greatest individual, he is the knower of all. He will perform service for me in everything he does, Scion of Bharata.

20. This is the most secret of the scriptures disclosed by me, sinless one. Being enlightened by this, one becomes enlightenment, and thus all his doings will be right, Scion of Bharata.

Chapter 16

1. *The Blessed One said:*

Fearlessness, being in truth, the state of being united to awareness, charity, mental focus, ritual, study of scripture, austerity, and simple living.

2. Non-violence, honesty, lack of anger, renunciation, peace, being non-judgmental, compassion for all living beings, lack of greed, gentleness, humility, and determination.

3. Enthusiasm, forgiveness, endurance, cleanliness, lack of jealousy, and not seeking fame are the qualities of one who is born into divine nature, Scion of Bharata.

4. Pride, arrogance and vanity, anger and intolerance, as well as ignorance; these are the qualities of one who is born into dark nature, Scion of Partha.

5. Divine qualities assist in attaining liberation. The dark qualities are considered to lead into bondage. Do not worry, Scion of Pandu, you are born into divine qualities.

6. There are two kinds of living beings created in this world: the divine and the dark. I have spoken of the divine with great detail, Son of Partha. Now hear from me of the dark.

7. People who are of dark qualities do not know the difference between right and wrong action. Nor is there cleanliness, saintliness, or truth in them.

8. They say that this world is untrue, with no purpose, cause, or controller. It has merely come to be, due to no reason besides lust.

9. Accepting this vision, having lost their souls, the unaware revel in activities that bring painful consequences (Karma) to them and others. This leads to the harmful destruction of the world.

10. Seeking comfort in unfulfilling lust, absorbed in the vanity of pride and prestige, due to their delusion they cling to impermanent things. They revel in their dedication to the unclean.

11. They seek comfort in countless fears and anxieties until the time of their death. They seek comfort in the pleasures of the senses, believing that these are the greatest.

12. Being bound by these hundreds of hopes, they are always entangled. Lust and anger are always on their mind. They seek out lust for the sake of sense pleasures; they accumulate wealth by unethical means.

13. "Today I have gained this, and I shall gain more as I desire it. This is mine; that is also mine. And my wealth will only increase in the future."

14. "I have killed this enemy, I will kill that enemy and others too. I am the lord, I am the one who experiences, I am the mage, powerful and happy."

15. "I am wealthy and surrounded by noble relations. Who else is like I am? I will sacrifice, give charity, and rejoice." In these ways one is deluded by ignorance.

16. They are confounded by many worries, surrounded by a web of illusions. Attached to the lust of the senses, the unclean slide down into hell.

17. With a slothful soul and stubborn, absorbed in the illusion of wealth and fame, they perform rituals in name only. They sacrifice only for show, without practicing for genuine knowing.

18. Seeking comfort in false ego, strength, pride, lust and anger, they despise and envy myself and other living teachers.

19. Those who are envious of me and miscreant I cast into the ocean of the world as the lowest of humanity. I put them always into dark and unfortunate wombs.

20. The foolish gain birth after birth in dark wombs. Son of Kunti, without reaching me they sink into a damned place.

21. There are three gates leading into the hell that destroys the soul: lust, anger and greed. Thus, these three must be given up.

22. Son of Kunti, being liberated from these three gates of ignorance, a person cleanses their soul. After this he goes to the greater goal.

23. One who gives up the wise teachings will be stuck in foolish actions born of lust. He will never attain power, never achieve happiness, never reach the greater goal.

24. Thus the teachings reveal to you the way to discriminate between right and wrong action. Being aware of the wisdom declared by the teachings, you should take action in the world.

Chapter 17

1. *Arjuna said:*

Krishna, those who give up the wise teachings, but practice in their own way with full trust, in what element are they? Sattvas, Rajas or Tamas?

2. *The Blessed One said:*

Trust is divided into three kinds among those with bodies, depending on their dominant element, whether they are in the element of Sattvas (truth), Rajas (passion) or Tamas (ignorance). Now hear what I have to say about this.

3. Scion of Bharata, a person's trust will vary according to each person's reality. One who lets himself trust will certainly become filled with trust.

4. Those who are in the element Sattvas will practice toward the divine spirits. Those who are in the element Rajas will practice toward the spirits of nature. Those people who are in the element Tamas will practice toward the ghosts, empty spirits.

5. Those people who undergo unwise abstinences that are harmful to themselves and others, they are bound by pride and arrogance. They are driven by lusts and attachments.

6. Torturing the natural impulses of the body because of a lack of true consciousness, understand that although I am within their individuality, they have also filled themselves with demons.

7. There are three different kinds of foods that will be appealing to each of the kinds of people; as well as three different kinds of ritual, disciplines, and charities. Now hear of the differences between these.

8. The food that is appealing to one who is in Sattvas is positive to one's health, strength and long life. It brings more satisfaction and pleasure. It is juicy, fatty, filling and fulfilling.

9. The food that appeals to one in Rajas is bitter, sour, salty, spicy, pungent, dry, and hot. It causes sorrow, misery, and disease.

10. The food that is the favourite of one in Tamas is old, tasteless, foul smelling, rotting and left over from the meals of others. It is untouchable.

11. The rituals that are performed according to wise guidance and without lust of result could only be performed by someone who focuses their mind in the element of truth (Sattvas).

12. Best of the Bharatas, be informed that ritual performed for the sake of some goal is done in the element of passion (Rajas).

13. And ritual performed without wise guidance, for greedy purposes, without the vibrating of mantras, without sharing or service, and without trust is to be considered as being in the element of ignorance (Tamas).

14. Practicing service to the Divine, to the initiates, to the Guru, and to others worthy of service; cleanliness, simplicity, directing all desires to Brahma, and non-violence are said to be proper bodily disciplines.

15. Words that are not disturbing, truthful, appealing and helpful and which do not contradict the teaching of the Masters; these are said to be discipline of speech.

16. The gifted mind, without deceiving others, seriously focused on the soul, purifying one's being, is said to be practicing discipline of mind.

17. Having committed with greater trust these threefold disciplines, men who have no ulterior motives or lust of result are said to be practicing in the element of Sattvas (truth).

18. Practicing worship for the sake of gaining honour or being respected by others, and practicing disciplines in this world out of pride are said to be done in the element Rajas (passion). Their results are wavering and temporary.

19. Those who foolishly strive against their own souls, who perform disciplines of self-torture, or who wish to do harm to others, they are said to practice in the element Tamas (ignorance).

20. Giving charity to those whom it is worth giving to, with no desire for return, in the right place and time and to the right person, is considered to be charity in the element Sattvas.

21. But charity done for some ulterior motive, lusting for a certain result, or given reluctantly, is considered to be charity in the element Rajas.

22. Charity done in a wrong place, at a wrong time, toward unworthy recipients, or without respect or proper attention, is said to be charity in the element Tamas.

23. Om, the real, symbolizes the threefold Brahma. The priests had used it in the past, in their scriptures and rituals.

24. Thus, Om symbolizes acts of ritual, charity and discipline. The practitioners of the way of Brahma always begin any of these acts with it, in accordance with the teachings.

25. Thus without lust of result, various acts of ritual, charity and discipline can be done by those who sincerely seek liberation.

26. The real beings, the initiates thus bring the real into their sincere acts, and the sound of the real is used, Scion of Partha.

27. In ritual, in discipline, in charity the real is vibrated. That work is meant for the real, and so certainly the real is represented.

28. That which is given with no trust, whether in ritual or discipline, is said without the real. Scion of Partha, it has no purpose in this life or the next.

Chapter 18

1. *Arjuna said:*

Mighty warrior, I want to understand the truth of Sannyas and how it is like and different from renunciation, Master of Sensing, Mighty Killer of Demons.

2. *The Blessed One said:*

Renouncing the desire for activities is what the wise know as real Sannyas. The renunciation of all the results of activities is what the experienced call true renunciation.

3. Thus great thinkers will say that some types of work must be renounced as wrongdoing. But ritual, charity, discipline and other works should never be renounced.

4. Hear from me definitely thus regarding renunciation, Best of the Bharatas. Tiger among men, I declare that there are three types of renunciation.

5. Acts of ritual, charity, and discipline must be done, they should never be renounced. And ritual, charity and discipline purify even the great beings.

6. But in all of these kinds of activities one should renounce one's attachment to results. Scion of Partha, it is my definite opinion that these acts are best done only as a duty.

7. But the renunciation of natural activities is never correct. To declare that these activities should be given up is to be in the element of ignorance.

8. One who renounces such things out of fear will create misery for himself and problems in his body. Such renunciation is in the element of passion, and will not gain the results of true renunciation.

9. Thus, actions which are natural to you must be performed, Arjuna. Certainly, one should give up attachment to the results of these acts. To me, this is renunciation in the element of truth.

10. A clever and true renunciate, free from doubts, will neither hate unfortunate work nor become attached to fortunate work.

11. It is impossible for anyone in a body to totally renounce all actions. But anyone who renounces the result of actions is said to be a renunciate.

12. There are three kinds of action: action that moves one upwards, action that moves one downwards, and action that has mixed results. These results (Karma) will affect one who has not renounced them at the time of death. But they will never affect a true Sannyasin.

13. Mighty warrior, understand from me the five causes listed in the wisdom teachings, said there to lead to power in all actions.

14. They are: the place of action, the performer of action, the different kinds of instruments used for action, and the motivations of the person acting; and the influence of the Divine is the fifth.

15. It is these five factors that determine whether a person takes action with his body, words or thoughts; and whether the action is right or wrong.

16. One who believes it is his soul that takes action is being foolish and not enlightened.

17. One whose enlightenment is never blocked by his ego could do anything, even kill without truly killing. He will not become attached.

18. Awareness, the subject of awareness, and the one who is aware are the factors that determine the three types of action. The senses, the action itself, and the performer of the action are the three ingredients that result in Karma.

19. Through the gunas, there are thus three kinds of awareness, actions, and performers of action. It is said that they can be in three different elements (gunas). Hear of these now.

20. One who sees that in all living beings there is an absolute oneness, indivisible yet infinitely divided, that one is aware in the wisdom of the real (Sattvas).

21. But one who, because of dividedness, is only aware of the various divisions, and sees all living beings as falling into different classifications, that one is aware in the wisdom of passion (Rajas).

22. And one who sees only their own attached actions as the be all and end all, with no deeper cause, is without true wisdom and very petty. That one is said to be in the element of ignorance (Tamas).

23. All action that is done with centeredness, without association, without desire or reluctance, and by one who has no lust of result, is called action that is real (Sattvas).

24. But action performed by one who has lust of result, or ego, or action that is done with great striving, is said to be action that is passionate (Rajas).

25. And that action which is born of illusion, self-motivated, without taking responsibility for the consequences, causing destruction or misery to others and which leads to further bondage is said to be action that is ignorant (Tamas).

26. Performing action free of association, without ego, justified with drive and enthusiasm, trying equally though powerful or powerless, the performer of such actions is said to be real (Sattvas).

27. Doing action with great attachment to desired results, greedy, jealous and unclean, affected by joy and sorrow, the performer of such actions I declare to be passionate (Rajas).

28. Doing action that is unnatural, driven by material motives, stubborn, insincere, insulting to others, slothful, depressed, and hesitant, the performer of such actions is said to be ignorant (Tamas).

29. Now hear from me in detail about the different levels of centeredness in enlightenment that are determined by the three gunas, great champion.

30. Being wise about action and inaction, what should and should not be done, fear and fearlessness, attachment and liberation, this is enlightenment at the level of Sattvas.

31. Being informed by a teaching about what should or should not be done, this is imperfect enlightenment at the level of Rajas.

32. Being deluded and not knowing the difference between true and false teaching, and thinking always in the wrong direction, this is enlightenment covered by Tamas, Scion of Partha.

33. The will that focuses the mind, energy, senses, and actions, by the unwavering practice of Yoga, that will is in the element Sattvas, Scion of Partha.

34. But the will which focuses the way of lust and material effort, Arjuna, because of lust of result, that will is in the element Rajas, Scion of Partha.

35. And the will by which one never stops fantasizing, fearing, regretting, feeling sorry for one's self, and illusion, that foolish will is said to be in the element Tamas, Scion of Partha.

36. Best of the Bharatas, now hear from me of the three levels of joy one can enjoy by practice, through which one can also gain the end of misery.

37. That practice which can be compared at first to the taste of poison, but at the end is like the taste of nectar, is said to be joy in the element of the real. It is born out of the grace of the enlightenment of the soul.

38. The joy that is born of the combination of the senses and sensation, which in the beginning is like nectar but later like poison, is said to be joy in the element of passion.

39. And that which is in the beginning and end alike a joy that is due to the clouding of the soul, born of sleep, sloth, and illusion, is said to be in the element of ignorance.

40. There is no being in material existence, on this earth or in the heavens, even among the divine spirits, who is free of the influence of these three gunas.

41. Vanquisher of Enemies, the four types of men: godly (brahmanas), noble (ksatriyas), worldly (vaisyas), and unclean (sudras) are classified by their actions, born of their relation to the gunas.

42. Peacefulness, balance, discipline, purity, openness, sincerity, awareness, wisdom, and spirituality are the godly actions of a natural man.

43. Bravery, strength, will, cleverness, fearlessness when challenged, generosity, and a noble nature, are the actions of a noble being.

44. Stewardship of the earth and animals, as well as business, are the actions of a worldly man. And an unclean man should dedicate his soul to acting in service, for this is the natural role of the unclean.

45. For each type of man, following his own type of actions will lead him to reach a higher power. Now hear how by acting in practices according to one's nature this power is achieved.

46. A man can achieve this power by serving, by dedicating his own natural actions, to that which is the source of all life, which is within all things.

47. It is better to follow one's own natural path, however imperfectly, than to follow the path of another, however perfectly. By performing actions correct to one's own nature, one will never commit wrongdoing.

48. Son of Kunti, one should never give up the actions that come of one's own nature. Certainly all actions will have their imperfections, just as smoke will cover a fire.

49. With an enlightened perspective to all things, focused on the soul, free of material wishes, through the greatest magical power, detachment, one attains Sannyas.

50. Achieving this power, one achieves Brahma. Try to understand me when I say this. Son of Kunti, it is essentially that state which is the highest.

51. Enlightened, fully practicing purification, with determination driving the soul, abandoning the senses and sounds, putting aside attachment and hate.

52. Living in a lonely place, eating only what is needed, controlling the speech of the body and mind, constantly united in the highest meditation, seeking comfort only in detachment.

53. Doing these things one will be freed from false ego, strength and pride, lust, anger and greed. One will be peaceful, knowing one owns nothing. Thus one will be ready for the nature of Brahma.

54. Within the nature of Brahma one has a joyful soul. One never regrets nor desires. Equally open to all living beings, one gains my greater devotion.

55. One can know devotion to me in as much as I am true in this body. The part of me that is beyond truth can only be entered through awareness.

56. Although constantly performing actions, through my care and by my grace one can achieve the eternal never ending abode.

57. Consciously renounce (Sannyas) all kinds of actions unto me, under my care, seeking comfort in union with enlightenment. Just be in my consciousness at all times.

58. In my consciousness you will be able to overcome all obstacles by my grace. But if, due to your ego, you do not hear, then you will be lost.

59. If you seek comfort in your ego, and thus think "I shall not fight," know this to be false. Your nature is to strive, with determination.

60. Son of Kunti, your natural self is being conditioned by your Karma. You are deluded to believe that you do not wish to follow your nature. But though you are reluctant, you must act.

61. The divine master of all that lives is found in everyone's heart, Arjuna. It is what leads all living beings to seek, behind these bodies of illusion.

62. Scion of Bharata, you must surrender unto him completely. By his grace, you will find great peace and the eternal home.

63. Thus have I shared with you this awareness, the secret of secrets. Consider this, do not take it lightly, and then do what thou wilt.

64. Hear from me again the greatest of secrets, the highest teaching. Because you are very dear to me, I will share it for your sake.

65. Take on the nature of my mind, become my devotee, my priest, offer your respects (namaste) unto me. Then you will come to me. This I promise to you, because you are dear to me.

66. Abandon all religious teachings, surrender unto me alone. I will free you from all wrongdoing, do not be worried.

67. This teaching must not be given to one who is not disciplined, nor to one who is not a devotee, ever. Nor also to one who is not practicing, or to anyone who is jealous of me.

68. Anyone who explains this, the greatest of the secrets, to my devotees, will be performing the greatest devotion unto me and will certainly come to me, with no doubt.

69. There is no one among men who will be dearer to me than he, nor will there be any dearer than he in all existence.

70. Also, whoever studies this sacred conversation of ours is performing a sacred ritual of awareness. In this way I judge that he is showing service to me.

71. Any man who hears this conversation with trust, and without envy, will become free. He will be fortunate in the world, attaining to righteousness.

72. Scion of Partha, have you heard all of this with total concentration of your consciousness? Has your deluded awareness been cleansed, Great Conqueror?

73. *Arjuna said:*

My illusion is washed away, my memory is restored by your grace, ideal one! I am free of doubts, and will follow your commands!

74. *Sanjaya said:*

Thus have I heard the debate between the greatest of spirits, Krishna, and Arjuna, also a great soul. Having heard such an awe-inspiring thing, my hairs stand on end!

75. By the mercy of the spirit, I have heard this greatest secret of Yoga, from the master of Yoga. Directly from Krishna, who spoke it himself.

76. My king, remember! Remember this awe-inspiring spiritual debate of Krishna and Arjuna. I am enthralled, again and again.

77. And also, remember! Remember the most awesome form of the Lord. My amazement is so great, my king, it enthrals me more and more!

78. Where Krishna the master of Yoga, and where the Scion of Partha, expert of the bow and arrow, are together, there is nobility, victory, strength, and righteousness. This is my feeling.

"Inner Self"
Ma Leela Prem – 2007

Commentary on The Bhagavad Gita

Chapter 1
The Yoga of Grief and Attachment

1. *King Dhirtarashtra said:*

In the place of pilgrimage, the place called Kurukshetra, there has assembled desiring to do battle my army, and the army of the sons of Pandu. What did they do O Sanjaya?

v. 1

Kurukshetra literally means the 'Fields of righteousness.' It was a holy place. So terrible was the war of the Mahabharata that it had come to this, the largest battle ever fought, being fought in one of the holiest places.

When the self is not operating in unity, this is what it produces: it creates a battle within you, a battle in the holiest of places, your very being.

. . . .

2. *Sanjaya said:*

After studying the deployment of the soldiers of the Pandavas, King Duryodhana [son of Dhirtarashtra] was approached at that time by his holy teacher, Bhisma. The King addressed him.

3. Look upon the armies of the sons of Pandu, holy teacher, great spirit. They have been arranged by the son of Drupada [Dhirstadyumna], your own best student.

4. Here in the army are great warriors, mighty bowmen like Bhima and Arjuna, who are equal in prowess to Yuyudhanah, Virata or Drupada, also great fighters.

5. There are also very strong heroes like Dhirstaketu, Cekitana, KasiRajas, Purujit, Kuntibhojah and Saibya. They are legends among our people.

6. Yudhamanyu and mighty Tamaujah, and the very mighty son of Subhadra; as well as the sons of Draupadi are all certainly great charioteers.

7. Take note of those in our forces now, Best of the Teachers, and tell me which among the captains of my armies are particularly powerful.

8. Your good self, Bhisma, and also Karna and Kirpa have never lost in battle. Ashvatthama, Vikarna and the son of Somadatta are certainly great warriors as well.

9. Others also, many heroes are prepared to risk their lives for my sake. They are equipped with a variety of terrible weapons, and all of them are experienced strategists.

10. Our strength is beyond accounting, totally defended by you, Bhisma, while the forces of the Pandavas are only well defended by Bhima.

11. In the key fronts of the battle, also everywhere, all of us must give our respect and support to you, and assure our victory.

v. 2-11

Bhisma was a great teacher of war, a great master of combat. He was at that time considered the greatest strategist. In the king's analysis, they cannot lose the battle because it is known that Bhisma is a superior general to Bhima, who commands the Pandavas.

However, he fails to consider the presence of Krishna.

Krishna is not there as a warrior, he is only the charioteer for prince Arjuna.

But the presence of his enlightenment provides a spiritual strength that the forces of King Duryodhana utterly lack.

The final battle of this war between cousins, the Kauravas and the Pandavas, was a battle to determine the future of humanity.

The Kauravas were materialists, they were incapable of seeing past the body.

They saw the forces of the Pandavas, counted only the numbers and quality of the soldiers, and felt secure that they were superior.

They could not count – their spiritual darkness made them incapable of counting – the deeper qualities that existed.

They could not consider the passion of the heart, nor could they sense the power of Krishna's Buddhafield, because they chose to remain asleep to those things.

SO they could not sense, they chose not to sense, the benefit of awakened perception.

When you are undertaking a task with all of yourself, not separate but united, in Yoga, in yourself, you will be capable of far more than someone who is not doing this.

Because that other person will be stopped by their own conflicted nature.

They will not be able to act fully. They will be defeated by their own sense of limitation.

This is why Kurukshetra was such a crucial battle; it would determine the future between a humanity influenced by a mighty force of materialism, or by a mighty spiritual force.

If the Pandavas did not defeat the Kauravas in this battle, then the work of all subsequent Enlightened Teachers, and their ability to help progress the collective enlightenment of humanity would have been severely limited.

. . . .

12. Thus to bring joy to his army, Bhisma, grandsire of the Kuru dynasty blew his conch shell. It vibrated loudly, like the roar of a lion.

13. In response, the Kurus rang out with conch shells and large drums, small drums and kettledrums, as well as horns. These were suddenly sounded all at once, and that combined sound became deafening.

14. On the opposing side, on a great chariot with white horses were Krishna and Arjuna. In response, they sounded their divine conch shells.

v. 12-14

It is noteworthy that when Bhisma, commander of the Kauravas, sounds his conch shell, the response from the other Pandavas comes not from Bhima (who is commanding), but from Krishna and Arjuna.

Thus the Pandavas demonstrate that they are placing their first priority on spiritual command, and not on military materialism.

. . . .

15. Krishna blew the conch shell named Pancajanya, and Arjuna blew the conch named Devadatta. Also, Bhima, famous for feats of strength and a voracious appetite, blew the conch named Pundra.

16. The conch named Anantavijaya was blown by the son of Kunti, King Yuhdhisthirah. Nakula and Sahadeva blew the conch hells named Sughosa and Manipuspaka.

17. Also the King of Kasi and great archer Sikhandi, and the great warriors Dhirstadyumna, Virata and Satyaki, who had never been defeated in combat.

18. Drupada, the son of Draupadi as well, my king, and the son of Subhadra the great-armed. Each and all blew their conch shells separately.

19. That vibration shattered the hearts of the sons of Dhirtarashtra and the sky and the earth were all resounding tumultuously.

v. 15-19

At Krishna's lead, all of the Pandavas, beginning with Arjuna, sound their conch shells.

In this way, they all demonstrated harmony and unity.

In verse 13, you hear that the Kurus all ring out with drums and shells, a cacophony.

They are not united, not focused. They are just a noise that is deafening, that takes away awareness.

But the Pandavas all blow their conch shells, separately, each as individuals, but with one common purpose and common vibration.

This is how a Mystery School operates.

Each person must ring out their own music, their own vibration; it is not a question of conformity.

But each person, as an individual, is singing out, vibrating, with a common will, a common purpose.

The result in the battlefield is that the hearts of the Kauravas are shattered, their confidence is broken, because they see how united and focused the Pandavas are, and all of earth and heaven is shaken.

If you are united in your will, then all of earth and heaven vibrates with you.

. . . .

20. At that time, positioned as to be looking upon the sons of Dhirtarashtra, was he whose flag was marked with Hanuman the monkey-god, Arjuna the son of Pandu. He was preparing to fire his arrows, taking up his bow, when he suddenly spoke these words to Krishna, my king:

21. *Arjuna said:*

Most accurate one, please keep my chariot in between both of the armies, so that I might look upon all whom are ready to do battle in this place.

22. All those with whom I will have to try to oppose in this terrible battle.

23. Let me see those who will be fighting, those gathered here, wishing to aid the dark minded son of Dhirtarashtra.

24. *Sanjaya said:*

O Son of Kings, thus addressed by Arjuna, Krishna placed the great chariot right between both of the armies.

25. In front of Bhisma, Drona, and all the Kings of the land, he said: behold all of them, the gathered Kurus.

26. There Arjuna saw standing his fathers and grandfathers, teachers and uncles, brothers and sons and grandsons. Friends too, and in-laws and past allies. All of these were gathered in both sides, both armies.

v. 20-26

Arjuna is suddenly struck by a moment of hesitation, before the beginning of the battle.

This is doubt.

And to look at it, at first, you could suspect that this might be a weakness; everyone else in the army was ready to fight, but suddenly Arjuna hesitates.

However, doubt is a powerful strength.

Had Arjuna not doubted, he would have fought at the battle without full understanding. Krishna would never have given his discourse, and Arjuna would have fought as he was, not awakened.

Doubt is only harmful if it is not real.

Many times, people say "I doubt", when what they mean is "I choose to believe something different than what I see before me."

This is not doubt.

Doubt is not a belief. It is the absence of understanding.

Recognizing that you are uncertain about something, that you are hesitant, is vital and important.

If you recognize this, you will be able to look at your uncertainty and seek out a way to resolve it, whereas if you were to deny this doubt, you would simply remain incomplete.

Had Arjuna decided not to say anything, to just shut up and fight, he would have fought with that uncertainty within him, and all would have been lost.

If doubt is presented with a sincere desire to have those doubts resolved, clarified, then doubt is one of the most powerful virtues a human being can hold.

Doubt is only negative if it is not really doubt, if it is really just an unwillingness to recognize what is before you.

. . . .

27. After seeing them all, the different relatives of the son of Kunti, moved by a higher compassion and overwhelmed by grief, Arjuna spoke:

28. He said: after seeing all these, my people, all ready for battle, it makes my limbs shake and my mouth go dry, Krishna.

29. My body trembles and my hair stands on end, my bow slips from my hand, and my skin feels as if it's aflame.

v. 27-29

Note that Arjuna is moved by a higher compassion; what is really driving him is his compassion.

However, he is also overwhelmed by grief.

These are two different things.

The fact that he is overwhelmed by grief, by his emotions, makes it impossible for him to sense his higher compassion.

The Gita is not saying that these two things are the same. The Gita is saying these two things are confused inside Arjuna, and it is causing his ignorance. This is the diagnosis of his issue.

Higher compassion is the compassion that understands that what you must do you must do for the ultimate good, for what is most helpful in the world in the greater sense.

Grief is what motivates an immediate desire to feel better, a quick fix.

Giving a bottle of booze to an alcoholic might make him feel better in this moment, help ease his suffering in a moment, but few would say it is compassionate in the larger sense. Most would say that it is the opposite of compassion.

Giving a piece of bread to a poor man might be a momentary act that calms your own grief and guilt, but it doesn't actually do anything to help the poor man, and only lengthens his period of poverty.

Teaching the poor man how to help himself, on the other hand, is an act of compassion.

. . . .

30. Also, I cannot continue, I cannot just forget what is on my mind. Krishna, I see only disasters.

31. Nor do I see any good in killing my own people in combat. Nor do I desire victory, Krishna, or the joy of ruling a kingdom.

32. What use to us is the kingdom, Krishna? What enjoyment from living either? What happiness is there in doing this for the sake of ruling a kingdom?

33. All of them, those here on the field of battle, would be losing their riches and lives: my teachers, fathers, grandfathers, uncles and great-grandfathers.

34. Uncles, fathers-in-law, grandsons, brothers-in-law – all these relatives I would never wish to kill. I would have to kill them, Krishna.

35. Even if I could exchange their deaths for the Three Worlds, never mind this kingdom of the earth, what joy would there be for me, Krishna, if I must kill the sons of Dhirtarashtra?

36. Certainly I would be in the wrong if I killed all of these opponents. I have no right to slay the sons of Dhirtarashtra, as well as my own friends and relatives. How could I ever be happy after doing such a thing, Krishna?

v. 30-36

Here Arjuna gives a convoluted series of explanations, of excuses, to justify his grief.

Here he is arguing with Krishna, though Krishna has not yet said a word. Arjuna's ego is already spouting all kinds of reasons as to why Arjuna need not change, why he should stay with doing what he is already thinking.

The ego works in this way, justifying itself to you, justifying your own limitations, trying to make you sound like a good person for doing things you know deep down are not good for you.

Arjuna here is planning to flee the battlefield, not because he is a coward, but because he has foreseen disaster.

He has realized that even if his side wins, the devastation will be so terrible that what is left will not be worth owning.

And indeed, the battle of Kurukshetra would rage for 18 days, and by the end, virtually everyone who had fought, all of the nobility of India, would be dead.

What is more, Arjuna does not want to have his teachers, Bhisma and Drona, who are fighting for the Kauravas, despise him.

Arjuna loved his teachers very much, and here they were, arrayed against him. To get the kingdom he wanted to possess, he would have to kill these men.

So now, Arjuna is thinking mainly of himself, and what he wanted.

Arjuna wished to impose on reality a world where he and his brothers could easily gain the throne, easily rule, and things would be peaceful and lovely.

He had decided that this was how he personally could be happy, and this was what would be best for the world.

However, life has not agreed to his terms; and instead the things that he had defined as what he believed best will not come to pass, and Arjuna has realized that.

So now, seeing that he cannot get what he wants, and fearing that he will never be able to be happy, he is rejecting, he wants to fight against life, by running away and hiding in the forest as an ascetic.

In everyone's life, there are moments when one is confronted with this, with the realization that the things you would like reality to be, the things you would like to force on life, force on God, force on your environment, are simply not going to happen.

And in those moments you can rage, or you can run, or you can change.

It is a choice.

. . . .

37. Even if they do not see, overpowered by greed in their hearts, that killing a relative or attacking a friend are wrong acts.

38. Why should we not know that these are wrong acts? Would not the destruction of a dynasty be a criminal act if done by those who can see the evil of it, Krishna?

39. The destruction of a dynasty destroys the way of that society, it disrupts the eternal religion, and all the families are warped by unlawful activities and decadence.

40. When decadence has taken place, Krishna, do not families become unhealthy? Women of the families become polluted and produce unwanted children.

41. These unwanted children create a lawless society, destroy families. And if the family falls apart, then offerings of food and water to the ancestors stop being performed.

42. Such flawed people, the destroyers of society and unwanted children which they create will devastate social laws and family laws forever.

43. Krishna, I have heard from the priests that men who ruin the family ways will reside forever in hell.

v. 37–43

Arjuna continues to try to justify his readiness to run; his first verses were the most honest.

In those first verses, up to verse 36, his concern was with his own happiness.

His ego was telling him "you will never be happy, you will not get what you want if you cannot force things to be the way you imagined. Its better not to do anything, if you can't get what you want!"

But the Ego is very sophisticated, and Arjuna knows that in the end that first argument sounds childish, so now he moves on to a more philosophical argument, talking about society and religion.

Suddenly, his ego has convinced him that it isn't really about him at all, that it isn't just his own unwillingness to accept reality that makes him want to run; instead, the ego has convinced Arjuna that really he is taking an honourable moral and religious stance by not fighting.

The ego works like this in everyone.

First it will react with the true fear you hold, but very quickly it will jump to more convoluted excuses, to false excuses of morality or politics or philosophy, quoting scriptures or dogmas to try to convince yourself and others that what you are doing or failing to do is actually right, and not just right but altruistic.

That you are not being selfish, that you are actually trying to help others through your own crapulence.

. . . .

44. I regret our strange choice to commit such terrible acts; we were driven by greed, by my desire to become a king. This has led us to try to kill our relatives.

45. Even if I did not resist, unarmed, as the sons of Dhirtarashtra killed me on the field, it would be a better thing.

46. *Sanjaya said:*

Thus having spoken, Arjuna sat down again on the chariot, on the battlefield, putting aside his bow and arrows. He was distressed by grief in his heart.

v. 44-46

Led by his ego, which is fed by his fears (not of death in battle, but of not getting what his ego has told him he 'needs' to be happy), Arjuna has let his mind take him to the utterly wrong conclusion.

Now he is calling his previous righteous actions a 'strange choice,' now he is fully asleep and cannot understand why before he would have done those things.

The things that mystics do always seem strange and incomprehensible to someone who isn't open to the heart, because so much of it cannot be explained intellectually.

Intellectually, it seems crazy.

What is more, Arjuna is now claiming that his previous acts were just driven by a desire to become King, by greed.

This is not true at all; Arjuna has now sunk, through his ego, to the point of lying about his own previous acts.

Why is he doing all this?

Because he is unwilling to let go of a single idea.

This idea is the idea that ultimately allows the ego to govern everyone.

It has a million different forms and expressions, but in everyone it is the same.

It is the most fundamental difficulty of the human experience, and represents the heart of darkness of humanity.

This idea is the idea that life has to do what you want it to do or be what you want it to be; that you know what is best and that you want to impose your notions on life.

As long as one clings to that idea, then one can never escape suffering.

It is the core definition of attachment.

Chapter 2
The Buddha-Yoga

1. *Sanjaya said:*

Thus he was overwhelmed with compassion, his eyes full of tears and regret. Krishna spoke to him these words:

2. *The Blessed One said:*

From where has this dirtiness of regret come upon you, at this very critical hour? This is practiced by those who don't know the true essence. This line of thought doesn't lead to a higher dimension; it will only lead you to disgrace, Arjuna!

3. Do not take to helplessness, you who are the son of Partha. This behaviour does not suit you. It is a petty weakness of sentimentality, give it up! Get up, you who are the punisher of your enemies!

v. 1-3

Here Krishna is demanding that Arjuna pay attention. To become aware of his regret, to understand that regret over that which you would want but is not real is a worthless emotion to become attached to.

This is why Krishna calls it 'dirty,' because it stains your ability to be in the moment.

Sentimentality is a petty weakness: it is not emotion that is a weakness – human emotion is a gift.

Sentimentality is when one clings to an emotion, lets oneself get swept away by that emotion, and exaggerates the significance of that emotion; where one becomes self-centred and tries to imagine that whatever he's feeling right now is terribly significant not just to himself but to life, and that it's much more important than it really is.

Sentimentality is the enemy of the mystic.

. . . .

4. *Arjuna said:*

How can I attack with arrows men like Bhisma and Drona, who are worthy of my veneration, o Krishna?

5. They are my superiors. Certainly I should not kill such great beings. It would be better to live as a beggar in this very life, than to desire to gain by killing my superiors in society! It would be too difficult to enjoy any such pleasures if they are tainted with blood.

6. Nor do we even know what would be better; we can't know if we shall conquer or they will. But I know that by killing those before me, the sons of Dhirtarashtra, I would not wish to live.

v. 4-6

Arjuna is repeating his initial expression of Ego: that if he has to fight now, and destroy everything he sought in order to win, he will not be able to enjoy his victory. He would not be able to live with himself if he had to kill his beloved teachers in order to win.

. . . .

7. I am afflicted now by hesitation and weakness. I ask you to help me – my spirit is confused in my heart. Tell me what would be right. I am your disciple; I surrender unto you. Tell me what can be known.

8. I do not see how I can be free of that which fills me with grief and clouds my senses. Even if I were to gain a Kingdom in this world as great as the heavenly kingdoms, and power as great as the Gods', it would not free me from this.

9. *Sanjaya said:*

Saying this to Krishna, Arjuna the punisher of his enemies declared: "Krishna, I shall not fight." Then he fell silent.

10. O my King, descendant of Bharata, Krishna then smiled and spoke to the grieving Arjuna, right in the midst of the two great armies.

v. 7-10

Arjuna here asks Krishna, his Guru, to help him.

He says that he surrenders. However, in reality he does not do so. Immediately after his false surrender, he begins to place conditions again. He tells Krishna what he believes to be true (that there is no answer to his dilemma), and he tells Krishna what he has already decided is right (not to fight).

Real surrender to a Guru cannot come with conditions. Trying to say "I will surrender, but..." is like saying you are a "little bit pregnant." Surrender isn't a question of degrees; either you surrender, or you do not, you cannot "Partially surrender."

Even so, Krishna smiles. He smiles because although Arjuna has not really surrendered here, he has made clear his wish to be helped. He has expressed that he wants to surrender.

This means that Krishna will try, he will do whatever is possible, to open Arjuna's eyes; not by doing what Arjuna wants, which is to tell him that he is right, but by presenting Arjuna with a reality that is completely outside of what Arjuna's perceptions allowed him to see until now.

. . . .

11. *The Blessed One said:*

You are grieving for that which is not worthy of grief. Speaking from wisdom you would say that no life is lost, now or ever. You would not grieve over death.

12. There has never existed a time when I was not, or you were not, or these were not, any of these kings. Nor shall there ever be a time when we will not be.

13. Any who lives a mortal life in a body will experience childhood, youth, and old age. Likewise, they will achieve other forms of life beyond this one. One who is focused will not be blind to this.

14. Son of Queen Kunti, it is only the senses that see the winter and summer of suffering and joy. They come and go, but are in no way permanent. One must accept them all, Scion of Bharata.

15. Finest of Men, one who isn't disturbed by these things, who is the same in happiness and suffering, he has discovered patience. For one like this, the nectar of liberation is obtainable.

v. 11-15

Here Krishna begins to unveil the Yoga of Assessment to Arjuna. This Yoga is a kind of self-inquiry. It begins with the understanding that no life is ever created or destroyed, that everything is life, and that the only things that truly 'die' are those things that are based on momentary experience.

The moment is an eternity; it is also a constant change.

If we try to freeze-frame this eternal change, then what we perceive will seem like death.

If we roll a ball along the floor, and decide that when the ball is rolling that counts as 'life' and when it stops that is 'death,' then when the ball stops, you will believe that 'death' has occurred.

In fact, it is only because you have chosen to perceive a made-up reality. The ball is still there, the floor is still there, everything is still present; even the kinetic energy that made up the motion of the ball still exists, in another form now.

The only thing that has changed is in your imagination. You imagined that one thing was life and another death, you classified.

It is the same with our lives.

You are no longer the same person you were 2 years ago, much less 20 years ago. That person is already dead. Yet you create a fixed span of time and call it all one life, one being.

That being does not exist.

What exists is a consciousness, in this moment.

And just because this particular consciousness' connection to this particular body will come to an end, it does not mean that life comes to an end. All of life persists, nothing is lost, but everything always changes.

. . . .

16. There is nothing in this world that lasts forever as it is. The only thing that is unchanging is the eternal. These two forces, the essential and the nonessential, have been studied by the seekers of truth.

17. Know the essential to be indestructible, and to be found throughout your entire body. No person or thing can harm it.

18. Our physical bodies are easily destroyed, but the essence within them is said to be eternal. It is beyond all measure, and indestructible. Therefore, you may fight, Scion of Bharata!

19. One who thinks himself the slayer, or one who thinks himself slain, is in delusion. The essential cannot destroy nor be destroyed.

20. Nor is it ever born, nor does it ever die. It has never been created, nor will it ever be created, nor is it being created. It is unborn, eternal, permanent. That which is eternally ancient is not killed, even if its body is being killed

v. 16-20

The moment consists of the combination of the eternal and of constant change. These two forces, 'the world in which nothing lasts' and the 'essential' combine to create reality.

You have within you, this eternal reality, what is essential.

In your life too, you should remember what is essential and what is not.

Anything that is a product of outside influences is non-essential.

That which is the product of that eternal inside of you, is essential.

The Yoga of Assessment requires that you be able to differentiate between these two, because often to the unenlightened person something that seems to be from inside of you, or an essential truth, is really unbeknownst to them the product of their deep-rooted external conditionings. This is done by self-inquiry.

. . . .

21. If you know this essence to be unborn, unchangeable, indestructible, and always existing, then how can you believe that you can cause harm or death to anything essential, Son of Partha?

22. Just as one gives up old worn out clothes, and accepts and wears new clothes, in the same way does the embodied essence give up old or worn bodies, and take on new ones.

23. This essence can never be cut with a blade or burned by fire, nor will water make it wet, nor will wind dry it.

24. This essence cannot be broken, burned, dissolved, or desiccated. It is certainly immortal, omnipresent, immutable, unchangeable, and eternally as it is.

25. It is invisible, and beyond the understanding of the mind. This essence cannot be altered. Thus, if you are aware of this, you should not feel regret.

26. But even if you think that this essence is one that is always being reborn and dying, there is still no reason to grieve.

27. For anyone who is born is sure to die. This is known for certain. Thus there is no reason to grieve for that which was bound to occur.

28. That which in the beginning has no form, gains form in the middle, and then is destroyed and once again becomes formless. All things are such, Scion of Bharata, so why grieve?

v. 21-28

The quality of something essential is that it cannot be affected by outside forces.

Truth cannot be affected by the whims of individuals.

If you are doing what is essential, what is natural, then you cannot do wrong.

Likewise, if someone else is being unnatural, acting in a way that is focused on the unessential, you cannot change them, but you cannot allow them to change you either.

For Arjuna to do something unnatural and allow evil to win in the world, because his beloved family and teachers are being unnatural too, will not solve anything.

If he is forced to kill them, what is essential about them will not die, only the unessential.

. . . .

29. Some will see this essence as awe-inspiring. They will describe it as a Mystery. It is likewise awe-inspiring to one who hears of this Mystery. For to any who hear of it, it will be beyond all comprehension.

30. The essential self is eternal and cannot be killed. It is the Mystery. It is within all beings, Scion of Bharata. Thus you need not grieve for any living things.

v. 29-30

What is the Mystery? The Mystery is a force that is everywhere, and that is indescribable. Some call it the Tao, some call it other names; but it is beyond comprehension. It is a force that we know in our hearts exists everywhere, and yet that cannot be described by any non-essential quality. This great unknowable fills us with awe; we know it is something beyond the limits of the mind or the body.

. . . .

31. One's own spiritual nature must also be considered. You should never hesitate, for to your spiritual nature, there is nothing that suits you better than being a warrior. It is your destiny to be a warrior. You have no other choice.

32. When it naturally occurs, conflict such as this can open the doors to higher consciousness. For those who are kings, this is a very fortuitous event.

v. 31-32

How is it possible that a horrific war can be a great opportunity? It is because a conflict like this is a crisis.

Human beings only have the chance to connect to that which is beyond themselves, to get out of their comfortable routines, when there is a spiritual crisis pushing them to it.

That is why the Guru's task is to create spiritual Crisis in his students.

Crisis is an event that creates change, by breaking down one's routine and assumptions.

A horrific war like the Mahabharata created a situation where all those who were fighting in it had a choice, to break free of their usual ways of acting, to change, to grow.

The opportunity to grow is the greatest gift in life.

Some took it in small ways, some would take it in greater ways; and others would refuse to take it, and the crisis would destroy them. For Arjuna's own case, despite all his resistance he would be pushed to the ultimate transformation due to this war.

When Krishna says that this war is fortuitous for Kings, he is not referring to regular monarchs of kingdoms. Why would it matter to them any more than anyone else?

What Krishna calls 'kings' are specifically those people who are ready to open the 'doors to higher consciousness.' The 'kings' of Krishna are meditators, those who are ready to be mystics, and have a little more awareness open to them than most of the people, thus they are more ready to make the choice that a crisis like this war presents them.

. . . .

33. Thus, if you see this as a spiritual duty, to avoid fighting now will go against your nature and lead to the loss of your prestige. You will gain only further disturbance in this way.

34. You will be shamed before all the people, and they will speak ill of you forever as one who was not true to his nature. For a man of insight, such a fate is much worse than death.

35. If you quit the battle out of fear, your fellow warriors who currently honour you will judge you as unworthy of any respect.

36. Your enemies will be able to speak terrible slanders against you. This will be more terrible to you than anything else.

37. If you die here, you will gain a higher state of consciousness. If on the other hand you are victorious, you will have the world. Thus arise, Son of Kunti, be secure in the determination to fight.

38. Joy and sorrow are equal in gain and loss, as are victory and death. Thus if you approach any of these without attachment, you will never incur distress.

v. 33-38

Joy, sorrow, victory, death, all of these are part of the nonessential. All are equally meaningful and meaningless. It is we – human beings – who concern ourselves with creating a difference, from our point of view. But someone who is truly wise understands that all of these things are the same.

. . . .

39. I have described all of this to you intellectually, but you must understand this from the perspective of enlightened consciousness, beyond the limits of intellectual thought. If you can enter into enlightened thought, you will be free of the restrictions of karmic consequences.

40. Even in attempting this form of understanding you cannot go wrong. Even if you can reach a limited form of enlightened understanding, it will help to decrease your distress.

41. If you are determined to be conscious, to be enlightened, you will achieve greater unity to reality, my beloved friend. There are various paths by which you can reach this enlightenment, and thus be free from internal division.

42. All of these flowery words have been said before by those who had not actually achieved this enlightenment, by those who claim to be religious. But there is no substitute for the actual experience.

v. 39-42

To read this book, to read my commentaries, none of that is enough to do anything at all to you.

There are an astounding number of spiritual 'seekers' who believe in the power of books as some kind of magic charm, that by having them, owning them, they are already gaining something. Others who think that by reading them, it's just like they're living what they are reading.

But obviously, if you go to a car mechanic, would you rather go to the mechanic who has read 2000 books on engine repair and never actually repaired an engine; or would you prefer the mechanic who has read 2 books on engine repair and successfully repaired 2000 engines?

To understand mystic truths intellectually is utterly worthless, it is not a real understanding, not unless one goes out and does the practice.

Krishna reassures that if you do the practice, even a little, just by attempting you will be moving ahead.

But someone who studies and reads and absorbs quotes of scripture and never bothers to attempt, never gets anywhere.

. . . .

43. Being filled with desires, including the desire for consciousness itself, but also for material comforts, these false religionists engage in elaborate ceremonies in the hope of gaining material goals.

44. Those who are attached to such things are actually deluded. They cannot focus their consciousness on enlightenment; they will never transcend their minds.

45. The old scriptures mostly relate to the states of material being, the gunas. But you should attempt to transcend these gunas altogether, Arjuna. Go beyond duality, in a pure state of existence, free from notions of desire, centred in your soul.

46. That which can be found in a drop of water can also be found in the vast ocean. Likewise, all that can be known in studying religion can be understood in a true way by a man who has become aware of the Brahman, the supreme consciousness.

v. 43-46

Religion, and all religious study, is like a drop of water. But it is only that: a drop. Those who misinterpret the scriptures as the be all and end all, or who mistake listening to and learning the quotations of great teachers as being the real understanding are mistaking a raindrop for an ocean.

Books on religion are products of intellect; and mainstream religions are mostly concerned with intellectual discussions about morality (the gunas), about right and wrong behaviour, not about awareness.

Only awareness, not intellect, is the ocean.

Only in practice of sadhana, of one's spiritual path, can you find the ocean; the ocean is not in a book.

. . . .

47. It is certainly right of you to follow your duties in society, but do it without lust of result. You should not perform actions for the sake of some desired result, nor should you seek to avoid action for the sake of some desire.

48. Act according to your true nature, in a balanced state. Give up your attachments to desires of success, or fear of failure, Arjuna. Being balanced, taking all things equally, this is Yoga. This is being united.

v. 47-48

Being United is the same, in its mystical definition, as mastering Yoga, and both are the same as the state of spiritual Love.

To obtain this spiritual Love, one must be in balance in their life, in their material pursuits and works, in their mind, in their heart, and in their spirit.

. . . .

49. Leave all of your harmful Karma far behind, by becoming united to Enlightenment. This is called Buddha-Yoga, Conqueror of the World. Try to surrender to this consciousness. Do not try to hold on to false desires for that which is unreal.

50. One who is in consciousness can be freed, even in this very life, from concern about all good or bad results. Thus, for the sake of being united, follow this art of Yoga in all you do.

51. Great mystics can give up all Karma and its consequences by entering this state of consciousness. They are freed from the restrictions of birth and death, and reach a state that is beyond any suffering.

52. When your consciousness takes you beyond the dark forest of illusion, then you will no longer need to rely on seeking knowledge or on what you already think you know.

v. 49-52

When you are in a closed room with no windows, you cannot know if it is sunny or dark outside, if it's raining or clear.

You can make up all kinds of fantasies in your head about one thing or the other, and even if your guesses end up being correct, they were still only fantasies. The correctness was only by coincidence, because you didn't really know. You were only guessing.

But the moment you actually open the door and step through it, you know. Then there is no need for guesswork, you will be able to experience directly whether it's bright or dark, cold or warm, sunny or raining.

Likewise when you let yourself be united to awareness, and can see reality in the moment as it truly is. Then the need for intellectual 'answers' or your own personal guesswork about what life is like will become completely unnecessary, and you will realize how untrue those things are compared to simply observing the Real.

. . . .

53. When your interest in religion is no longer motivated by your desires, you will achieve absolute transcendental enlightenment. Then you have achieved union.

v. 53

For most people, their religion is motivated by desires. It is desire to be special, or be powerful, or to know an answer, or to feel safe, or to escape their suffering, or to have a place to belong, or countless other reasons.

It is only when you are doing mystical practice for its own sake, with no lust of result (no expectation that you will get what you personally are seeking out of it) that you will start to be able to truly see.

. . . .

54. *Arjuna said:*

How do you recognize someone who is in this state, Krishna? How does one in this state speak? How does he sit? How does he walk?

v. 54

Here Arjuna asks a classic question of a mystical seeker. How to know what kind of man is awake? How can one tell? How does he walk?

. . . .

55. *The Blessed One said:*

One such as this is free of any kind of investments, Son of Partha, and free of mental notions. Purely centred in his soul, fulfilled. One who obtains this is said to have achieved awareness.

56. One who is surrounded by miseries without himself being distressed, one who is surrounded by happiness without himself being invested, free from desire, fear or anger. He whose awareness is steady, he is called a mystic.

57. One who avoids sentimentality, regardless of the situation, takes good or bad results without pride or envy, he is in a state of awareness.

58. When he can draw inside himself, like the turtle draws its limbs into its shell, separating the senses from the sensed, he is in a state of awareness.

59. Some abstain from the material sources of pleasure for the sake of appearing religious, but will secretly keep lusting for these things. But one who actually gives up the lust for these things, he will experience a vastly greater pleasure.

v. 55-59

Krishna's answer is that an awakened person is free of notions besides what is real. He is centred. And such a person is thus able to be present and do what is necessary in any given situation, without bringing himself and his own ideas into it. His awareness is steady.

But Krishna also warns, because he realized that Arjuna would fail to understand, that what he is not saying is that an awakened person is an ascetic, a renunciate. That is not it at all. An awakened person is someone who is fully in the world and in life, doing exactly what pleases him, but without any vested interest or lust of result.

On the other hand, those who tell you that they are renunciates, who are trying to make a big show of how they don't 'need' any material things, they who have not given these up, are only fakers.

Those who are hypocrites are not aware.

. . . .

60. Son of Kunti, even while trying to be a man of consciousness, the senses can become agitated and the mind can throw you off track.

61. Keep all these senses under control. They should all be focused upon me. One who can thus dedicate all his senses to a single focus is in a state of awareness.

v. 60-61

Krishna tells Arjuna to make use of him, to rely on him, as Arjuna's Guru. The Guru is present to be used to help keep you on track, and centred.

. . . .

62. One who is undisciplined in the senses will develop attachment. Attachment leads to desire. Desire leads to anger.

63. Anger leads to deludedness. Deludedness leads to false perceptions. And one who perceives the unreal cannot be aware. Such a person will fall.

64. One who has become free of desire and repulsion, who does not allow his senses to be wildly led by outer lusts, he has come under the control of his own soul, and has attained freedom of the soul. He has obtained a divine blessing.

65. Achieving this blessing leads to the end of all misery. For one who is in such bliss, enlightenment will soon follow.

66. Enlightenment cannot happen if you are not unified. Nor can bliss. Nor peace. And how can there be joy without peace?

v. 62-66

If you are not total, then you can't possibly be fully aware of the moment. To be total, you must unite yourself. If you are not trying to unite yourself, you will get distracted by your own conflicting desires. You will be frustrated by not getting what you think you want, and you will start making up stories and excuses for yourself, to try to hide from or justify your failure to choose unity.

Uniting is not easy. It is very hard.

It is a hard choice mainly because it requires giving up all the pretty fantasy stories, all the sentimentalism that you had created for yourself in your mind.

. . . .

67. If one is being led by the senses, constantly distracted by one's mind, one's awareness is lost. One becomes like a boat on a windswept ocean.

68. Thus, Great Warrior, one who can make the distinction between the senses and the sensed, he is in awareness.

69. When others are in the dark of the night, such a person is awake and in control. And what others consider being awake, the mystic knows to be nothing but the dark of night.

70. As the oceans are constantly being filled by water flowing into them, so is one constantly being filled with desires. One who is trying to fulfill all his desires will never be at peace.

71. But in giving up desires, living free of lust or a sense of material possessiveness, you lose the ego. You attain peace.

72. Son of Partha, one who is unaware of the real can never gain this spiritual state. But if you can obtain this state, even at the very end of life, you will reach the divine Nirvana.

v. 67-72

If you let yourself be governed by those pretty fantasies, you are lost in a turbulent ocean of your ego. You cannot possibly force life to make the world be what you would think it should be based on those fairy tales of your head.

And your head will keep producing more fairy tales, more thoughts of 'If only.' If only you could have a certain thing, or do a certain thing, or be a certain thing, then you would be at peace.

This is nonsense! It is materialism.

You must stop seeking these fantasy things, and look at the real world, naked as it is, and not become lost by your fairy tales.

To do this, you must be able to make a distinction between the senses and the sense, between what you would like to see, and what is actually there.

Focus on what is here, in the moment; on what is real, and you will have peace.

Chapter 3
The Yoga of Action (Karma)

1. *Arjuna said:*

If you think that awareness is better than actions born of desire, Krishna, why are you trying to cause me to commit such horrid acts?

2. Your words are clear yet they confuse me. So please tell me now directly, what must I do that will benefit me?

v. 1-2

Arjuna does not yet wish to admit that his actions have ulterior motives, that he is not wishing to leave the battlefield out of some kind of altruism, and that in fact he wishes to leave only because he is angry that he will not be able to get what he personally desires out of it.

Arjuna wanted a kingdom, a peaceful prosperous kingdom to rule in; but it was clear to him that after the battle was over there would be nothing left worth calling a kingdom, the devastation would be so total.

That is why he was fighting; he had no real concern with the deeper reasons why this battle needed to be fought, to save the world from the darkness of the Kauravas.

So he was fighting for himself, not in harmony with the Divine, but he was trying to pretend that his concerns were altruistic philosophical concerns.

3. *The Blessed One said:*

As I have already told you, my faultless friend, there are two paths to follow in this world. There is the Yoga of awareness followed by the spiritual philosophers, and the Yoga of devotional acts followed by the mystics.

4. You cannot become free of Karma by avoiding actions. Nor can you gain success by mere renunciation.

v. 3-4

Krishna replies to Arjuna that his claims are nonsense, they only hold up to the unenlightened mind. So many of the excuses people use to justify their own falsehoods are based on meaningless drivel. An awakened person, or even anyone with some measure of awareness, can quickly see through these things, and see that people are mainly trying to lie to themselves.

. . . .

5. For there is not even a single moment in this life when you are free from some kind of action. You are forced to be in constant activity of some kind, merely by virtue of being alive. This is the reality of the gunas.

6. Even if you control all the five senses through mental willpower, you are still constantly engaged in thoughts and desires. Anyone who believes he can truly do nothing is a foolish soul, a false religionist.

v. 5-6

Krishna makes it clear that there is no way to 'escape' from the body, or from materialism, or from action in the world.

Most institutional religions of the world try to claim that there is a way to do this, that somehow the problem of humanity is found in their possessions, or their bodies, or their actions, anything but themselves.

There is no way to escape action. Even not doing anything is an action in this world, by nature of your very being.

Thus Arjuna's arguments are poppycock.

. . . .

7. One who starts to control the senses with the mind, Arjuna, by focusing the senses upon uniting, will reduce attachment and be by far the better.

8. Take whatever action is required. To take action is better than to avoid it. You cannot even maintain your body without taking action.

9. Actions done for spiritual purposes are better than any other form of actions. Son of Kunti, action to this end will serve excellently to free you from attachments.

v. 7-9

Taking action is better than pretending to be inactive. You can never actually be inactive. Even total inaction is an active choice. Thus, why bother pretending? Krishna says to do whatever you are meant to do and get on with it.

But he also adds: actions that are done for spiritual purposes are better than regular actions, because they are even more total.

The problem with inaction is that it is never total.

Regular action is also not total, however, because part of you is focused on the action, and part is focused on your intended result.

Spiritual actions, thus, are actions where you are dedicating your action to life, doing the action for its own sake, and not for any motive, without any lust of result.

. . . .

10. In the ancient times, having performed the spiritual rituals, the god Brahma said, "By these rituals you shall be increasingly prosperous. Let the spirit bring to you all good things."

11. The divine spirits are pleased by ritual sacrifices. These spirits will reward you in return. By this mutual service, you will obtain the greatest of blessings.

12. The spirits will provide you with all of the necessities of life, being in turn given what they need by your rituals performed in gratitude. But one who receives what is given in life by the spirits, without in turn giving thankful ritual, is certainly a thief.

v. 10-12

What is Krishna talking about here, when he speaks of spirits, and of ritual sacrifices?

He is quoting the god Brahma from ancient scriptures, and trying to help Arjuna understand what they really meant, and what their real purpose was, and how they were corrupted over time and by religions.

Krishna was not in favour of the Vedic priests of that era, just like teachers in most times and places find themselves against the priesthoods of organized religions, because these priesthoods take real teachings and turn them into false teachings.

The priests were claiming that Brahma (God) had said that if you perform formal rituals, you will end up being rewarded with material prosperity.

Krishna is very clever in his statement – he does not just deny. Instead he redirects that quoted scripture to mean something totally different than what the priests say, and closer to reality.

He says that the way you live your life must be a ritual, it must be an act of devotion. That the 'ritual sacrifices' you must make are not burning incense in a temple, but how you sacrifice lust of result. In that way, each action you take, free of lust of result, is a devotion to God.

The 'spirits,' life, God, give you everything you need. If you respond with this devotion of Karma Yoga, making your actions free of lust of result, then you will benefit.

But taking what the spirit gives you, and then still refusing to make that sacrifice will make you a thief.

What is more, it will mean you will not be able to appreciate their gift. Because what you are really stealing from is your own peace. You are stealing from yourself, by refusing to accept the gift of life, and trying to steal away your own fantasies from life instead.

. . . .

13. Devotees who eat food that has been purified by the ritual of devotional gratitude are relieved of any guilt associated with that food. But those who eat gluttonously and without gratitude or awareness are committing terrible deeds.

14. Our bodies grow from food. Our food grows from the rain. The rain is thanks to the spirits. We must act to honour them.

15. You should know that all actions come from Brahma, they are a direct manifestation of the Divine. So Brahma is everywhere, and will always be present in our rituals.

16. Therefore one who does not follow the way of ritual in this life, one who lives shamefully only for the pursuit of desires, is wasting his life, Son of Partha.

v. 13-16

If you are too busy pursuing your desires to be able to appreciate the food you eat, the rain, the life you have before you, then you have wasted the greatest of all gifts.

Brahma exists in the world around you. If you claim to want to find him, you must look to these things, as they are, here in the present. Not in how you would wish them to be in your mind.

. . . .

17. However, anyone who finds bliss in his soul will enlighten his soul. A man who is satisfied with his own being will not have to perform any outer spiritual actions.

18. Certainly the performance of his duties would have no purpose, but also there is no purpose for him to avoid the performance of his duties. For in all of this world he need not seek any purpose whatsoever.

19. Thus, always without attachment, do whatever duties you will. By doing all work without attachment, a man achieves the highest.

v. 17-19

Thus the formal rituals of the Vedic priests are not any more or less meaningful than the ritual of eating your food. If you practice Karma Yoga, then you are free to do your will.

. . . .

20. By doing such work it is known that King Janaka and other lords achieved their great spiritual powers. And you must also consider that the lesser people will be observing how you act; you must consider them.

21. Whatever a man in a position of respect does, certainly the common people will see it as an example. Whatever he does, all the world will follow.

22. Son of Partha, there is no duty in all the Three Worlds that I must perform. There is nothing that I want, nothing I could gain. But clearly I too take action.

23. If ever I did not take action, or perform actions carelessly, all men would follow my example in every respect, Son of Partha.

24. All of these worlds would be put into ruin if I did not set an example. I would be the cause of undesirable births, and all life would have to be destroyed.

25. The ignorant are greatly attached to taking karmic action. Scion of Bharata, the wise must do the same. In this way, they can slowly lead the common people to detachment.

26. They must strive not to lead the foolish away from awareness; they should not give the foolish cause to avoid working. Instead, the wise must give them some work that will lead them in the right direction.

v. 20-26

Krishna is saying that even masters continue to exist, to be in the world, and to keep living their lives in a way that can serve as an example to others.

To someone who is aware, any action is as good as any other action. However, it is important to be able to interact with people in regular society, so as to be able to communicate truth to them.

. . . .

27. In the material world, the gunas cause all kinds of activities to occur. Deluded by the ego, the soul believes that he is the one who is acting.

28. But the one who knows truth, Great Warrior, he understands the gunas and Karma, and the difference between the senses and that which is sensed. With this perspective he will avoid attachment.

29. These elements of reality (gunas) will delude people, and they become attached to actions and desires in the material world. These people are either lacking in wisdom, or they are lazy. One who is wise should not try to disturb them.

30. Surrender all actions unto me by being conscious, aware of the self. Be without lusting for any result, be without possessiveness, and free from reluctance, fight.

31. Those who follow my instructions regularly are human beings performing divine acts. With devotion and without desire, they all become free from the bondage of Karma.

32. However, those who out of jealous desire do not follow my instructions regularly, they are foolish in every way. Know this well, they are all ruined without consciousness.

33. Even an intelligent man, though he may try otherwise, is still controlled by the elements of the material world. All living beings are subject to this, so what good will self-restriction do?

v. 27-33

If you try to be an ascetic, to restrict yourself or pretend that you do not have desires, then you are leading yourself to ruin. You cannot reach truth by starting from falsehood. You must start from whatever truth you have. The first truth is that you do have desire. There is no way to escape this.

If people are able to follow the Guru's instruction, to admit their desires but practice awareness, then they will be able to achieve a state where they are freed from the attachment to their actions.

If on the other hand they do not listen to what the Guru advises, and half-heartedly 'follow' a Guru while still clinging to their own ideas of spirituality, they will be lost.

. . . .

34. Of the senses and the sensed, of what you desire and also what you wish to avoid, you should put all of these under some control. You should never be controlled by them, or else these things will distract you from being conscious.

35. It is better to follow your own discipline, even badly, than it would be to follow someone else's discipline even if you did it perfectly. Even if your own path leads you to death, it is better. For following the path of others is more dangerous than death.

v. 34-35

How do these lines make sense with what Krishna just said before? First he is saying, "follow the instructions of the Guru", and then he is immediately afterwards saying it is better to follow your own way!

The key to this is to understand that you do not know your own way; it is the Guru's job to show you the means to learn this way.

At the beginning, you are full of 'ways' that are given to you by others: these are dogmas. If you seek to follow these, thinking them your own way, you will end up acting in resistance to the Guru's instructions, because the Guru's job is to shatter your dogmas.

The very best situation is if you know yourself.

But until you can, then the next best thing is to work with the Guru at uncovering yourself.

However, if you cannot surrender your own dogmas and really listen to the Guru, it is better to follow your dogmas, follow them through to their conclusion, than to half-heartedly listen to the Guru and half-heartedly follow these dogmas at the same time.

Then you are divided, and resisting yourself.

If you cling to an idea that tells you that you will be rich, or loved, or spiritual, and the Master shows you how to let go of it, if you can let go of it you will benefit greatly!

But if you cannot, and keep trying to listen to the Guru, in the back of your mind you will still be holding onto your idea thinking "if I'd just done that it might have worked."

If you are stuck in that frame of thinking, it's better to go and try your idea.

If you realize later, by experience, that your idea will not work, then you can finally drop it and come back to the Guru.

Do not be half-and-half.

. . . .

36. *Arjuna said:*

Then what is it that motivates a man toward false action? Even if they do not wish to, it seems that men are drawn to it by force, Scion of Virshni.

v. 36

Arjuna asks a very important question, and it is clear that he is finally beginning to be able to listen to Krishna. Arjuna asks why it is that men carry their dogmas.

. . . .

37. *The Blessed One said:*

This is desire and anger, born out of the Raja guna (the element of all-consuming passion) that leads men to great error. Know that in this world, it is the great enemy.

38. Just as fire is concealed within smoke, or a mirror concealed by dust, or as an embryo is concealed in the womb, so does reality become concealed in desires.

39. By this is consciousness hidden from the self. It is the eternal enemy. Also, Son of Kunti, one is never fulfilled in the fire of lust.

40. The senses, perceptions, and the mind are called the thrones of desire. Lust deludes all of these, hiding the true awareness of the embodied being.

v.37-40

The 'Lust' that Krishna is talking about is not sexual lust; it is attachment. Desire. The Lust of Results.

In life, human beings who are asleep are disconnected from God.

They are desperate to find that connection again, to come back to the source.

This separation has happened because humans have a divine level of perception but an animal body and brain.

We are an intermediate step in evolution.

And the result is that we can sometimes sense free action, but we are easily bound by animal patterns of instinctual behaviour.

Society encourages these patterns, creating Conditionings that allow people to be productive and controlled.

In that desperation to connect to the Divine, we attach ourselves to the things our attachments tell us will make us happy.

We become attached to the idea that we can make life conform to the way we would imagine 'perfection' to be.

We can understand the concept of perfection, but we have no real familiarity with it, and end up defining this perfection via our conditionings of what we imagine we'd like life to be.

This is the cause of human ignorance.

. . . .

41. Thus you must begin by disciplining the senses, Lord of the Bharatas. You must curb this great symbol of falsehood, which destroys both awareness and knowledge of the self.

42. The senses are said to be superb, but the mind is said to be greater still, and awareness is even greater than the mind. But the centre is even greater than awareness.

43. Thus awareness leads to centred consciousness, by focusing and steadying the mind. Great Warrior, you will conquer the greatest enemy if you conquer desire.

v. 41-43

The Discipline Krishna speaks of here is not restriction. It is not trying to repress your feelings or your desires. It is the discipline that evolves naturally, when you first witness your senses with your mind, then practice that witnessing with awareness.

Krishna explains the hierarchy of enlightenment here: the senses must be processed by the mind, observed through awareness, and this will lead to the centre. You cannot get to the Centre as step one, you must follow a process of techniques that will lead you to first examine the mind (through self-inquiry) and to practice awareness (meditation).

Then you can focus the centred self on the moment, and in that way overcome your lust for result.

Chapter 4
The Yoga of Discerning Wisdom (jnana)

1. *The Blessed One said:*

I taught this Yoga to the Sun, Vivasvan, and he taught Manu, the father of humanity. Manu then taught it to King Ikshvaku.

2. Thus, one after the other received this teaching, understood by Kings. But in time this knowledge of the great Yoga became scattered, Defeater of your Enemies.

3. This very same ancientmost Yoga I am speaking to you today. You are my devotee, you are my friend also, thus this Mystery is transcendental.

v. 1-3

Krishna is saying here that this Yoga, taught by the Enlightened Master since the beginning of human history, is one and the same, in all cultures and times. The essential teaching of mysticism is the same in every place, and every teacher is trying to say the same thing.

The nature of how his teaching is delivered always varies, based on the culture and place he is in. Each teacher will deliver the teaching wrapped in the context that is most useful for the type of students he will attract, based on their culture and conditionings.

Also, in every time and place, the teaching will become deformed after a teacher has died and his school gets turned slowly into a hollow movement or religion.

4. *Arjuna said:*

You were born much later than the Sun, so how am I to understand that in the beginning of time you had taught him?

5. *The Blessed One said:*

I have had many births, and you as well Arjuna. I know them all, but you do not remember them, Defeater of your Enemies.

6. Though I was unborn, my undiluted soul existed as the transcendental form of myself within the great Lord. Being in this state, it is my choice when I incarnate my soul into this world.

7. Whenever and wherever true spirituality has become deteriorated, Scion of Bharata, and there is a predominance of false religion, I will appear at that time.

8. I will help the true students, and I will cause strife to the wrongdoers. I will remind people of the true way. I will appear age after age.

9. Anyone who realizes the reality of my transcendental birth and actions will never take birth again in this form. Instead he too will connect to me, Arjuna.

v. 4-9

Krishna is saying that the teacher is always the embodiment of the same Truth that appears in every time and culture. There is never a time in human history, or a society, where there is not a Guru present to provide the experience of the Real.

And from the point of view of the awakened being, it is not his 'reality' or his 'truth,' it is the one and same truth, and he is one with all of the other teachers of history.

An enlightened being will innately be able to understand the real teaching behind the corrupted versions of history or religion, and may express understandings or interpretations of other teachers or teachings, that may not come from any scripture or history book.

Everyone who attains to awakening becomes one with all of these teachers.

. . . .

10. Free of attachment, fear, and anger, fully connected to me, in me, by awareness purified of many wrongdoings, he will obtain spiritual love with me.

11. All who surrender unto me, them I surely reward. All men follow my path, Son of Partha, in every respect.

12. Desiring great power and success in their material actions, men make sacrifices to the spirits. Those who do so are certainly rewarded in their limited material ambitions.

13. The four divisions of human society were created by me, so that any man would do the work best suited to his dominant element. Although you may realize me to be the father of this, you must also realize that I am the eternal, which is free of action.

14. I am never affected by any actions, nor do I have any ambitions. Thus any who realizes me will never become attached to the Karma of actions.

15. Thus, knowing that actions were done by past masters who indeed attained awakening, take action now, as the ancient ones did.

v. 10-15

Every person in this world is seeking Love, that is Union, with the Divine. The things they pursue in the world, what they believe to be their desires, are merely symptoms of that spiritual longing. Each person will naturally be engaging in the type of activity that is possible, and that is limited, by the level of his or her awareness.

. . . .

16. Even the intelligent are deluded as to what is action and what is inaction. I will explain action to you, so that in being aware of this you will be free from misfortune.

17. You must understand which action is right and which is wrong. You must understand when not to act, and when to enter action.

18. When you can see non-doing in doing, and doing in non-doing, then you have gained awareness in the world. You will be in unity, even if you take all kinds of actions.

v. 16-18

The greatest difficulty to one who is not aware is the inability to be natural, because such a person no longer understands which action is natural and which isn't. Sometimes you will do things thinking that you are being 'Natural,' when in fact you are being driven by your ego. Other times people will avoid action for the same reasons, thinking it is their awareness that is guiding them, but in fact it is their fears or conditionings.

To be able to discriminate between natural action and inaction and unnatural action and inaction, you must be able to see in what cases your actions are actually purely unmotivated, and in which cases your actions or inactions are guided by other external factors.

. . . .

19. One whose efforts are free of lust of result, who gives his actions as sacrifice to the Divine, he will be called wise by the awakened ones.

20. Having given up the lust of result, being satisfied without any false security, such a person will be in non-doing, even though he takes many actions.

21. Focusing the mind and the soul, without lust of result, giving up all sense of possession, only working for what is needed to maintain the body and soul, one doing so will never go wrong.

22. Fulfilled by the good things that come of their own accord, beyond duality, free of jealousy, equally steady in success or failure, one doing so may take action and remain free from reaction.

23. One who is detached from the elements, who is free, whose wisdom is in awareness, who acts for the sake of gratitude, his work is entirely unified.

v. 19-23

If you can do without doing, you can take action or inaction for its own sake without ulterior motives, then you are being natural. Then you can act not from fears and concerns of security, or looking to gain some further thing. Then your very actions, your life in the moment, are their own security and their own reward. This is freedom.

. . . .

24. Brahma is found in the sacrifice, and Brahma is found in the fire (where the sacrifice is performed). And Brahma is found in the one who makes the sacrifice. Brahma is certainly attainable to any whose actions are united with Brahma.

25. Some worship the spirits through ritual, but mystics worship perfectly through the fire of Brahma, thus making sacrifice of sacrifice.

v. 24-25

In the Vedic religion, sacrifices were performed with fire offerings. Krishna is saying that Brahma, the Divine, exists equally in the sacrifice being offered, in the flame that receives the sacrifice, and in the person who is making the offering.

So Krishna is saying the Divine isn't found in religion. It's found everywhere, in everyone.

You can worship with the rituals of religion, but offering up a calf, or flowers, or incense, or money, or prayers is not the same as offering yourself. You can offer yourself by making every act you take an act of awareness, an act free of ulterior motives, free of lust of result.

. . . .

26. Others practice restraint of the senses, offering their senses, like hearing, to the fire. But others offer the sound that is heard by the senses to the fire.

27. Also, others control the actions of the senses, and the breath. But others practice the focusing of their soul to union; they offer their urge for awareness in the fire of sacrifice.

v. 26-27

Some people try to practice self-denial, or rigorous physical or mental disciplines. A mystic will instead offer his very desire for spiritual attainment, giving that up to the moment.

. . . .

28. Others sacrifice their possessions, their comforts, in the vows of the eightfold discipline. Others take the strict vow of sacrifice in wisdom, in the advancement of awareness.

v. 28

Some people will try to give up material possessions. But a mystic will understand that this gets you nowhere if you do not instead give up your ignorance, and offer up the willingness to keep trying to increase your awareness of the moment.

. . . .

29. Others offer the ingoing and outgoing breath, or stopping the movement of the ingoing to the outgoing breath. Others are drawn to the trance of stopping all breath, or giving up food and offering the ingoing breath as sacrifice to the outgoing.

30. All of these methods of sacrifice and what are understood as purification rituals may appear different. But those who gain some success in any of these do come closer to the eternal space of Brahma.

31. For those who follow no practices there is nothing on this world or the other, Best of the Kurus.

32. Thus various kinds of practices have been spread by word of mouth from the priests. Learn of all of them, because awareness of one will lead to freedom.

33. But greater than the sacrificing of material possessions is the offering of being aware, punisher of your enemies. Son of Partha, all actions reach their end in totality.

v. 29-33

There are all kinds of spiritual disciplines. And trying to practice any of these is better than doing nothing at all. Someone who does not have any spiritual awareness will not offer anything at all, and will gain nothing.

Someone who is seeking might look in many places, many of these places will be imperfect or only offer a beginning, but everyone has to begin somewhere. The place where all of these paths lead, if one does not get stuck in them, is to the place of being aware; of letting your life and your everyday activities in the moment be your sacrifice to the Divine.

. . . .

34. Try to understand these things by approaching one who is wise, by humbly asking him, and providing service to him. He can initiate you into awareness, because he is aware and can see what is real.

v. 34

For most people, a Guru is a vital help in being able to understand how to keep moving, to keep getting closer to this state of awareness.

. . . .

35. Son of Pandu, you shall gain freedom from ever being deluded again. You will see the great soul (Atman) that is in all things, or in other words that is in me.

36. Even if you are the greatest sinner of all sinners, with the boat of awareness you will be able to go beyond all such sins and completely cross the ocean of suffering.

37. Just as firewood in a blazing fire turns to ashes, Arjuna, in the fire of awareness all material Karma similarly turns to ashes.

38. There is nothing that exists in this world that can be compared in holiness to awareness. He who gains experience in Yoga over time will enjoy the bliss of the soul.

39. A dedicated man will gain awareness. He will be very drawn to it, and focus his senses in it. Having gained awareness in his senses, he very soon gains a deeper spiritual peace.

v. 35-39

There is no person in the world who cannot benefit from awareness. There is no action one can take that will lock you away from awareness forever. Some people are in a little darkness; others are in great darkness. But awareness is the light that banishes all darkness.

. . . .

40. For a fool who rebukes this path, with no dedication, or one who is filled with doubts and cannot trust, it will be very difficult for him to find happiness in this world or the other.

41. One who renounces lust of result through Yoga will cut down his doubts with the sword of awareness. When you are centred in your soul your actions will never bind you, o Conqueror.

42. Thus cut off your doubts with the weapon of the soul. They are born of ignorance, and cover your heart. Centred in Yoga, Scion of Bharata, stand and fight!

v. 40-42

Your doubts are like darkness, but to try to repress the doubts, or try to deny the doubts, or to wallow in doubt are all paths that lead nowhere.

There is one simple thing that will cut through all doubt, and that is the experience of the real.

If you have a sealed box in front of you, and do not know what is in it, your mind could make up all kinds of ideas about it.

You could explore the outside of the box, you could read labels, you could shake the box.

You could have a lot of doubts about what is inside, or you may try very hard to convince yourself you've figured it out.

But the only way to dispel all doubts forever is to open the box.

Awareness is opening that box, and directly experiencing truth.

Chapter 5
The Yoga of Awareness in Action
(Karma samkhya)

1. *Arjuna said:*

Krishna, first you are giving praise to the renunciation of activities, then you give praise to Yoga. Please tell me definitively which one is more beneficial.

2. *The Blessed One said:*

Renunciation of work or the work of Yoga, both of them lead to the way of openness. But of the two, the work of Yoga is better than the renunciation of all work.

3. He should be understood always as the renouncer, who neither rejects nor desires. Free of duality, Great Warrior, he is always happily liberated from bondage.

v. 1-3

Renunciation, 'Sannyas,' has falsely come to mean someone who abandons all his material wealth. Krishna teaches that the real renunciate is someone who renounces attachment and revulsion. If you neither reject nor desire.

And rejection and desire are the same: two sides of the same coin. The things you reject, that you hate, your rejection is always motivated by something you desire.

If you reject something, it is because of your desires or your fears.

So there is no renunciation in rejection, just a reverse kind of attachment, a reverse kind of desire.

To really renounce you have to give up being attached one way or the other.

. . . .

4. The ill-informed say that Yoga is different from witnessing. When you are involved in one, you are completely enjoying the results of both.

5. Whatever achievement is gained by witnessing, one can also attain through Yoga. You can attain unity through either method, if you have eyes to see.

v. 4-5

Witnessing and 'Yoga' (the spiritual discipline of uniting to the Divine), are one and the same thing. You can only renounce attachment and unite with the Divine by first observing yourself.

. . . .

6. But simply renouncing all things without taking up Yoga, Great Warrior, can afflict you with misery. One who practices Yoga will be engaged. He can attain Brahma easily that way.

7. A pure soul practicing Yoga is centred in his soul, having conquered the senses. He will have compassion to all living beings, and though he acts he will never become attached.

v. 6-7

Renouncing without practicing awareness, without being a meditator, is worse than useless, it is harmful. If you renounce material things or pleasures out of religious dogma, or to impress people, or for whatever other reason, you will end up unbalanced.

Why is this? Because a meditator knows what is really necessary to renounce and what is not. How can someone who does not practice awareness for themselves, that is being told what to think by outside sources (be it scripture that he read or what he was told by someone) know what is right for they themselves to give up?

A meditator, someone who practices Yoga, is engaged, says Krishna. He is connected to life.

If you are not connected to life, how will you know what is natural? Doing anything else before practicing witnessing and meditation is only a recipe for leading yourself further astray.

People who practice Yoga will be centred in their senses. They won't renounce things that are not worthy of renunciation; they won't reject anything out of revulsion or hate, because they are comfortable with their bodies and their feelings.

Before renouncing anything, first you must be comfortable with yourself, with your body, with your senses; otherwise, what you do is likely to be a by-product of some kind of self-hate.

Someone who is practicing Yoga will have compassion for all living things. A person renounces without being a meditator, they will be acting out of selfish motives. They'll lack a real compassion. And you see this all the time, as the so-called religious renouncers try to force their dogma on other people, try to make other people suffer because those people don't believe in the same things the renouncers do.

These renouncers are still attached in every way that matters: They are attached to their actions. They are doing things with ulterior motives. Krishna teaches that this is not the way, that this is utterly counterproductive.

. . . .

8. One who knows reality will think: 'I am never involved in doing, even though I am seeing, hearing, feeling, smelling, eating, defecating, dreaming and breathing.'

9. Let one always consider thusly, although they may be talking, giving, taking, opening and closing, and generally involving the senses in activities.

10. Dedicate all works to Brahma. One who takes actions, but without attachment, is always free of wrongdoing, like a lotus leaf is not touched by the water upon which it rests.

11. Purified of body, mind, awareness and the senses, practitioners of Yoga perform all actions while giving up attachment. This purifies the soul.

12. One thus practicing, giving up the lust of result, achieves unswerving peace. One who does not practice this, acting with desired results in mind, will always become attached.

v. 8-12

Lotus leaves rest on top of the pond, but they are not wet. They are part of the water, but unique. They are participating, but do not forget themselves. This is why the Lotus is seen as the sign of meditation throughout the east.

The Lotus is not 'above it all.' It has not run away from the water. And its roots are in the water. It is in every way a part of the pond, it is just not submerged. The fact that it's a part of the pond is just as important as the fact that its surface remains dry and floats on the top of the water.

. . . .

13. Renouncing all activities of the mind, one who is so focused will always be blissful. In the city of nine gates (the body), one must be embodied in such a way that you desire no action nor any result.

14. The master of this city will claim no possession of it, nor cause its people (parts) to take actions. Nor will he be connected to the results of any activities, but only act naturally.

15. Likewise the greater king of all the cities (Brahma) will not accept any saintliness or sin. It is only individual beings who are deluded to believe so, their awareness clouded by ignorance.

16. However, when ignorance is destroyed by awareness, the awareness of a living being becomes like a golden dawn, revealing the highest.

v. 13-16

There is a saying in spirituality, "As above, so below." Just like the Universe does not judge, so must you not judge. The universe, life, God, accepts all that is in it. It is a delusion to think otherwise. Likewise, if you can accept what happens in your life, not in a passive way of attempting to avoiding action, but in the active way of seeing life itself as the richest gift and taking what has been given to you and using and enjoying it, then you will have a peaceful, natural existence.

. . . .

17. One whose consciousness is always thus focused, one whose soul is always thus focused, one whose trust is always thus focused, one whose total comfort is only in this, he achieves unity. By awareness all doubts are swept away.

18. Well armed with true wisdom and gentleness, the learned will see no difference in the priest, the cow, the elephant, the dog, or the outcast.

v. 17-18

Man always wants to think he is special. In particular, religious seekers want to think they are special. The dog or the elephant would not argue with you if you suggested they were of the same value as one another. The outcast, the poor person, from the lower class, might or might not argue with you; if you said (not as an insult but as an observation), that his existence is worth just as much as the existence of a dog or an elephant, that he is just as important and no more important. But a Priest?! A priest would always argue against that! If he did not, it would only be out of hypocrisy, he might agree so that people wouldn't call him arrogant, but under the surface he would be hurt. So would most rich people, so would most educated people, so would most meditators. Because all of these people, they do what they do, they seek what they seek, out of a wish to be a 'special' person.

But the Divine does not play favourites. Its Love is infinite and equal. To Brahma, from the point of view of life, the dog isn't more important than the elephant, and the priest isn't more important than the outcast.

Someone who is able to see that and truly understand that will learn how to really be wise and how to really be gentle.

. . . .

19. Those whose mind is focused on seeing the unity will certainly conquer birth and death, even in this lifetime. As Brahma is perfectly united, so shall the united be in Brahma.

20. One who is completely aware of Brahma is in Brahma. He will neither rejoice when good things happen nor will he become unhappy when bad things happen.

v. 19-20

As above, so below. If you are completely united within yourself, as Brahma is a complete unity in itself, then you will be completely united with Brahma. If you are completely aware, just as Brahma is complete awareness, then you will be completely within Brahma.

. . . .

21. One whose soul is not clouded by nonessential pleasures will enjoy the bliss of the soul. By uniting to Brahma you unite to your soul, and enjoy unlimited bliss.

22. The senses are certainly the source of pleasures, and also of suffering. All of these things shall come and all things shall pass. Son of Kunti, the enlightened never revel in such things.

v. 21-22

You only have as much room for the Divine as you are willing to make for the Divine. What you give is what you get. The more cluttered your awareness is by what you desire, the less room there is for God. Good things and bad things come from the world; you should not reject, but you should not get lost in these things. You should let go of your priorities if you want to make room for the Divine.

. . . .

23. One who is able to tolerate desire and anger born of lusts, in this very body before it dies – he who can accept it all will find happiness in his humanity.

v. 23

You cannot escape desire, anger, or lust. If you are able to tolerate it, not fight it, not cling to it; then you can find peace. Peace isn't found when you run from anger. Peace is found when you can tolerate anger within yourself without letting it overwhelm you, and without trying to rebuke it. If you can do this before you die, then you will understand how to be human, and you will learn happiness. Not the thing you are chasing that you think is happiness, but real happiness as it exists in embracing the Real.

. . . .

24. One who has inner happiness, focusing inwardly and enjoying the inner world, he is certainly a mystic. Being aware of the reality of Brahma, he obtains enlightenment in Brahma.

25. Those who are inwardly active achieve enlightenment in Brahma. They are free of any wrongdoing. They have destroyed duality, are focused on the soul, and are doing a service to all living things.

26. Those who are free of desire and anger, the saintly ones who have control of consciousness, the ones who have become aware of the soul, they are assured to gain enlightenment in Brahma.

v. 24-26

If you have destroyed duality in yourself, only then can you serve Life. All living things benefit by being around one who is whole, because in his wholeness he creates the space for others to become more whole in themselves.

Real service, divine service, is when you act as an aid to give others the chance to become more aware in themselves. Anything you do to this end is service. If you do not achieve this, then whatever you do is not a service at all.

. . . .

27. Suspend nonessential sensory forces, like sound and eyesight, in the space between the eyes. Keep the incoming and outgoing breath in the nostrils.

v. 27

Here Krishna is detailing a method of meditation, of awareness. He is saying, watch what you see and what you hear, witness your breath.

If you can remember to do even one of these two things, you will be meditative.

Just remember, as you are observing things, looking at things, or as you are hearing things, to watch yourself too, as you hear and as you see.

Or watch yourself breathing, in and out. Do not force your breath, do not hold your breath, just watch it.

This is all you need to be meditative.

. . . .

28. In this way controlling the senses, awareness, and the mind, the seeker will be destined for liberation. He will discard desires, fear and anger. He will certainly be forever free.

29. The receiver of offerings and sacrifices, the great lord of all the worlds and their rulers, the benefactor of all living beings, one who knows me as this will achieve peace.

v. 28-29

If you are being meditative, if you are watching the breath, then you cannot get lost in unnatural behaviour. As long as you are being meditative, you cannot act except in each moment.

Thus, you become free.

If beyond that, you can see the Divine in all things, from the Guru to your family to strangers to animals, all the way to the rocks and the sand, then you will also be at peace. If you see the Divine in yourself, and the Divine in everything else, how can you not be at peace? If you are watching these things, then you are united, and you know that you are part of everything, and everything a part of you, and there is no need for inner struggle. Everything you are and everything you do becomes a part of God.

Chapter 6
The Yoga of Meditation (dhyana)

1. *The Blessed One said:*

He who acts according to what must be done, without being drawn into lust of result, he is a Sannyasin and a mystic. Not so, he who does no work and thus no devotion either.

2. What they call Sannyas (renunciation), you must know as uniting (Yoga), Son of Pandu. Certainly, no mystic can become anything without giving up the divided desires of the self.

v. 1-2

It is not enough to call yourself a Sannyasin or a mystic to be one. It's not about what you wear, or about changing your name, or about cutting your hair, or growing it long. Reading many books about religion will not do it. The only thing that will make one a mystic is to do what must be done, to do work and devotion.

3. For the beginner at Yoga, practicing a discipline is said to be the means. For one who has attained in Yoga, the cessation of all such activities is said to be the means.

4. When one does not involve himself in the senses or in activities, renouncing all desires, at that time one is said to have reached the height of Yoga.

v. 3-4

If you are starting the process of mysticism, then developing regular work and discipline is vital. When you have done absolutely everything you can, you are an adept.

An adept is one who has attained some awareness, some ability in mysticism, but has not yet awakened.

For the adept, the only way is the way of ceasing all his disciplines, because in the end, the final desire that must be overcome is the desire to be enlightened.

. . . .

5. One must free the soul from the mind, never allowing the soul to be clouded. The mind can be the great friend of the soul, but the great enemy as well.

6. For the soul that is in control of the mind, the mind is certainly the friend. But for the soul who has failed to be in control of the mind, due to dividedness, the mind is the greatest enemy.

7. One who has triumphed over the mind has obtained peace. He has completely entered the supersoul. He will be the same in heat, cold, happiness, sadness, honour, and dishonour.

8. By awareness and experience, a soul is focused in his senses, centred, and fulfilled. It is said such a mystic is greatly advanced. He will see that pebbles, great stones, and pure gold are all the same.

v. 5-8

The mind makes a wonderful servant and a horrible master. If your mind is the servant and not the master, then you will see that everything outside of the moment is the same. A piece of rock, a nugget of gold, in your mind they are precisely the same. They're illusions.

. . . .

9. One who is highly advanced will be able to see enlightenment in allies, patrons, enemies, neutral parties, messengers, those who envy him, his relatives, those said to be saintly, and those said to be sinners.

10. A mystic must constantly be meditative, his entire soul in a place of aloneness. Alone, always watching the mind, not drawn toward anything, free of possessiveness.

v. 9-10

If you can recognize the Divine in everyone else, then you can obtain awareness. This is not easy; it's very hard to see the Divine sincerely in people your mind has told you are ignorant, or that they are inferior, or that they are evil. It is not easy to see the Divine when the mind wants you to think that you are more special than everyone else, because if everyone else were just as divine as you, you would not be special.

But if you can do this, then you will become aware.

. . . .

11. On holy ground, his soul seated firmly. Neither too high nor too low, on sacred grass covered with soft cloth and deerskin.

v. 11

Sitting neither too high nor too low means to be at the human level. Remember, Krishna has said "the soul must be centred", he is not talking about physical meditation advice.

For years, meditators in India have sought out what they thought was 'holy ground': the tombs of saints, places where gods fought battles, dead places and fairy tales.

But this verse is actually Krishna teaching you how to create holy ground. He says you must create it with your soul. You do this by not trying to think too highly, to get distracted in fantasies, or too low, being distracted by self-pity or base emotions.

He says that holy ground is sacred grass, with soft cloth and deerskin. Sacred grass means the natural world, the divine creation. Deerskin is the animal world. And soft cloth, woven by the hands of man, is the world of men, human civilization. To be a meditator your soul must be seated on all three levels. If you try to be divine without being animal or human, you will fail. If you try to be human without recognizing the animal and the divine in you, you will be stuck. If you try to be animal without being human or divine, you will be lost.

. . . .

12. Thus, with the mind focused on a single point, regulating the mind, senses and activities, sitting in a fixed position, one should practice Yoga techniques to clear the soul.

13. Keep the head, neck and body straight and unmoving, still. Looking only at the tip of your own nose and not in other directions.

14. The soul will be at peace, free of fear, innocent. Totally overcoming the mind, focusing it on me, the practitioner being situated in me is the ultimate goal.

15. Constantly practicing with the entire soul in this way, the mystic will attain peace, the great Nirvana, the endless sky.

v. 12-15

What Krishna is advocating here is a very simple practice. Just sit straight and focus the senses on the tip of the nose, and the mind on the Guru. He is not advocating any complex practices or magical rituals. He is not saying you will gain superpowers – what you will gain is Nirvana, peace.

. . . .

16. One who eats too much is not united, neither is one who fasts too much. Nor one who sleeps too much, nor one who stays awake, Arjuna.

17. Practice the work of balanced eating, playing, and working to maintain yourself. The one who is balanced in sleep and wakefulness through Yoga will see less and less suffering.

18. When the mind is particularly focused, it certainly becomes centred in the soul. Freed of the desire for all kinds of things, at that time it is said to be united.

19. Just as a lamp does not flicker when there is no wind, so does a mystic whose mind is focused remain constant in the unity of the soul.

20. In that state where mental activities cease, being distinguished from the essential through Yoga, a pure soul aware of the soul becomes fulfilled by the soul.

v. 16-20

"A pure soul aware of the soul becomes fulfilled by the soul." It is all the same thing. The work of Yoga is just a recognizing that union was always there, that you were always united. The soul is what wishes to be united, the soul is what you must discover in order to unite, and the soul is what you are uniting to. This together is the Supersoul.

. . . .

21. The supreme bliss that can be attained by transcendent enlightenment is such that one in it will never again move from it.

22. What is gained by this attainment is nothing more than that state, whereby even the greatest misery will not move you from it.

23. You must know this: all of the suffering of the world can be overcome by the trance of Yoga.

v. 21-23

Enlightenment is a permanent state. It is the end of the dream. While you are asleep, you are dreaming, and you might experience different depths of sleep, but it is all still sleep. When the moment comes that you really wake up, you snap out of it, and the sleep is over. There is no going back.

. . . .

24. The practice of Yoga must be done firmly, without deviation. You must completely give up all the turmoils of the mind, born of desires. Focusing the mind and all the senses, all the time.

25. Gradually, step by step, one should concentrate the mind by awareness and with determination. When you are centred in the soul, thoughts will no longer trouble you.

26. All kinds of things can disturb the mind, making it flicker from one thing to another with no centre. One must release attention from all of these distractions, returning into the centeredness of the soul.

27. The mystic whose mind is in great peace will attain the highest bliss. His passions made peaceful, liberated by Brahma, he is beyond all his past errors.

28. Thus engaged in his eternal soul, the mystic is beyond all impurities. In bliss, constantly connected to Brahma, he obtains the greatest joy.

29. The soul that exists in all beings is also in your soul. One who has united the self by Yoga will see everything with the same eyes.

30. Whoever sees me in all things and all things in me is not far from me, nor am I far from him.

31. He who is devoted to me is in the oneness that is in the heart of all beings. He is entirely in that oneness, in spite of himself; the mystic remains in me.

32. He who sees that his soul is everywhere and the same, Arjuna, whether in happiness or misery, such a man is considered a perfect mystic.

v. 24-32

When you have united to the Supersoul, you are your own true self, and you are also an indivisible part of all other people and things. In fact, everyone is that already, but they do not see it or understand it. The awakened person knows that he is never apart from the Divine, or from other people, and yet he is completely himself. Thus you are authentically natural in all situations and cannot be divorced from nature.

. . . .

33. *Arjuna said:*

This system you have broadly described, Great Warrior, seems impossible for me. I know I am too restless and unsteady.

34. Krishna, the mind is an unstable thing, constantly in strong turmoil and uncontrollable. I think that to focus it would be as difficult as trying to catch the wind.

35. *The Blessed One said:*

Great Warrior, there is no doubt that the mind is unstable, and difficult to focus. But through practice, Son of Kunti, and detachment, it can be focused.

36. In my opinion, unity is extremely difficult to obtain without disciplining the mind. But a centred soul is a realistic goal that can be achieved, if you know the right means.

v. 33-36

To most people, when they have thought about it at all, the idea that one could discipline the mind seems impossible. You consider how much your mind directs everything you do, to think that you could make it serve you rather than you serving it, this seems practically impossible, as it did to Arjuna. But Krishna insists that this must be attempted.

. . . .

37. *Arjuna said:*

What of one who had the trust, but could not achieve unity due to a troubled mind, and thus fails in mysticism? Krishna, what is the fate of such a person, who has failed to reach the highest?

38. Krishna, mighty warrior, being thus unsuccessful in both material and spiritual ambitions, such a person could belong to neither realm. Lost from the path of the Divine, will he not perish like a scattered cloud?

39. This is my doubt, Krishna. I ask you to satisfy my doubts. Other than you, I am sure no one else could do this.

v. 37-39

Arjuna here voices another common doubt to one on this path: what if it is all for nothing? People think of this as an all-or-nothing game; that either you must become enlightened soon; in a few months, or in a year, or in ten years, or at the very latest before you die, or else you will have wasted your entire life. If you are thinking in that way, then you are still being driven by motives of desire, and you are missing the point.

The person who thinks like this is thinking exactly what Arjuna is saying: Arjuna here says "I should just pursue material ambitions... because if I pursue mysticism, then I definitely will not do as well as I could in my career, and since Mysticism seems really hard, if I don't become enlightened I will have wasted my life completely. I won't be a material success and I won't be a spiritual success."

In fact, both of these are 'material success': Arjuna is thinking like a materialist in both instances – there is no such thing as 'being a spiritual success.'

40. *The Blessed One said:*

Son of Partha, nothing is destroyed in this world or the other. Thus no one is truly lost who had started on this path.

41. One who has done this work but not completed it will reach higher realms, and after dwelling there for many years will again take birth in a wealthy or spiritual household.

42. He might take birth in a family of mystics, who are wise. But this type of birth is very rare.

43. He will be able to regain the level of enlightenment that he had in his previous form, and after that may continue on the way of perfection, Son of Kuru.

44. Due to his past work, he will be drawn automatically to this practice. He will be curious about Yoga, and will see past the dogmas of ritualistic religion.

45. Working in discipline, such a mystic is cleansed of wrongdoing. After many births, having achieved the great power, he attains the highest.

v. 40-45

Krishna responds to Arjuna's concern by explaining to him, first of all, that Arjuna's premise is completely wrong. There is no either-or, no all-or-nothing. The 'material world' and the 'spiritual world' are just one world. Thus Arjuna's entire idea is based on a groundless fear.

Second, Arjuna's desires are senseless. The purpose of practicing mysticism is not 'to become enlightened.' The purpose of practicing mysticism is to be more human, and this is accomplished by the very act of practicing mysticism. Every step you take on the path of mysticism is a step toward your humanity and away from inhumanity, and thus every step is a victory. There is no loss, even if you give up, or even if you turn away, because with each step you have glimpsed a little more awareness. Once you have that glimpse, it can never be taken from you.

When Krishna speaks of moving to higher realms, even if you do not accept this idea of reincarnation, you must accept that either way nothing has been lost. If this life is all there is, then nothing you could have done would have been any better or worse than being a mystic.

And what's more, being a mystic would still be better, because mysticism is not like religion, where you practice it hoping for some reward in another life. Mysticism is its own reward. You will have lived a life of more awareness, more humanity, and that is the reward.

But in reality, know that your awareness and the gains in your awareness will continue to have useful repercussions, will continue to do good, long after you are finished this lifetime. All of your existence, and all of existence in general, benefits from your increased awareness.

. . . .

46. The mystic is greater than the ascetic, and also greater than the wise. He is considered greater than those who succeed in the material world. Thus, Arjuna, simply become a mystic.

47. And of all the mystics, those who are within me, within themselves, in total trust, giving devotional service, they are considered by me to be the finest.

v. 46-47

Being a mystic is the best way to reach humanity. And if you are going to be a mystic, you may as well not do half a job of it. You may as well be a mystic with all of your heart!

Chapter 7
The Yoga of Wisdom and Transcendence (vijnana)

1. *The Blessed One said:*

With your mind directed to me, Scion of Partha, practicing Yoga in awareness of me, try to hear how you can become completely aware, and free of doubt.

2. I shall fully explain to you this awareness and this knowledge, which once known, there will remain nothing further in this world to know.

3. Out of thousands of men, one will struggle for the higher power. And of those thousands struggling, only one will know me in reality.

v. 1-3

The awareness of the Divine is the ultimate attainment. Nothing else can truly satisfy. Of all the men in the world only one in a thousand look for it, and only one out of every thousand of those who seek it will find it in a given lifetime.

---

4. Earth, water, fire, air, the ether, the mind, awareness and the false ego; all of these are my own eightfold energies in division.

v. 4

Krishna here classifies all the substances of the world into eight qualities: the four elements (earth, water, fire and air) are the first four. Then there is the ether, which is that which exists with no material qualities and no consciousness. Then there is the mind, which exists with no material qualities and a limited consciousness. Beyond that, there is awareness, which consists of the senses and the ability of the mind to receive information. And finally there is the (false) Ego, the force of one's individual personality created by the Mind's limited ability to process the information received through awareness, of the interaction of the four elements plus the ether.

. . . .

5. These are inferior forms. But besides these there is another form. Endeavour to understand this superior form of me. This superior form is life, the living beings, Great Warrior, who make use of these elements of matter.

v. 5

Above all of these, there is the divine energy. Krishna correctly identifies this energy as life itself, the source of that greater awareness that processes all of these other elements, material and mental.

. . . .

6. In this way, know that there are these two forms whose intermingling produced all things. I encompass all creation and destruction in existence.

v. 6

The Divine exists in both the divine energy of life, and the material and mental energies. It exists everywhere, in both of these things and in how they mix.

. . . .

7. Conqueror, beyond me there is no greater thing. Everything that you see, all that is, is in me; like pearls strung on a thread.

8. Son of Kunti, I am the flavour in water, I am the light of the sun and moon, I am the sound OM that is in all mantras, I am the vibration in the ether, I am the genius in man.

9. I am also the original fragrances of the earth, I am the heat in fire. I am the life of all things. I am the austerity of the ascetics.

10. Mine is the seed of all living beings. Son of Partha, try to understand that which is eternal. I am the awareness of the aware. I am the skill of the skilful.

11. I am the strength of the strong, free of lust or attachment. I am the natural sexuality of all beings, Lord of the Bharatas.

v. 7-11

Krishna says "I Am" – he is speaking of himself as divine awareness. He is speaking from the point of view of the enlightened being, completely united with the Divine.

And he is trying to emphasize that the Divine is found in everything, absolutely everything. It is found in water, in light, in sound, in intelligence, in qualities of strength, in sexuality, in absolutely all things.

. . . .

12. And all of the elements of beings: Sattvas (truth), Rajas (passion), and Tamas (heaviness), all of them come from me. Do not try to know me in their light. You must instead understand them in my light.

13. There are three gunas (elements of being), and by these is the whole universe in delusion. It cannot see me above these, greater and never-ending.

14. It is very difficult to transcend this maya (illusion) of the gunas, but it is actually my own energy. Thus those who surrender unto me will go beyond this illusion.

v. 12-14

In India the three alchemical forces, the Gunas, were described as being Truth, Passion, and Heaviness (or coarseness). Would-be Indian alchemists of that time believed that you could reach a state of perfection by somehow purifying yourself of the two 'inferior' qualities, Tamas and Rajas, and becoming purely Sattvas (truth). But Krishna is saying that in reality the Divine exists within all three of the alchemical states, and that the key to wisdom was found not in trying to overcome the lesser states but to balance and understand them all in a divine context.

. . . .

15. The foolish, the lowest of men who do not surrender unto me, have had their understanding stolen by this illusion. They have accepted being in darkness.

v. 15

People who identify with any of the particular Gunas, who behave as if controlled by any of the three, are trapped in the darkness of illusion.

. . . .

16. There are four kinds of people who will trust and render service unto me, Arjuna. They are those who are in distress, those who are curious, those who desire material gain, and those who understand the real, Greatest of the Bharatas.

v. 16

People will become mystics for various motives. Some do so because they are suffering greatly, and their state of suffering has pushed them to seek God. Others do so out of curiosity, because they desperately desire to know deep truths, to seek some kind of answer. Then there are those who want some kind of material gain: they want to be powerful, or they want to be respected, or they want to be famous, or they want to be listened to, or just want to be special. Finally, there are those who have had a glimpse of something real.

. . . .

17. Of them only those who understand the real, and the devotees, are special. I am very close to those who understand deeply. And they are very close to me.

18. All of these are certainly great, but it is my opinion that one who understands the real has the same soul as me. He is certainly in the state of the united soul, in me, which is certainly the highest goal.

v. 17-18

Everyone who pursues the path of the mystic, for whatever reason, is on the right track. Krishna is not judging the other motives to be wrong, but he makes clear that once you are on the path of the Mystic, you must come to understand that seeking the Real – not power, or knowledge, or an end to pain – is the only sincere motive to practice mysticism. These are the people who are closest to awareness.

. . . .

19. After many births and deaths, one who is aware surrenders unto me. Thus everything becomes the divine consciousness, and this supersoul is the most rare of experiences.

20. One who is lacking full awareness will surrender to other spirits, and will follow the corresponding disciplines according to their natures.

21. Whichever and whatever form of spirit a devotee wishes to be devoted to with trust, I will certainly grant him the opportunity.

22. Being inspired by his trust in the devotion to that spirit he is drawn to, he will obtain what he desires from it. This is in fact arranged by me.

23. But these results are only transitory, appropriate to those of limited knowing who go to the spirits. But those who are directly my devotees will reach me.

v. 19-23

Everyone who enters the path of the mystic will eventually attain Awakening. It is inevitable. However, this work can take more or less time depending on what one is seeking. It can take several lifetimes before one is ready to surrender completely. Along the way, one might be drawn to other spirits, to other motivations within mysticism. If you seek out these other things, they will be what you get. Jesus said that those who follow the Father to be seen as holy have already gained their reward; Krishna means the same thing. If you practice mysticism for some inner peace, for a lessening of suffering, that is what you will get. If you practice mysticism to get blissful states, that is what you will get. If you practice mysticism in order to be part of a movement, that is what you will get. If you practice mysticism in order to be seen as wise, then that is what you will get. Whatever spirit you surrender to, the Divine will grant you that. And when you are ready to surrender directly to the Divine, without motivation, then the Divine itself is what you will gain.

24. Those who have limited consciousness believe me to be an impersonal force. They do not know me as the great work, the force of life, never-ending and most sublime.

25. Nor do I make myself visible to everyone. Those persons who are foolish, clouded by their connection to illusion, cannot understand me as the unborn and never-ending.

v. 24-25

Likewise, your understanding of the Divine will be limited by your own definitions of what you think the Divine consists of. If you think of the Divine as 'energy,' then you will only be able to understand the part of the Divine that is energy. If you think of the Divine as a God, then you will only be able to understand the part of the Divine that is God. If you think of the Divine as immaterial, then you will only be able to perceive the part of the Divine that is not material. But if you are free of ideas and notions, if you are free of your own definitions, only then will you be able to see the Divine as absolute, as existing in a never-ending presence in all things, as material and nonmaterial, as never created and never absent, as present in people and things, as present in mind and in energy.

. . . .

26. I am completely informed of the past, present and future, Arjuna. I also know all living beings, but none of them know me.

v. 26

The Divine is beyond all intellectual understanding and definition. You cannot become united to the Divine by trying to think it through, and trying to define what the Divine consists of.

. . . .

27. Scion of Bharata, the duality of desire and hate is born of illusion. All living beings fall into this delusion upon taking birth, Conqueror of your Enemies.

28. But those persons who have by trust erased all their past wrongdoings, they have become freed from duality, and thus delusion. They will devote themselves to me with great will.

v. 27-28

If you are free of definition, you are also freed from the desire for certain things and the hatred of others.

. . . .

29. All of those who seek to take shelter in me, for escape from the cycles of birth and death, such persons are actually Brahma. They know all that are transcendental acts.

30. Those who know the laws of life, that govern all spirits, know me. Even at the time of death they know me, and their minds unite to me.

v. 29-30

If you are free of your own ideas and notions, then you can truly understand that you are already a part of Brahma, of the Divine, and you become united to the Divine.

Chapter 8
The Yoga of the Divine
(askhra brahman)

1. *Arjuna said:*

What is Brahman? What is the self? What is Karma, greatest of beings? What is it to be alive? And what are the beings called the spirits?

2. Who is the Lord of Devotion and how is he here, in this very body, Great Warrior? And how can you be known at the time of death by those who are not unfocused?

v. 1-2

Arjuna, his consciousness being slowly awakened by Krishna, is beginning to ask questions that he previously assumed he knew the answers to. He is not asking to have his own ideas confirmed, he is asking out of sincerity, recognizing that he is confronting the unknown.

. . . .

3. *The Blessed One said:*

The highest infinite is called Brahma. It is the eternal self. It is the source of all life, and its creations are called Karma.

4. Its physical form has an ever-changing nature. It is the universe, and all the spirits. I am certainly part of this supersoul, incarnated in this body, great one.

v. 3-4

The body of Brahma, of God, is the Universe. All the universe is a part of God, everything is a part of God. There is no place where Brahma is not. Every person is a part of the supersoul, incarnated in a body.

. . . .

5. At the end of this life, he who leaves his body remembering me will go into my being. Of this achievement there is no doubt.

6. At the end of your life, whatever you are remembering, that will be the state of being you achieve, Son of Kunti.

7. Thus, at all times, remember me. Fight for me. Surrender your mind and awareness unto me, and you will attain with no doubt.

v. 5-7

Whatever is in your awareness at the moment of death, that is where you will be directed. If you spend your life practicing meditation, focused on the moment, then you are very likely to be able to be in the moment at the time of your death. If that happens, then you will find eternity.

If you are thinking of God as a concept, or the Guru, or spirits, or any of those things, you will find a union with those concepts, and might reach to enlightenment sometime after.

If you are afraid, or clinging to the world, then you will find fear, or the world, all over again.

. . . .

8. By the practice of Yoga, without distracting the mind, through constantly thinking of it the supreme and divine individuality will be attained.

9. Always focus on the all knowing, the most ancient, the master of all, smaller than an atom, the maintainer of all things, beyond intellectual understanding, whose form is brighter than the sun and overcomes all darkness.

v. 8-9

How can you truly 'think' of something smaller than an atom, or brighter than the sun? Krishna is not saying you should play make-believe here, or pretend you can think of these things. He is offering a Zen koan; saying you should try to conceive of these things, and reject them as you realize that whatever you are imagining cannot possibly be TRULY like a brightness brighter than the sun. As you go along, rejecting your false imaginings, you will reach a state that is beyond thought, and there you will discover the supersoul. The supersoul cannot be achieved by regular thinking, it can only be reached when you can move beyond the regular intellect.

. . . .

10. At the time of death, without being distracted by the mind, in full devotion, practicing the mystic Yoga, focusing all life-energy on the space between the eyebrows, one will achieve the transcendent individuality in the Divine.

v. 10

Be single-mindedly focused at the moment of death, leave behind all of your fears and concerns, direct all of your attention to the moment you are experiencing, and you will awaken. But you are only capable of doing this if you have been practising for it. This is why you must die before you die, if you are a mystic.

. . . .

11. That which the priests call the OM, entered into by the great sages, the hermits; that which is practiced by those who desire innocence, that which they struggle for in their lives, I will explain to you now very simply.

12. Controlling all the doors of the body, securing the mind inside one's heart, fixing the life-energy of your soul on the top of your head, this is how to practice Yoga.

13. Thus this one word, OM, becomes Brahma. Anyone who leaves their body while remembering me and vibrating this word will achieve the great goal.

v. 11-13

The OM is not a written word; it is not even a sound a human being can make by himself or herself. It is the sound of the vibration of the universe. The divine sound that exists in the background of all existence that can only be heard when you are in absolute silence.

. . . .

14. Without distracting the mind, anyone who regularly remembers me will very easily reach my state, Scion of Partha, by regularly practicing Yoga.

v. 14

If you regularly practice Yoga, meditation, you will be able to hear the OM in the moment of absolute silence. It is a roar in the absolute silence.

. . . .

15. Achieving me, being reborn, the great souls will not return to this plane of the temporary, this place of miseries. They have achieved the great power.

16. They are raised up to the world of Brahma-being. Arjuna, they return to me, they arrive, but will never take birth again.

v. 15-16

Someone who becomes enlightened – when they leave this body, it is for the last time.

. . . .

17. They know that one day of Brahma is like a thousand ages. Those who understand know also that at the end of one thousand ages of night, there comes the day.

18. All living beings are born from the unborn, at the beginning of the day. At the coming of the night, all is once more absorbed into that which is called unborn.

19. This is the sum of all living beings, being born and born again and also inevitably destroyed at the coming of the night, Son of Partha, being born once more at the arriving of the dawn.

20. But in that great nature, there is the uncreated behind all that is created. It is eternal. As all that is created is destroyed, that which is uncreated is never destroyed.

21. That which is said to be the uncreated and perfect is known as the ultimate goal, which, once gained, one never returns from. This is my supreme home.

v. 17-21

Everything that exists goes through cycles of creation and destruction: Something is born with the dawn, and dies in the night, over and over again, taking temporary form. But when you discover the eternal form – which is constant change because it is infinite – you no longer need to limit yourself to identifying with any single temporary form, and become eternal.

. . . .

22. It is the greatest individuality, Son of Partha, which can be achieved by absolute devotion. For it is located within this very life that surrounds all that we see.

v. 22

The eternal exists all around us. Everything has the eternal within it, thus the eternal hides in plain sight. When you can see the eternal, you are freed from the idea of being attached to anything you believed to be temporary or fixed.

. . . .

23. Different kinds of mystics return and do not return at different times, depending on the time that they have left. I shall explain this to you, Greatest of the Bharatas.

24. Fire, the light of day, under the waxing moon, during the six months that the sun is in the north; in these times, those who leave the body will go to Brahma, if they know Brahma.

25. In smoke, at night, under the waning moon, during the six months that the sun is in the south; in these conditions the mystic will achieve the light of the moon, and will return.

26. There are certainly these two ways of passing, in light and darkness; such is the opinion written in the scriptures of the world. Going by the one, you will never return, but going by the other you will come back again.

27. Son of Partha, even if he is not aware of these things, the true mystic is never confused. Thus, just be constantly focused on Yoga, Arjuna.

v. 23-27

These verses are not a literal teaching; it is not saying that if you die in the summer you will be awakened, but if you die in winter you will not be. What it is saying is that if you are fully aware when you die, you will not return. If you have a certain level of awareness, if you are present at the moment of death but still attached, you will return again for another lifetime. If you are in darkness at the time of your death – not a physical darkness but a darkness of consciousness – then you will continue to return. But Krishna also mentions that you need not be concerned about this sort of thing as a goal; what is important is to simply practice Yoga, practice meditation, and the rest takes care of itself.

. . . .

28. Studying the scriptures, performing rituals, practicing self-denial, giving charity, and performing other works that show your faith; all of these things are surpassed by the learned yogi, who just naturally achieves the highest resting place.

v. 28

Just by naturally practicing meditation, without concerns, you will accomplish more than a person who is obsessed with techniques, rituals, worship, secret truths, or proving his goodness or his spirituality.

Chapter 9
The Yoga of the Great Secret Teaching (rajavidya rajaguhya)

1. *The Blessed One said:*

I am singing this great secret unto you. For you are not jealous. And so this taught knowledge will become true understanding. Knowing which, you will be freed from this limited world of suffering.

v. 1

Jealousy, the desire to compare yourself to others, the need to feel superior, is a great barrier to mysticism. If you can approach spiritual learning without letting your ego get in the way with its expectations and demands that you hold onto your sense of 'specialness,' then you will be able to really learn. If not, whatever you receive or experience will end up twisted by your own sense of comparison.

2. This is the King of Knowledge, the King of Secrets, the Purest, Transcendental. It is understood only by directly experiencing. It is the way. It brings great bliss in its practice, and lasts for all time.

3. Such people as are without trust in this way, mighty fighter, without attaining me they will continue coming back from death to the paths on the wheel of suffering (Samsara) the world of illusion.

v. 2-3

If you are attached to your desire to compare, to try to keep yourself separate from life in order to feel superior or special, then you will be stuck inside of yourself, repeating the same cycles of suffering over and over again.

. . . .

4. The entire world is filled with me in an impersonal form. Although not all living beings are in me, I am in all of them.

5. Although not all beings can see that they are in me, if you witness you will find the union in my divinity. I am the force that maintains all life, though I am not myself part of life, for I am the source behind it.

6. Just as wherever the wind blows it is part of the great sky, so are all living things part of me. Try to understand this.

v. 4-6

If you can set your ideas of your self aside, then you experience the Divine, and can understand it belongs to everything and is in everything just as the wind is everywhere in the sky.

. . . .

7. Son of Kunti, all living things enter my nature at the end of time. And again, at the beginning of time I create them anew.

8. Entering into my nature, I will create again and again all of these things that live. By my will, life automatically springs.

9. I am not bound by any of these actions, Conqueror. I am neutral to all of these actions, not attached.

10. Through me, through my attention, all life emanates, both the animate and inanimate. Son of Kunti, it is for this reason that the world exists.

v. 7-10

The Divine is not bound by motives or actions. The Divine doesn't exist for a 'reason' human beings can comprehend, and whenever human beings have sought out those reasons all they have done is impose their own personal likes and dislikes on their ideas of God. So 'God' to them ends up being a very limited being, with hates and likes that serve only to fit their own motives.

. . . .

11. Foolish men reject me when I take on a body. They do not know my higher life. I am the great deity of all that is.

12. They are fools in their hopes, fools in their actions, fools in their lack of understanding. They are deluded, demonic and wicked, and the things they seek comfort in are nothing but illusions.

v. 11-12

People that like to imagine God in a set image will not be able to see God in the person next to them. They will not be able to accept teachers, much less accept the Divine in their neighbour. They are more comfortable holding onto a fantasy they've called God, a fantasy that keeps them apart from life.

. . . .

13. But the great souls, Scion of Partha, have taken shelter in my divine nature. Without being distracted by their minds, they perform service, being aware that the source of existence is never-ending.

14. They are always singing devotionally of me, working with determination, offering signs of respect (namaste), and always practicing devotional ritual to me.

v. 13-14

The truly great souls, the ones who have set aside their own notions and motivations, make their every action a devotion to the Divine. Please note that Krishna is not saying that to be a 'great soul' you must spend all of your time singing devotional songs, doing namastes, or doing devotional rituals. This is the misunderstanding that has led foolish people to misinterpret these verses for so long.

Rather, what Krishna is saying is that people who are not tied to their ideas, who do not think of God as a limited being that fits their notions and definitions, will turn everything they do into a devotion! When they eat breakfast, or go to work, or play a game, or speak with a friend, it is like they were singing devotions or doing ritual. It is better, in fact, because it is the true essence of what those other practices were supposed to be about! Such a person might never enter a temple in their life, and still be more sincerely devotional, more sincerely spiritual, than someone who spends all of their time singing kirtans to God.

. . . .

15. Others, by cultivating awareness, practice rituals to me as the dual, the non-dual, the infinitely diverse, or the single universal form.

16. I am the ritual of the priests. I am the performing of sacrifices. I am the offering. I am the healing herb. I am the mantra. I am the ritual fuel, I am the ritual fire, and I am the ritual itself.

17. I am the father of this universe. I am the mother, the friend, the grandfather. I am what can be known, and what purifies. I am the OM. I am all of the great scriptures.

18. I am the goal, the caregiver, the Lord, the watcher, the home, the safe place, the best friend, creation and destruction, the earth, the place of rest, the undying seed.

19. I give warmth and cold. I give rain, and drought. And I am immortality, death, spirit, and matter, Arjuna.

v. 15-19

When someone is sincere in their practice, be they practicing with the structure of a Dualistic god, a non-dualistic god, a god with an elephant head, a god with no image, a god with a female form or a male form, a pantheon of gods or a single god; whatever form they take, their practice is sincere.

What Krishna is saying is that it doesn't matter WHAT you are doing, it matters WHY you are doing it. Your intentions are what matter, not the outward appearances.

The Divine is in everything, and can thus be found in anything. What matters is that one have the right eyes to see.

What matters is that you cultivate awareness.

. . . .

20. It is my will also that some will know the threefold teaching. Those who drink the soma juice, or purify themselves of wrongdoing by prayerful worship to gain passage to the realm of the god Indra, they enjoy the celestial divine pleasures of the gods.

21. When the vast pleasures of these heavens are exhausted, these holy beings fall back down to the world of mortals. Thus those who follow the threefold teaching to seek the pleasures of heaven will ultimately only gain repeated birth and death.

v. 20-21

The Soma juice was a drug that the ancient priests of India would drink to gain visions. So Krishna here is talking about people who use methods, be they drugs or be they ritual purifications, ecstatic techniques, etc., to try to experience bliss. Whatever your means of doing it, be it drugs or prayers, if your goal is to get lost in bliss, that is what will happen. You will experience the 'Pleasures of the realms of the gods.'

But inevitably, you will fall back down.

If your practice is done only to experience altered states, to 'bliss out,' then you will just keep repeating a cycle over and over again.

. . . .

22. Those who have no such goal, but only focus their mind on me, they are practicing properly. Those who are always focused in this way will be united, protected, and supported by me.

23. Those who are devotees of other gods, who are trusting in their worship, they too worship me though they may not know it, Son of Kunti.

24. I am surely the one who enjoys all rituals. I am the Lord. Those who do not know the reality of me will fall down.

v. 22-24

If you do not try to seek out bliss, if you just practice for the sake of practicing, then your practice will be sincere and you will experience union. It doesn't matter what 'god' you direct your practice to; be it meditation itself, be it a deity of some kind, be it the idea of the Tao or the Force or any other notion, as long as you are practicing without attachment.

. . . .

25. Those who worship the Gods will go to the Gods; those who worship the ancestors will go to the ancestors. Those who worship ghosts will go to the ghosts. Those who are my devotees will go to me.

26. A leaf, a flower, fruit, or simple water. Anyone who offers these in devotion unto me, I will accept them, so long as they are offered with pure spirit.

27. Whatever you do, whatever you eat, whatever you offer, whatever you give, whatever disciplines you practice, Son of Kunti, do so as an offering to me.

v. 25-27

If you get stuck on the notion, you will only find the notion, but if your practice is free of motivation, you will find what is beyond that. If you are practicing free of lust of result, then any simple offering, any kind of practice, the simplest thing will suffice. So let your everyday life be your devotion, let your every action be offered up to life without expectations.

. . . .

28. In this way, you will be free of the Karma of being bound to good or bad results. Having your soul firmly focused on the Yoga of renunciation (Sannyas), you will attain my freedom.

v. 28

The Yoga of Renunciation is the renunciation of lust of results. If you free yourself of the expectation that you must be special, that you must be rewarded, that things have to go the way you want them to, then you are truly renouncing, and you will find freedom.

. . . .

29. I am equal to all living beings. I hate no one, nor do I hold any dearer than others. But those who practice service with devotion unto me are in me, and I am certainly in them.

30. Even if one commits the most abominable acts, but is practicing service unto me without fail, he is certainly to be treated as a saint, because he is certainly determined in his intentions.

31. Very soon he becomes natural in his soul, and gains a lasting peace, Son of Kunti. I declare that no devotee of mine will ever perish.

32. Scion of Partha, those who specifically seek shelter in me, whether they are from a low background, or women, or merchants, or untouchables, even they will go to the highest place.

33. How much more certainly will the priests, the righteous, the devotees, the honourable kings! So while you are in this transient world, full of suffering, gain the gift of service unto me.

34. Become my devotee, always thinking of me. Worship me; give motions of respect (namaste) to me. You will come completely to me; your soul will unite with me totally through devotion.

v. 29-34

No one is more or less special in the universe. No one is closer to the Divine than anyone else. Those who are sincere in their practice just understand that they are part of the Divine, and the Divine in them.

There is no question of judgment in the Divine. Just as no one is special, no one is abominable to the Divine; anyone can follow the path of awareness, and no matter what they were or what they did before that, they can come to be transformed.

Nor do you have to become a good or a perfect person before you can practice spirituality. This is a falsehood. Do not let this idea fool you into avoiding practice; just practice awareness and keep doing whatever you feel to do; because awareness is the medicine that heals you itself, without any special requirements. If you are sincere in your awareness, over time you will change, just by yourself, to becoming more natural and more at peace. Trying to become 'peaceful' in appearance, or 'holy' in appearance, or even 'good' in appearance before it is natural to you is pointless. Only the holiness that emerges naturally from having awareness is worth anything, everything else is equally ignorant.

Devotion frees, all by itself.

Chapter 10
The Yoga of the Divine Manifestation (vibhuti)

1. *The Blessed One said:*

Mighty warrior, just hear me once more, in this great teaching which I will give you for your benefit, because you are my friend.

2. The spirit beings will never know my majesty; the great sages will never know. For I am the source of everything that makes up the spirit beings and the great sages.

3. Anyone who knows me as uncreated, without beginning, he knows me as the great divinity. He is without delusion. Among all those destined to die, only he will be freed from wrongdoing.

v. 1-3

Not even holy men or spirits would be able to know, to intellectually fathom, the majesty of the Divine.

How could you ever possibly know God if everything that is God covers every fibre of your existence, and then goes far beyond that?

Your mind can only 'know' to the limit of every fibre of your existence. It can't possibly know anything beyond.

This is why intellectual methods cannot lead one to enlightenment. It is impossible.

Nor does enlightenment mean that you now 'know' the true nature of God or the secrets of the universe. Enlightenment means that you understand that these things are unknowable by the mind.

You are only able to experience these things, but you cannot know them, cannot assess them. It would be like trying to hold a hundred litres of water with a teaspoon! The mind doesn't have the capacity.

All you can do is dive your whole being into the Divine. You cannot expect the Divine to fit into the smallness of you, but your smallness can easily fit into the infinite inviting largeness of the Divine.

. . . .

4. Enlightenment, awareness, freedom from doubt, forgiveness, truthfulness, disciplined senses, disciplined mind, joy, suffering, birth and death, fear and courage.

5. Non-violence, balance, fulfillment, guilt, giving, fame, infamy; all of these different natures of living beings are arranged by me.

6. The seven great sages, and the four originators of humanity, were all born of me. They were created by my mind, as were all of the people of this existence.

7. Anyone who knows this reality as miracles of Yoga will be able to practice Yoga without fail. Of this there is no doubt.

v. 4-7

Existence itself is a miracle. It is the miracle of a union – a union of two parts of one whole.

The Divine is an absolute, perfect emptiness that became a fullness because of its perfection. This fullness can only be defined as having two natures within it that counterbalance each other. These two create synthesis – a third quality that contains elements of both its predecessors. With the consideration of these two absolutes and the synthesis of these two, you end up with infinite forms.

But all of these forms are one single reality. Thus it is a miracle.

If you understand the miraculous nature of the universe you will be able to practice this union, to return to the source of all existence.

. . . .

8. I am the source of all creation. From me come all things. Knowing this, the enlightened become devoted to me with great fervour.

9. Their minds focused on me, their lives dedicated to me, they share this enlightenment with one another. They will constantly talk about me, finding joy in divine bliss.

10. They are always practicing service from their devotion. They are filled with the ecstasy of love. I give to them that unity of enlightenment by which they come unto me.

11. To them I give a particular grace. Any ignorance caused by darkness within their hearts, I can destroy with the bright lamp of awareness.

v. 8-11

Note that Krishna does NOT say that by constantly talking about the Divine, or practicing service, or being ecstatic, you will become Aware. He says that people who are aware have these qualities.

Someone who is aware, his every word will be filled with awareness. Thus, even if he is only saying something mundane, even if he only says "pass the butter please", the Divine is in his every word.

Even in the mundane things he does, he is practicing service to the Divine.

Even when he is just alone, or resting, or watching TV, or speaking with people, or driving in a car, he is ecstatic.

But imitating these things, talking constantly about the Divine if you do not know anything about the Divine, or practicing what you think is service when you do not yet know how to serve, or trying to force yourself to be ecstatic, this will not make you an Enlightened person.

This is like someone seeing that all police officers wear a metal badge, so they start wearing a metal badge thinking this will make them into a police officer.

The part to focus on is your awareness, not your exterior behaviour. Krishna says, "I am the source of all creation." Whenever he says these 'I am' statements, he is referring to his enlightened self as the embodiment of God. It has nothing to do with Krishna specifically; it has to do with understanding the source of all creation.

If you understand that the Divine, what you seek, is what created everything around you, and that absolutely everything comes out of the Divine, without exception, then you will have learned a secret that will be of use to you in your practice. You will be able to discover, if you really understand what this means, the 'obviousness' of devotion! How could you not be devoted then?

Then any darkness, any ignorance you may have had, will be burnt away by the light of awareness.

. . . .

12. *Arjuna said:*

The Great Brahma, the Great Force, the Pure Greatest Being. The First Individuality, Transcendent, the Lord of the Spirits, Uncreated and Most Miraculous.

13. The sages all say these things of you. Even the divine sage Narada, and Asita, Devala, and Vyasa all say this. Now you are yourself explaining this to me.

14. I accept all of these claims that you are making, Krishna. No one can know you in your fullness, Blessed One, not even the divine or demonic spirits.

15. You know, personally, your soul through your soul, Greatest One. Creator of Everything, Lord of Everything, Spirit of Spirits, Father of the World.

16. Tell me in detail of how you have earned this divine and miraculous soul, the miracle by which you can remain within all dimensions at once.

17. Great Yogi, how shall I know you and think of you always? In which various natures are you to be thought of by me, Blessed One?

18. Describe again to my satisfaction the miraculous uniting of the soul, Destroyer of Doubt. Although I have been hearing you, I have not yet attained the nectar.

v. 12-18

Arjuna understands what he has been hearing, but he has not yet experienced. Instead of trying to interpret Krishna's words in his own way, and take that away with him filled with his own notions, Arjuna remains and requests to hear more.

There is a tremendous difference between hearing a teaching, and experiencing one truly. If you are honest with yourself, it is obvious.

If you are just hearing, then you will take the words, play with them in your mind, try to interpret them in the context of your already-held notions and beliefs, and walk away with some new 'talking point,' some new factoid for you to show off.

If you are experiencing a truth, the reception of this truth will create some kind of a change in you: You will feel it! You will realize that it has altered the way you see things, the way you understand things. You will not categorize it within your accepted criteria; rather, it will remove some of your accepted ideas!

This is the difference between accumulating knowledge and actual learning!

. . . .

19. *The Blessed One said:*

Yes, I will speak unto you of the divine miracle of the soul. I will explain the main points, Best of the Kurus, for there is no limit to how far I could expand on this.

v. 19

The ways that one could attempt to describe the nature of reality, of the soul, of spirit, are infinite. They are such because none of them would really be able to intellectually communicate the reality.

Lao Tzu said "The tao which can be spoken of is NOT the Tao."

Here Krishna says the same thing; here he can only try to explain the main points, try to create some idea of something similar to the Truth, in the hopes that it might open your eyes to the truth.

Thus, if you get hung up on the particular expressions a teacher uses, his particular words, you will miss out! You will end up becoming dogmatic, and you will not get the real purpose. Nothing any teacher ever says is actual truth. How a teacher exists is Truth. The things a teacher says or writes are only efforts to push your consciousness open a little, so that you can then receive truth.

Remember this, and remember that it applies even now, in these commentaries! These commentaries are not truths; they are an attempt to get you to open to the experience of truth. You won't find truth by analyzing these words. You'll find truth by opening yourself to the experience these words are trying to move you toward.

. . . .

20. Arjuna, I am the soul. I am within the heart of all living beings. I am the beginning, the middle and the end of all life.

21. Of the Gods I am Vishnu. Of all lights I am the glowing Sun. Of all the winds I am the solar wind. Of all the planetary bodies I am the moon.

22. Of all the scriptures (Vedas) I am the Samveda (the first). Of all the divine spirits I am the king of heaven. Of all the senses I am the mind. And of all living beings I am the living force of consciousness.

23. Of all the demigods I am Shiva. And of all the lesser demigods I am the Lord of the Treasures. Of the elementals I am fire, and of all mountains I am Mt. Meru, the holy mountain.

24. Son of Partha, know me to be the prince of the priests, the hierophant. Of all the commanders I am the General. Of all the sources of water, I am the ocean.

25. Of all the great sages I am Bhirgu (the son of God). Of all the vibrations I am the voice in the silence. Of all rituals I am chanting. Of all immobile objects I am the Himalayas.

26. Of all the trees the Banyan, of all the divine sages Narada, of the divine choir Citraratha, of the magicians the wise Kapila.

27. Among horses know me as Uccaihishrava who was made from the tempestuous ocean. Of the noble elephants Airavata, and among human beings the King of Kings.

28. Of all weapons I am the thunderbolt. Of cows, I am Kamadhuk. Of the causes for begetting children I am true love. Of serpents I am Vasuki.

29. I am also Ananta of the hydras. Of all mermen I am the demigod Varuna. Of the ancestors I am Aryama. And of all the judges I am Yama, the lord of death (who judges the time of your death).

30. Of the demons I am Prahlada. Of all the conquering forces I am time. And I am the lion of all the animals, and the divine Garuda, of all the birds.

31. Of all the purifying forces I am the wind. Of all warriors I am Rama. Of all fish I am the shark. And of all rivers I am the Ganges.

32. Of all creation I am the beginning, the middle, and the end, Arjuna. Of all forms of knowledge I am the experiential knowledge of the soul. Of all forms of argument I am logic.

33. Of letters I am the letter A. Of compounds I am the dual compound. I am the eternal aeons, I am the fourfold creator.

34. I am the death of all that is, and the source of all that will be. Of the virtues of women I am fame, beauty, fine words, memory, intelligence, firmness, and patience.

35. Of the songs in the Samveda I am the Brihatsama. Of all poems I am the Gayatri. Of the months of the year I am harvest month. Of all the seasons I am spring.

36. Of all forms of vice I am gambling. I am the splendour of everything splendid. I am victory. I am risk. I am the might of the mighty.

37. Of the descendents of Vrishni I am Vasudeva. Of the Pandavas I am Arjuna. Of the wise I am Vyasa. Of the philosophers I am the philosopher Usana.

38. Of all the legal structures I am just punishment. I am the righteousness of those who seek noble goals. Of all the secrets I am silence. I am the awareness of the aware.

v. 20-38

In these verses, some of the most beautiful of the Gita, Krishna expresses that the Divine is found in the first of all things. All of the various things he named would have been recognizable in the culture in which Krishna was teaching as the first and foremost of each quality.

. . . .

39. Whatever there may be of all living things, I am the seed, Arjuna. Without me, there is nothing that can exist, no living being, animate or inanimate.

v. 39

Krishna is saying that the Divine is the 'seed'; the first ideal expression of all things, out of which everything else evolves and emerges. Absolutely everything exists only as a part of the Divine.

. . . .

40. Nor is there any limit to my divine miracles, Conqueror of Enemies. All of these are only some examples I have spoken out of a vast expanse.

41. Whatever miracles are real, most beautiful and glorious, you must realize that they are only born of a part of my splendour.

42. What could you possibly gain by understanding these things one at a time, Arjuna? I pervade this entire world, while being within one part.

v. 40-42

All of infinity is born out of the source, the Divine. And everything else that you experience in life is only one part of the Divine. So it is clearly worthwhile to approach the Divine, First of all things. If you want to understand, you must begin at the very root, at the very seed of everything. Only then can you understand the proper context, the natural place, of all other things. Each little thing in the world contains the Divine, and the Divine contains all things in existence.

Chapter 11
The Yoga of Seeing and Transforming
(darshan visvarupa)

1. *Arjuna said:*

Just out of your friendship you have spoken to me these great secrets of the soul. Your words have removed my illusions.

2. I have heard from you in detail about the creation and destruction of all living things, Lotus-Eyed One. And I have experienced infinite wonders.

3. Thus what you have spoken is of the real spirit, greatest of divine Masters. Now I wish to see your real divine form, Finest of Individuals.

4. If you think it is possible for me to see this, my Lord, Divine Master of Yoga, show me your eternal soul.

v. 1-4

Having come to some understanding, Arjuna is now ready to glimpse a level of reality as it is, not reality as he has been choosing to see it up till now. This is what the Buddha called 'Right Seeing.' Usually you see everything from the point of view of the things you have experienced and the things you expect. This ends up limiting your actual vision extremely. You see, you experience reality though a very narrow peephole of your own ideas and notions. You wear blinders. Now Arjuna wishes to drop his blinders and see all of reality at once.

. . . .

5. *The Blessed One said:*

Scion of Partha, just see my forms; hundreds of thousands of combinations and countless colours.

6. Best of the Bharatas, see the twelve sons of Aditi, the eight Vasus, the eleven forms of Rudra, the two Ashvinis, the forty-nine Maruts, and many other awe-inspiring forms that you have never seen before.

7. In this one place you can see the entire world completely and immediately. Both the mobile and immobile are here in this body, Arjuna, and everything you could wish to see.

8. But you cannot see me with your own eyes. I will give you divine eyes to see my divine mastery of Yoga.

v. 5-8

In just one place, just where you are, you can see all of reality. If you see with spiritual eyes and not just your own perceptions blinded by your ideas, you will be able to see how everyday life, and everything around you, is filled with the awe of the Divine.

. . . .

9. *Sanjaya said:*

Thus, after saying this my King, the greatest Divine Master of Yoga, the Praised One, showed unto Arjuna the greatest divine form.

10. Many mouths, many eyes, many awe-inspiring sights, many divine ornaments, and many divine weapons wielded.

11. Divine necklaces (malas), wearing divine dresses, covered in divine perfumes, all awe-inspiring, godly, infinite and present all at once.

12. There were many thousands of suns in the sky all at once, as if their light was the very radiance of the supersoul.

13. Arjuna could see the entire world all in once place, divided into many. This was the God of gods, manifest in that very moment as the universe.

14. Thus Arjuna was overwhelmed with awe, his hair standing on end. He bowed his head in respect, with folded hands toward the Divine, and began to speak.

v. 9-14

In this moment, Arjuna was overwhelmed with an instant of Satori, of pure awareness, where he saw all the awesomeness of reality in one moment. If you could see without your blinders on, you would be amazed by the miraculousness of what is around you. What is being described in the Gita was not some magical vision. What Sanjaya was saying with his words was the feeling, the overwhelming impact, of seeing things just as they are. It is not that he saw a million suns, it is that he saw the real sun for the first time, and not just what he believed. And its power and majesty was like a million of what he had previously believed the sun to be – more than a million . . .an infinity.

. . . .

15. *Arjuna said:*

I can see all the Divine in your divine body. And all the living beings gathered. Lord Brahma and Lord Shiva sitting upon a lotus flower, and all the great sages and the divine serpents.

16. I can see many arms, torsos, mouths and eyes. I can see you in every direction, with no beginning, middle or end, Divine Master of All. I see you as the all.

17. I can see helms, maces, spheres, and radiance, glowing in every direction. I see you, but it is difficult to bear, like blazing flames everywhere or the light of the sun, beyond measure.

18. You must be realized as the absolute, the greatest foundation of the all. You are the infinite upholder of the way. In my opinion you are the eternal supreme individuality.

19. Without beginning, middle or end. Infinite glories, infinite arms, eyes like the sun and moon. I see you with blazing fire burning from your mouth, giving warmth to all existence.

20. From the reaches of space to this earth and filling all in between, are you alone, in all directions. By the sight of your awe-inspiring and terrifying form, the Three Worlds themselves tremble, great soul.

21. You are within the entire school of spirits. Some of them are folding their hands from fear, offering supplication. The great sages proclaim peace, the school of magicians sing their incantations unto you with invocations from the ancient rituals.

22. All of the forms of Shiva, the Adityas, the Vasus and the Sadhyas, the Vishvedevas, the Ashvinu, Maruts, and the ancestors, schools of divine choirs (Gandharvas), Yakshas, demons and mages are all looking upon you in awe.

23. The great form of you has many faces and eyes, Great Warrior. Many arms, waists and legs, many torsos, and many fangs; and upon seeing them all the worlds tremble. As do I.

v. 15-23

Arjuna is describing his experience. What he is 'seeing' in the text is really a description of what he is feeling, at having Krishna's guidance reveal to him the nature of absolute reality. The vision of absolute reality is not only the ability to see that in front of you there is a tree, or the grass, or the sky. It is the ability to see, all at once, what the majesty of the tree and the grass and the sky represent, as well as the presence of your own self in this moment, and your intellect, emotions and energies. All of these things exist, all of them are real, and all of them are around you. All of these things are connected to each other, and all of this exists with an infinite fullness and power running through them. It is enough to make all the world tremble; and anyone who speaks of a Satori experience without trembling has never had a Satori experience. You tremble because it is overwhelming. It is the vision that kills your ego, because you realize how tiny your understanding was up to that moment.

. . . .

24. There are many glowing colours reaching to the heavens, open mouths, great glowing eyes. Seeing you I am shaken within my soul. I have lost all balance and my mind is troubled, Vishnu.

25. Seeing your terrible teeth and faces, which are like the fires of death, I have lost all sense of direction. I plead for grace, divine Master, Comforter of Worlds.

26. All of these sons of Dhirtarashtra, and these warrior kings, Bhisma, Drona, Karna, as well as the generals of our armies, they are all within your jaws, mightiest warrior.

27. They are entering, rushing into your terrible fangs. I see some of them, devoured by you, their heads crushed in your teeth.

28. As the rivers flow into the oceans, so do all these kings of the world flow into your mouths, and burn.

29. As moths are drawn into a blazing fire to their destruction, so are all people drawn with great swiftness into your mouths.

30. You are devouring all the people from all directions with your burning mouths glowing. You are covering all the world with your radiance, your terrible rays scouring all, Vishnu.

31. Please show me grace, Lord of the Gods, and explain to me your fierce form. I wish to know you as you really are, for I do not understand your purpose.

v. 24-31

All your ideas and illusions are devoured by the experience of the real. It is just as darkness can be extremely deep, extremely dark, but it is destroyed at once when you turn on the light. There is no question of resistance of the false against the real – if you only just see the real, it overwhelms all of your fantasies about life and how you think things ought to be.

But the experience of Satori does not by itself equal an understanding and an integration. Thus, one can experience Satori many times, and it will bring you closer to truth, but if you do not melt into the experience, if you do not transcend the feeling of awesomeness, you will move back, forget and rebuild the shell of your ego.

Satori is thus a very powerful and important experience for a mystic, but a Satori will not always bring an enlightenment. A mystic can, by his efforts, reach to a Satori, and after a Satori, his shell of ego will always end up a bit more cracked, he will be a bit closer to truth. But by his own effort, a mystic cannot reach enlightenment itself. He will fall back into his ego.

Only grace, which Arjuna now asks for, will allow one to reach enlightenment. There is nothing you can do through your own effort that will grant you enlightenment. Enlightenment is what happens when you give up all efforts, when you surrender completely to this awesome, awe-inspiring, and often terrifying reality of Life, of the Divine. When you can give up completely – surrender all effort – then in that surrender you will reach full awakening.

. . . .

32. *The Blessed One said:*

I am Time, the destroyer of worlds. I am that which destroys all who are in the world. And all who are on this battlefield today are doomed to die, except for you.

33. Thus, rise up! Gain fame in conquering your foes. Enjoy the prosperous Kingdom you will gain. For all those here have already been destined to be destroyed by me. You will just be the vessel for this, Arjuna.

34. Drona, and Bhisma, and Jayadratha, and Karna, and all the other great warriors have already been killed by my will. You must destroy them, so be not troubled. Only fight and conquer your enemies.

v. 32-34

Krishna explains that the Divine is the force of endless change. Everything that exists is destined to change, destined to die in its current form. And Krishna guides Arjuna back to the key of his surrender, that he must accept his natural role in life, and he must fight in the battle of Kurukshetra, to be the agent of this divine change.

. . . .

35. *Sanjaya said:*

Thus hearing Krishna's words, with folded hands, trembling Arjuna offered respectful motions (namaste) many times over. Then he spoke fearfully to Krishna, his voice wavering.

36. *Arjuna said:*

Divine Master of the senses, by your glory the world is rightfully yours. It rejoices in union with you, and the demons are running fearfully in all directions. The whole school of mages is motioning respectfully as well (namaste).

37. Why should they not offer respect unto you, great soul? You are the Superior Brahma, the Divine Creator. Infinite, God of the Gods, Comfort of the World. You are never-ending, and thus beyond the real and unreal.

38. You are the God of gods, the oldest of individuals. You are the great comfort of this existence, you are the knower and the known, and the greater fulfillment. This entire existence is filled by you, infinite form.

39. You control the air, fire, water, the moon. You are the father, the great-grandfather, and I offer honours upon honours unto you. Let it be so a thousand times over, again and again I offer my respect unto you!

40. Before you and behind you I offer respect. I offer my respect unto you from all directions, because you are all things, limitless strength and limitless force. You envelop all things, thus you are all things.

v. 35-40

Here Arjuna accepts the reality that is shown to him.

. . . .

41. Having assumed you to merely be my friend, Krishna, my dear friend, whatever I may have said was out of foolishness or out of love, without knowing your true greatness.

42. Whenever I may have joked about you or dishonoured you, relaxing and sitting with you while dining together. Or when I was alone or with other friends, ideal one, I ask your forgiveness for all these unthinkable acts.

v. 41-42

In the moment of awareness, you realize how many of your prior actions were unnatural, based on your limited understanding of reality. Arjuna asks for forgiveness of his teacher, because, like any student, he did not truly understand the significance of his Guru, or what his Guru was trying to tell him. Arjuna is filled with guilt about his way of acting toward Krishna in the past, of all the times he failed to listen or to treat Krishna with the reverence and gratefulness he deserved, that he put his ego in front of his surrender to his Guru. Even so, this remorse is still a sign that Arjuna has not yet fully understood, or else he would realize that whatever he did in the past was just a product of his dreaming. An awakened one will never be concerned about what someone who is asleep will do to him, he will always pardon it instantly, because naturally he understands that those who are asleep 'know not what they do.'

. . . .

43. You are the father of all the dimensions, mobile and immobile. You are worthy of worship, the glorious Guru. There is none equal to you. How could there possibly be any who is greater in all the Three Worlds, most powerful lord?

44. Thus I offer up my whole body in respect for you. I beg unto you for mercy, the Divine who is worthy of worship. Like a father unto a son, like a friend unto a friend, like a lover unto his beloved, so I ask you to treat me, divine one.

v 43-44

Arjuna recognizes that up till now, everything he had done had sprung from the source of wanting life, the world, society, his Guru, and everything else around him, including God himself, to act according to Arjuna's desires. This is the fundamental truth of all unenlightened beings; they are trying to force their will on the world. They want, deep down, for life to meet their expectations and their demands. They try to negotiate and bargain with the universe. And the root of all suffering is in this unnatural expectation that life 'should' go the way you want it to, rather than you becoming an agent of life itself.

. . . .

45. I am filled with joy at seeing this which I had never seen before. But my mind is also shaken with fear. So please grace me once more with your divine form, Master of Gods, Comfort of the World.

46. With your helm, club, and wheel-like weapon (chakra) in your hand, that is how I wish to see you. Thousand-armed one, I wish to see you in your four-armed form, representative of all that is.

v. 45-46

Arjuna strives once more for Satori, for the experience of the real seeking to transcend the ego-killing experience.

. . . .

47. *The Blessed One said:*

Arjuna, I will gladly show you this great form, through the union of the soul. It completely radiates upon the entire universe, infinitely. It is my most real form, which no one has ever seen prior to you.

48. Never through the priestly rituals, nor by study, nor by charity, nor by any saintly acts, nor strict ascetic acts, has anyone else in this world of matter seen this form before you, greatest warrior of the Kurus.

49. Let it neither trouble nor confuse you to see this horrible form of mine. Free from fear, contented of mind, again simply witness this, my form.

v. 47-49

Krishna makes it clear that the full experience of reality, beyond even the feeling of ego-killing awesomeness, is unobtainable by any means available to human beings. It is not something you can work at, force, or strive to obtain by your own effort. No amount of reading, study, prayer, or even meditation can make you 'earn it.' It is only obtained when you are naturally ready to surrender. It is grace, the ultimate gift of the Divine.

This is the most difficult challenge for the mystic, because it requires giving up one's own spiritual work and effort. You must work hard, practice your sadhana (your work) diligently, to reach Satori. It is not easy. But once you have reached that state, then none of what you have done, none of that hard work, will help you to take the final step. The final step doesn't depend on any work or effort on your part at all. It depends on you being ready to completely give up all effort and all work.

. . . .

50. *Sanjaya said:*

Thus, speaking in this way to Arjuna, Krishna once again showed him his true form. This brought much fear to him, so once again the great soul returned to his more beautiful form.

51. *Arjuna said:*

Looking once more upon your beautiful human form, Punisher of Enemies, I am now relaxed in my mind, I am once again composed.

52. *The Blessed One said:*

This form of mine that you have seen is very difficult to bear seeing. Even the divine spirits constantly long to gaze upon it.

53. I have never made it possible, either by the study of scripture, or ascetic acts, or charity, or worship, to see me as you have seen me.

54. But through the direct experience of devotion, Arjuna, I have made it possible to see and be aware. In fact, in this way you can enter the real, Great Warrior.

55. Doing my work, see me as the great individual. Being devoted to me, free from intellectual attempts at knowing, one who is without enemies among all living beings will come into me, Son of Pandu.

v. 50-55

At the end of attainment, when one has obtained true reality and transcended even the awesomeness of the ego-killing experience, everything comes back to being ordinary.

This is what the Zen masters mean when they say, "first there is a mountain, then there is no mountain, then there is." It is the secret contained in the Tarot, where one's path along the major arcana takes one from being the Fool, to being the Universe, then back to being the Fool. It is what is meant when the Buddhist teachers say that first you cut wood and carry water, and at the end you cut wood and carry water. The end of the mystic path is not some awesome experience of the Divine – that is the middle of the journey. The end of the journey is when you can go back to the ordinary. When you learn to be fully human, and natural, without any pretence.

After you receive the grace of enlightenment, you do not become superhuman, you become truly human – more human than ever, and a natural part of the natural world.

Chapter 12
The Yoga of Devotion (bhakti)

1. *Arjuna said:*

Then who are the most true in union: those who are always engaged in devotion, properly venerating you, or those who have moved beyond the senses into the impersonal mystery?

v. 1

Arjuna is asking: is it easier or better to practice devotion as the means to awakening, or to focus on meditation without devotion?

. . . .

2. *The Blessed One said:*

Those who focus the mind upon me are always practicing veneration to me. They are granted a greater trust by me, they are considered to be most involved in practicing the real.

3. But there are those who are completely engaged in venerating the impersonal, formless mystery that is beyond all the senses, and is also ineffable, omnipresent, unchanging, and immovably fixed in the now.

4. Focusing all of the senses, they are equally open to all things. They achieve me by practicing out of compassion for all living beings.

5. There is much trouble for those who are attached to the impersonal with their minds. Certainly for those who are in a personality, progressing into the impersonal can be achieved, but with much difficulty.

6. But those who renounce all activities to me, who attach to me, without deviating from such Yoga, they can meditate upon me.

7. And I will deliver them from the ocean of constant death and rebirth. Very soon, those whose consciousness is focused on me, I will become them, Scion of Partha.

v. 2-7

Krishna's response is that both devotion and meditation without devotion are equally valid methods. However, because our minds are trapped in personifications, starting with the personality we have created for ourselves, and extending into our ideas about everything else, it is very difficult to sincerely begin in the impersonal form of meditation.

It is not impossible – Krishna describes the method in these very verses: you must focus on the now, your senses equally open to everything around you, having an equal amount of compassion for all living beings.

This is possible for some, but for many, it is simply not possible from the beginning. It is easy to imagine, but very hard to do, to be able to keep your senses equally focused on everything, to be able to care equally about all things.

So Krishna says that it is easier to practice through devotion, to instead focus everything you do, the things you care about a little and the things you care about a lot, into your devotion to the Guru and to the Divine. If you offer up everything you do to the Divine, practice just as you are but with awareness and giving up your lust of results, you can achieve just as well as if you are trying to dive into the impersonal from the beginning.

Both paths work, and in the end both become the same; but one is more likely to work for most people than the other.

. . . .

8. Fix the mind upon me. Apply your awareness to me. You will live in me thereafter – do not doubt it.

v. 8

In devotion, it is best if you are able to fix your attention completely, devote all of your actions, to your devotion, to the Guru and the Divine.

. . . .

9. If you are not able to focus your consciousness on me steadfastly, then by practicing Yoga you will in time develop the will to reach me, great champion.

v. 9

But if total devotion is too difficult, then Krishna says it is still acceptable just to keep to your practice, to do as much as you can, and over time you will improve.

. . . .

10. If you are even unable to practice, become dedicated to doing service for me. Even work done for my sake will let you achieve great powers.

v. 10

If your practice is unsteady, even then Krishna says you need not give up. Try to practice as best you can, and be sure to offer up your service. Helping the Guru, the school, and the teaching will lead you to become more dedicated to your practice, and in that way you will improve. So remember that if your practice is unsteady, you can still help the teacher and your fellow students.

. . . .

11. If you are unable to do this either, then perform the Yoga of Refuge in me. That is, give up the results of all actions, and become in that way centred in your soul.

v. 11

If none of these things are possible for you, then the least you can do – the place to start – is in surrendering yourself to the Guru, in declaring your wish to be a student. Some people seem to think this is the only thing they need to do, but in reality this is useless if you are not trying to move past it; at least into service, better yet into regular practice, and best of all into full devotion. Simply declaring that you are willing is only useful if it is the first step, if you can try by doing this to find the sincerity and the will to start making the effort. Otherwise, it is no different than religion.

. . . .

12. Awareness is certainly better than formal practice. Meditation is even better than mere awareness. But renunciation of the results of actions is better still. By such renunciation you will gain peace.

13. Be without jealousy toward any living being, friendly and kind, with no ego or sense of possession, equal in happiness or sorrow, forgiving.

14. Such a yogi is always fulfilled. Determined, focused on the soul. With the mind and awareness focused on me, such a devotee of mine is very dear to me.

15. People who are never disturbed, and who do not disturb others, and who are free from happiness, distress, fear and worry, such people are also very dear to me.

16. Anyone who is neutral, pure, mastered, carefree, free of misery, the renouncer of all efforts; such a devotee is very dear to me.

17. One who neither takes pleasure nor grieves, does not complain or desire, and renounces the fortunate or unfortunate; such a devotee is very dear to me.

18. One who is equal toward friends or enemies, and who is also so toward honour and dishonour, in cold and heat, happiness and misery, who is balanced and free from attachment.

19. Who is equal in fame or infamy, silent, fulfilled by any situation, who has no home, who is focused in determination; such a devotee is a true human being. And he is very dear to me.

20. Those who completely involve themselves in this, what is called the nectar of the way, with trust, knowing me as the greater; such devotees are very very dear to me.

v. 12-20

Krishna, like all true Teachers, does not want simple followers. It is more important to him what you do than what you say; it is better if you can work for the Sangha, the school, than if you just speak the praises of the teacher. It is better if you can practice, than if you simply work for the school. And it is better if you can be aware with devotion, than if you can simply practice formally.

Chapter 13
The Yoga of the Sacred Awareness (kshetra)

1. *Arjuna said:*

Life and the one who experiences life; the battlefield, and he who is aware of the battlefield. I want to understand all of this, and I want to understand awareness and the object of awareness, Krishna.

v. 1

Arjuna seeks to understand the relationship between life and the individual. In so doing, he seeks to understand the nature of awareness, because this is the link between the two.

. . . .

2. *The Blessed One said:*

Son of Kunti, this body is the battlefield; so is it said by one who knows. Thus, those who know this are called 'aware of the battlefield.'

3. And certainly know me as the one who is aware of the battlefield; of all fields, Scion of Bharata. The field and he who is watching the field; to realize the difference is true awareness, in my opinion.

4. I will explain that field, as it is, and what kind of changes it undergoes and how, and what influence it can have, in brief.

v. 2-4

"This body is the battlefield." Krishna is saying that the battle Arjuna must truly fight is within himself. It is not difficult for him to go and fight the battle at Kurukshestra, it is difficult for him to first win the battle within himself. The battle is the battle to overcome the limitations you have imposed upon yourself, within your body and your mind.

But Krishna does not advise to fight and struggle darkly, to be grim and dour and against the body. The body isn't the enemy, it is only the field of battle.

And you will not win by being very serious and cynical.

You will win when you understand that it is your nature to fight. As soon as you realize that, and participate fully in the battle, you have already won.

. . . .

5. It is in many ways described by the sages, by the various chants in various ways, by the sayings of the scriptures (Brahma-Sutras), as having very certain causes and effects.

6. The great elements, ego, enlightenment, the impersonal, the eleven sensations, the five sources of sensation.

7. Desire, hatred, happiness, sorrow, the school, the proof of life, determination; all of these are just some parts of the field, and examples of its interactions.

v. 5-7

The battlefield is described to include all of your being. When Krishna says the body, he doesn't just mean your physical body; he says the battlefield is your body, your emotions, your intellect and ideas, your senses and perception, and your energy. All of these things must be brought into balance.

. . . .

8. Humility, lack of pride, non-violence, tolerance, simplicity, service toward a saintly teacher, cleanliness, steadiness, focus on the soul.

9. The renouncing of the senses, egolessness, and witnessing the causes of birth, death, age, disease, and sorrow.

10. Being free of attachment, free of associating yourself as a father, husband, homeowner, and so on. And also having obtained constant balance, neither drawn to the desirable nor away from the undesirable.

11. Also by dedicated Yoga, and devotion unto me, without pausing, going into the quiet places, being unattached toward people in general.

12. Constant in awareness of the soul, for the sake of awakening the vision of awareness of the real. All of these things I declare to be awareness. All else is ignorance.

v. 8-12

All of the things Krishna describes are your weapons in the battle. They are the practices and techniques that create awareness in you.

. . . .

13. I will explain the possible subjects of awareness. And when one tastes the infinite nectar of this awareness, one will know my greater form, Brahma. Then one will be beyond all causes and effects.

14. It has hands and legs everywhere. Eyes, heads, and faces, with ears everywhere, filling all that exists in the world.

15. It is the original source of all the elements (gunas) of the senses, although it is itself without senses. Without being attached, it is the maintainer of all life. And without any physical form, it is the controller of all the physical elements as well.

16. Inside and outside of all living beings, mobile and immobile at once. Indefinable due to its multitude of definitions. Far away, and also near at once.

17. Indivisible, though apparently divided into all living beings. The maintainer of all living beings, that must be understood as the devourer as well as the creator of all.

18. It is in all radiant things, and it is also the source of all radiance. It is said to be beyond all darkness. It is awareness, it is the source of awareness, it is the longing in everyone's heart to be aware.

19. Thus the battlefield, and awareness, and the possible subjects of awareness have now been explained in brief by me. Any devotee of mine who understands all of this will attain to my nature.

v. 13-19

Awareness as described by Krishna is a force, it is a Mystery; it exists within everything, as the source of everything. It is that state of awareness, and it is also that state of seeking awareness, and it is the longing in between those two as well. It is in everything, everything is awareness.

. . . .

20. You must know the world of matter and the living beings in it as being eternal. Their transformations through the gunas are the result of the interactions of matter.

21. The interaction of matter is said to be the instrument that creates causes and effects. The interactions of living beings are likewise the instruments of the creation of joy and sorrow.

22. Living beings that exist in matter certainly have experiences of matter. These experiences are caused by the gunas. The guna that a living being identifies most closely to will determine his good and bad experiences in his lives.

v. 20-22

The 'gunas' is the term used in Indian symbolism to represent the building blocks of all the universe. In western mysticism, they are described as the alchemical elements: salt, sulphur, and mercury. They are described as heaviness, hotness, and swiftness. They are matter, energy, and vibration.

Modern science says that nothing can be created or destroyed, only changed into new states. Krishna is saying something very similar here, that all that exists in the universe is in a constant state of change: nothing is ever really destroyed, it is only changing; sometimes changing slowly, sometimes very fast.

Realizing those two things: that nothing is ever destroyed, and that everything is always changing in one way or another, are two very important keys to understanding reality and achieving awareness.

. . . .

23. The overseer who allows all of this, the master and true owner is the great divine master, the supersoul. And indeed it is said that the true experiencer within the body is this greater experiencer.

24. Thus, anyone who knows about the living beings, the material world, and the gunas, whatever his present state, he will never again be forced to take birth.

v. 23-24

If you become aware of this truth of the universe and universal change, you start to identify and become aware of the supersoul, the binding force, the mystery that links everything together in this constant river-like flow of change.

. . . .

25. By meditating on the soul, some will see the supersoul in the soul. Others will see it through self-inquiry, Yoga, or the works of union.

26. But others still, without any special training, by merely hearing of this from others, will begin to practice. They will also transcend the path of death, for these ones are predisposed to hearing the truth.

v. 25-26

There are many ways, Krishna says, to become aware of the supersoul. One is by meditating and understanding the soul itself. Another is to seek to understand yourself through self-inquiry, because by looking at yourself you will see this truth of constant change. Another is through techniques of Yoga, because in seeking to unite all things and see the union of all things, you will find that binding force. Some will even just come to find it in a spontaneous moment of understanding, if they are in the right state of consciousness at the right place and time.

. . . .

27. Whatever comes into existence of any kind, mobile or immobile, know that it is only a great combination of the observer and the subject observed, Best of the Bharatas.

28. Anyone who sees that the great divine master is equally present in all living things; that it is in all mortal things but is itself immortal, that one has true vision.

v. 27-28

If you see the interaction between these basic elements, you see the supersoul. You see that the constancy of change is the immortal itself.

. . . .

29. Seeing the divine master equally everywhere, one will find no limit to the soul within the soul. Then one will reach the greater goal.

v. 29

When you understand that this change is happening everywhere, and is present in all things equally, you realize the union of existence.

. . . .

30. Anyone who sees that regardless of which activities are done in the material realm, one's soul remains free of activity, that one has true vision.

31. When one endeavours to see the separate personalities of living beings as being in fact oneness, then one will attain expansion into Brahma.

32. This soul is eternal, transcendent of matter, infinite. Son of Kunti, though it is in the body, it never acts nor can action be taken upon it.

33. It is the astral force (akasha). It is within all things but can never be affected. Likewise, the soul is everywhere in the body but can never be affected.

v. 30-33

This supersoul is present everywhere and in everything. Look at the people around you, and when you can see that they are as much a part of you as your own body, you will see the greater truth of the supersoul. This Mystery is what exists in everything and is beyond any influence.

34. As the sun gives light to the whole world, this subject gives light to the whole body, Scion of Bharata.

35. Thus with the vision of awareness one can see the difference between the body and the one who witnesses the body. Those living beings who know this will gain liberation from material bondage, and will approach the greater.

v. 34-35

If you see the supersoul shining in all things like the sun, giving its light equally to all of life, you will become one with the light, and with the sun.

Chapter 14
The Yoga of the Three Gunas

1. *The Blessed One said:*

Again I shall speak of the greatest of all understandings, the supreme understanding. Knowing which, all of the great sages of this realm attained power.

2. Taking shelter in this awareness, having attained the same nature as my own, they are not born even in the time of creation, nor are they destroyed in the time of annihilation.

3. The womb of my material existence is Brahma. Into that womb I seed the possibility of all things, which is the source of all living beings, Scion of Bharata.

v. 1-3

What Krishna is explaining here is the nature of the Universe. Brahma, God, is the womb; it is the birthing place of all things. The divine is the force of all creation.

. . . .

4. Son of Kunti, all species of life, all forms that can exist appear. Brahma is the source of all their births, and I am the seed-giving father of them all.

5. Truth (Sattvas), passion (Rajas), and ignorance (Tamas) are the three elements (gunas) born of matter. They condition all eternal living beings who occupy temporary bodies, Great Warrior.

v. 4-5

The manifested form of all things is composed of a mixture of the three alchemical elements, the Gunas.

. . . .

6. There is the element of Sattvas, purest in this existence, that provides illumination and avoids wrongdoing. It conditions one toward happiness and awareness, Sinless One.

v. 6

Sattvas is the element of purity; it is essential truth and wisdom.

. . . .

7. Know the element Rajas to create desire in the soul. It conditions one to feel longing, which binds you to performing actions that produce Karma, Son of Kunti.

v. 7

Rajas is passion, longing, ambition. It is not any worse or any better than Sattvas. Just as Sattvas is truth, and vital to any thing in existence, Rajas is motion, and equally vital. It is not that one Guna is good, and another bad, it is that all three must be kept in balance.

. . . .

8. But know that the element Tamas is born of a lack of understanding of the real. It is the delusion of all living beings, producing madness, laziness, and tiredness, that binds one to an animal existence, Scion of Bharata.

v. 8

Tamas is 'heaviness,' 'ignorance,' imperfection. It sounds very negative, but it too is necessary. Without it, nothing could have form, there would be no room for anything to change. It is 'delusion,' because most things in existence only believe that they are that thing.

It is like if you take a rock, a rock that is mostly made out of base elements, but inside it, there are also precious metals. If you looked at it, you might only see a rock. You would need to break it down, melt it down, and filter out the precious metals to be able to see them, but they were always there in the first place.

. . . .

9. The element Sattvas attaches you to pleasure, the element Rajas binds you to lust of result, which conceals awareness of the real, Scion of Bharata. But the element Tamas is said to attach you to animal madness.

v. 9

Any of these three elements, if put out of balance, will lead to attachment and thus to suffering. It does you no good to try to gain an excess of one element at the cost of the others. Some mystics have mistakenly believed that the goal is to cast off those other 'lesser' elements and be left with the pure element of Sattvas, but this is not true.

. . . .

10. Sometimes Sattvas is in greater proportion than Rajas or Tamas, Scion of Bharata. Other times, Rajas is most prominent, or Tamas.

v. 10

At different stages in your life, different elements might be stronger in you. Krishna goes on to explain how these different imbalances will end up affecting you.

. . . .

11. When the element Sattvas is most prominent, all the gates of the body develop illumination and awareness. Thus is it said.

12. When there is an excess of the element Rajas, greed and the uncontrollable longing to act out of desires will develop, Best of the Bharatas.

13. When Tamas is most developed, then darkness, sloth, madness and illusions are certainly manifest, Son of Kuru.

v. 11-13

If Sattvas is the most prominent of elements, then you are in a state of wisdom. Thus it is better to have your most prominent element be Sattvas; but if you go too far, then you are left with an attachment to 'pleasure,' to your own grandeur. You get lost in your mind and in your own sense of self-importance. Sattvas is the spiritual ego. So the balance must be very careful; you must be able to associate with your wisdom without getting lost in it. You can get lost in your own sense of wisdom just as much as you can get lost in your own lusts or your base natures.

. . . .

14. But when Sattvas is most developed at the time of death, the embodied being then attains to the pure dimension of the great scholars.

15. One who dies in the element Rajas, he will take birth in the company of those who live in this world of activities. Likewise, one who dies in the element Tamas will take birth among the animals.

v. 14-15

Whatever your state is at the time of death, to that you will attain. It is better to be in a state of wisdom when you die, but the 'realm of great scholars' is not the same as enlightenment; eventually you must go back to the human realm and continue. Likewise, if you die in a state of base ignorance, you will be like an animal; and there too you must work your way back up to a state of humanity.

These statements do not only mean how you will be at the time of literal death; they also refer to what your condition is at any time in your life. If you are in an overabundance of Sattvas, you will be living in the realm of the great scholars, the realm of the mind. If you are living in Rajas, in your lusts, then you are living in the material world. If you are living in Tamas, you are living and behaving like an animal, like something less than fully human. None of these three states make you a perfectly balanced human being. The balanced human being is one who is in Wisdom, in Activity, and in his animal naturalness all at once.

. . . .

16. Activities taken in the element Sattvas are said to be saintly, and result in purification. But actions done in the element Rajas result in sorrow, and actions in the element Tamas result in delusion.

17. From Sattvas is awareness developed. From Rajas is greed developed. And certainly also from Tamas is madness and animalistic delusion likewise developed.

18. Those in Sattvas will move upward. Those in Rajas linger in the middle, and those whose actions are in Tamas fall downward to the abominable.

v. 16-18

These verses explain that it is best to be balanced in the three elements but focused on Truth, on awareness; rather than on your lusts or animal nature. It doesn't mean these other two must be rejected. In fact it is impossible to reject these other parts of your nature. Trying to do so will lead to suppression, and this will cause you to begin to act in unnatural ways, and lose your centre. So the way to be in Truth is not to concern yourself about the other things; allow them to exist but do not be attached to them.

. . . .

19. When one sees properly that only the gunas are responsible for action, and knows that there is a force greater than all the gunas, he will ascend to my state of being.

20. When one transcends all three gunas that are produced by one's physical existence, he will gain freedom from the miseries of birth, death and old age.

v. 19-20

When you understand that all three Gunas must be transcended; that these elements are not the place for you to struggle and focus on, then you can see that the goal is to balance out these material elements and move with them and through them to pure awareness of that which exists behind all reality, the Divine.

. . . .

21. *Arjuna said:*

Which qualities will be present in one who has transcended all three gunas, my Lord? What is the behaviour of one such as this, and how does he succeed in transcending the gunas?

22. *The Blessed One said:*

Son of Pandu, one who neither hates illumination, attachment or delusion even in their presence; nor does he desire them in their absence.

v. 21-22

Arjuna asks the right question. He does not assume that he already knows what someone who has transcended the Gunas will look like. And Krishna's answer might surprise some. Krishna says that someone who's transcended the Gunas won't hate awareness, or attachment, or illusion. He won't be concerned with any of the three. To transcend the Gunas, you must accept them as a part of your existence, all three of them.

. . . .

23. One who holds no position is never disturbed by the gunas, and thus witnesses their action. Such a one remains steady and does not waver.

24. One who acts equally when suffering and joy are present in him, who is equally disposed to a lump of earth, a lump of stone, and a lump of gold. One who is equally disposed to the desirable and undesirable, and equally steady when his soul is being praised or defamed by others.

25. Equal in honour and dishonour, equal to groups of friends and enemies, renouncing all efforts, he is said to be risen above the gunas.

26. Also, a person who practices service and the Yoga of Devotion unto me, he will transcend all of the gunas, and become raised to Brahma.

27. I am the foundation of Brahma, of the nectar of immortality, of the infinite and eternal. And of the way of ultimate joy.

v. 23-27

The real joy is found when you can accept all that life gives you, all that the Divine has made for you. You must accept what you perceive as your flaws as much as what you perceive as your strengths. You must accept that you are animal, man, and divine. That you are ignorant, intelligent, and wise at the same time. It is the joy of the Ultimate Yes.

Chapter 15
The Yoga of the Supreme Being (purusottama)

1. *The Blessed One said:*

It is said that there is an eternal banyan tree with its roots above, and its branches below. The leaves are the scriptures. And anyone who knows this tree is a knower of the scriptures.

v. 1

It is important to grasp exactly how Krishna is framing his metaphor. The Scriptures are NOT the tree, they are the leaves. Anyone who knows the tree knows the leaves. Anyone who knows the Tree of Life knows everything that is of value in the scriptures, even if he's never read them. On the other hand, one who knows only the scriptures knows only the leaves, and not the entire tree.

2. Its branches extend downwards and upwards. They develop from the gunas. Its twigs are the objects of the senses. The tree's roots extend downward, where they are entangled by action in the world.

v. 2

The tree is born of the elements, and its branches are all material existence. And its roots are cause and effect, Karma.

. . . .

3. The form of this tree is not visible in this dimension. Never does it end and never does it begin, and never does it have a foundation. This banyan tree with its strong roots must be cut down with the weapon of detachment. This takes great strength.

4. After cutting it one must be watchful to find that place where, once you go, you will never return. One must surrender to the original individuality, from whom all things have come in the beginning, aeons ago.

v. 3-4

Only detachment can break down the whole tree, which is really a construction. It is beautiful, it is the structure of all life, but as long as you are in the place of the tree you cannot see the Unity of the Divine. But fighting with material things, or studying the scriptures, or trying to value one element over another – none of these things will let you get past the tree, because all of these things are part and parcel of the tree. You can only cut it down with detachment, and then find the place of individuality, what you are that is not a part of the tree.

. . . .

5. Without false pride and illusion, having conquered faulty associations, eternally in the meditation of the soul, detached from lust, liberated from the duality of joy and sorrow, those who are like this gain eternal clarity.

6. My great abode is not lit by the sun or the moon, nor by any other energy. Those who go there never come back.

7. The part of me that is in the world as a living being is eternal as well. But it must struggle with the mind, and the rest of the senses, that work in the material.

8. As the body acquires various things, the body loses its inner Mastery. In taking all these things one moves away from Mastery, just as the scents will be carried away from a flower by the air.

v. 5-8

There is a place of pure unity; that is enlightenment. When someone achieves enlightenment, he can never go back to unawareness.

But it is not to say that one part is real and the other is not, one part is eternal and the other is not.

The material world is real too, in its own level. And the part of life that is material is just as eternal as the part that is immaterial.

But existing as a being identifying with the material world means that you will continue going through cycles of Karma and suffering. Over the course of your lifetime, you will gain conditionings and lose your individuality.

. . . .

9. Hearing, seeing, touching, tasting and smelling, and the mind. These are all the senses that one will experience.

10. Foolish people cannot see that anyone who is in a body will lose their body, eventually. They are too busy existing under the spell of the gunas. But those who have the eyes of awareness can see this.

v. 9-10

Foolish people are those who try to believe that nothing will change in their lives, or try to ignore it. The most significant example of this is in how many people in the world make themselves forget that they will die someday, they don't want to remember, so they ignore it.

. . . .

11. Those who work in Yoga can also see this, if they are centred in their soul. But those who have not yet realized the soul will not see this yet, as their consciousness is not yet developed.

12. The sunshine, that by its splendour illuminates the entire world, and the splendour of the moon, and fire; understand that all of this comes from me.

13. Entering the planets and all the living beings, I sustain them by my energy. I nourish the vegetables and all drugs, becoming the juices that make these nourishing.

14. I become the ability to eat in all beings. And the inward and outward breath, which together with the digestion of the four kinds of food keeps the body in balance.

v. 11-14

What Krishna is saying is that all natural cycles are a part of divinity. The process of breathing, of eating and defecating, the circulation of blood; just like gravity, chemistry, mathematics, all cause and effect. Karma is also just a natural phenomenon – it is cause and effect.

. . . .

15. I am in the heart of all living beings. From me come memory, awareness, and forgetfulness. And I am the writer of all the known scriptures, and the knower of their teachings.

16. There are two classes of beings in this world: the restricted and the unrestricted. It is said that all living beings in themselves are restricted, but in the oneness they are unrestricted.

v. 15-16

There is the material, and the immaterial. You are both of these; the question is whether you associate yourself with your limits, or with your unlimited nature.

. . . .

17. But it is said that there is also a third class, the greatest individual, the supersoul. He who is inside the threefold worlds, maintains them, and is himself the infinite Master.

18. I am transcendent to both the restricted and the unrestricted, the greatest. Thus I am praised in the world and in the scriptures as the greatest individual.

19. Anyone who views me as such, without doubt, as the greatest individual, he is the knower of all. He will perform service for me in everything he does, Scion of Bharata.

20. This is the most secret of the scriptures disclosed by me, sinless one. Being enlightened by this, one becomes enlightenment, and thus all his doings will be right, Scion of Bharata.

v. 17-20

Beyond our unlimited immaterial selves, there is the unity of all selves in the Supersoul, the Divine. Thus enlightenment is the process of first realizing the limitlessness in yourself, and then the unlimited all-connectedness of the Divine.

Chapter 16
The Yoga of Divine and Demonic Qualities

1. *The Blessed One said:*

Fearlessness, being in truth, the state of being united to awareness, charity, mental focus, ritual, study of scripture, austerity, and simple living.

2. Non-violence, honesty, lack of anger, renunciation, peace, being non-judgmental, compassion for all living beings, lack of greed, gentleness, humility, and determination.

3. Enthusiasm, forgiveness, endurance, cleanliness, lack of jealousy, and not seeking fame are the qualities of one who is born into divine nature, Scion of Bharata.

4. Pride, arrogance and vanity, anger and intolerance, as well as ignorance; these are the qualities of one who is born into dark nature, Scion of Partha.

5. Divine qualities assist in attaining liberation. The dark qualities are considered to lead into bondage. Do not worry, Scion of Pandu, you are born into divine qualities.

6. There are two kinds of living beings created in this world: the divine and the dark. I have spoken of the divine with great detail, Son of Partha. Now hear from me of the dark.

v. 1-6

It's very important to understand clearly what Krishna means in these verses. He says that people are 'born of' divine nature or 'Dark nature.' In fact, it doesn't mean that certain people are naturally good and others evil. 'Born into' here does not mean the state of physical birth, it means where you have come to be.

So 'Born into' means that you have formed yourself a certain way. Just like initiation is a kind of rebirth, so it is that you can go from your natural form in childhood to be 'born into' a darkened state, a state of ignorance and suffering. Pride, arrogance, anger, and intolerance are the products of experiences that shape you to develop these qualities, which work against your ability to connect to the Divine. They are the path to the 'dark side,' and it is important, if Krishna is going to describe the entire Spiritual experience, to talk about and look at this element of life as much as the 'divine' element of life.

If you cannot address and deal with the dark side of life, then you will never be able to fully integrate into the divine side.

. . . .

7. People who are of dark qualities do not know the difference between right and wrong action. Nor is there cleanliness, saintliness, or truth in them.

8. They say that this world is untrue, with no purpose, cause, or controller. It has merely come to be, due to no reason besides lust.

v. 7-8

The principle quality of being in the dark side is an inability to see what is good and what is bad. This isn't to say that people in darkness are evil; it means they literally cannot know – even if they intend to be good – what is good and what is bad.

This is why it is so important to be able to examine the 'dark side,' the darkness within yourself. If you do not, then there is no way you will know what is good, or what is natural. You might want to, want to be good, want to be natural, but you will be unable to do so because by yourself you won't know what is really good, what is really natural.

Someone who is being guided by their pride, or by their arrogance, or by anger or intolerance will commit to certain behaviours, ideas, or actions thinking that they are being good or being spiritual, they might try to work toward awareness and think they're making all kinds of progress, but without addressing those dark traits, their work will be warped and unnatural.

Ultimately, a person guided by darkness will reject the world. This is a very significant statement by Krishna: he is saying that those who claim this world is untrue are guided in this by their own arrogance and spiritual pride. It is not just condemning people who are stupid atheists, or condemning nihilists or hedonists; it applies just as much to so-called spiritual people who claim you must reject the world or life or being in the world for the sake of spirituality, religion or God. These people might speak a lot about God, but in reality they are being guided by nothing more than a hatred of the world and a reaction to their own unaddressed 'dark sides.'

. . . .

9. Accepting this vision, having lost their souls, the unaware revel in activities that bring painful consequences (Karma) to them and others. This leads to the harmful destruction of the world.

10. Seeking comfort in unfulfilling lust, absorbed in the vanity of pride and prestige, due to their delusion they cling to impermanent things. They revel in their dedication to the unclean.

v. 9-10

What are 'Unclean things' to Krishna? Vanity, pride and prestige are unclean. The 'unfulfilling lust' that these people pursue might be material pleasures, or it might be spiritual obsessions. In either case, what is really significant is that it is self-aggrandizement. Trapped by their pride, they seek to be 'special,' and will struggle and fight for the chance to be special people.

The spiritual man is not special, he is just ordinary. He doesn't believe he is someone extraordinary or better than others. That is not to say that Teachers are humble people;

rather that they are just themselves and unconcerned with standing out. On the contrary, many people guided by the dark side will express a false 'humility,' to try to show that they are very specially humble.

People guided by the dark side will seek to be the centre of attention, whether through physical lust, or through power, riches, or being admired and respected. They will be addicted, be it to drugs or other substances, or to experiences, or to being admired. They will want to be 'the greatest.' They will long to not be simple participants in life or in spiritual work, they will want to show off being very intelligent or very powerful or very spiritual. They don't want to learn, they want to teach. They don't want to enjoy, they want to own. They don't want to participate, they want to rule.

. . . .

11. They seek comfort in countless fears and anxieties until the time of their death. They seek comfort in the pleasures of the senses, believing that these are the greatest.

12. Being bound by these hundreds of hopes, they are always entangled. Lust and anger are always on their mind. They seek out lust for the sake of sense pleasures; they accumulate wealth by unethical means.

v. 11-12

Naturally a person driven by their 'dark side' will be filled with fears and anxieties, but these will not be just a side effect of where they are; rather it is something they will seek out, because it too is a sign of being exceptional. They want to be able to claim that no one has suffered like they have; that their problems are exceptional problems, that their difficulties are because they have been persecuted for their greatness, that no one understands them because no one is unique the way they are.

They will of course become entangled in this addiction, this need to be special, this need to be recognized. It will lead them into falseness, into false seeing and understanding, and into projecting falseness about themselves to others.

. . . .

13. "Today I have gained this, and I shall gain more as I desire it. This is mine; that is also mine. And my wealth will only increase in the future."

14. "I have killed this enemy, I will kill that enemy and others too. I am the lord, I am the one who experiences, I am the mage, powerful and happy."

15. "I am wealthy and surrounded by noble relations. Who else is like I am? I will sacrifice, give charity, and rejoice." In these ways one is deluded by ignorance.

16. They are confounded by many worries, surrounded by a web of illusions. Attached to the lust of the senses, the unclean slide down into hell.

v. 13-16

The 'lust of the senses' is the desire to be special, and the desire to control life. It is pride coming out of a desperate desire to validate your existence, when no such validation is needed.

. . . .

17. With a slothful soul and stubborn, absorbed in the illusion of wealth and fame, they perform rituals in name only. They sacrifice only for show, without practicing for genuine knowing.

v. 17

Jesus had said that it is better to pray in a closet. In the bible there is the story of the 'famously spiritual' man who made a big deal about praying out loud and thanking God that he was so wise and religious, unlike the poor man next to him. But that poor man was praying from his heart, and in silence, expecting no praise. The former attitude is the attitude of being spiritual 'for show,' and the reward is only the attention of others. Nothing meaningful is gained, and the person who does this ends up lost and without awareness.

. . . .

18. Seeking comfort in false ego, strength, pride, lust and anger, they despise and envy myself and other living teachers.

19. Those who are envious of me and miscreant I cast into the ocean of the world as the lowest of humanity. I put them always into dark and unfortunate wombs.

20. The foolish gain birth after birth in dark wombs. Son of Kunti, without reaching me they sink into a damned place.

v. 18-20

These falsely spiritual people may come to real teachers, but they do so to get confirmation of their own grandeur. When a real teacher refuses to play along with that game of theirs, they turn on him. Many students who eventually betray their teacher do so even after it seems, for a time, that they are the most devoted students, practicing the most, having the most 'experiences,' and working the hardest to promote the school. But they did all of that so that they would get some kind of special place in the school, so that they would be seen by all as being an especially spiritual and valuable student, so they would be recognized. If their recognition doesn't manifest, they will turn around and eventually claim that they have outgrown their teacher, that they are superior, or that their teacher was obviously false because he didn't see how wonderful they were. And their feelings for the teacher are the same as their feelings toward the Divine itself: they want to 'follow' the divine with the understanding that the Divine will reward them for it in one way or another. If they feel that life has disappointed their expectations, they will turn around and hate the Divine. And this will lead them down a spiral into darkness. This is the 'dark and unfortunate womb' that they will find themselves in. Unless this type of person awakens to grasp the mistake they are making in trying to force their will on the world, they will continue to sink deeper and deeper into a hole of their own making, their resistance and reaction and escape from life becoming more extreme at every turn.

. . . .

21. There are three gates leading into the hell that destroys the soul: lust, anger and greed. Thus, these three must be given up.

22. Son of Kunti, being liberated from these three gates of ignorance, a person cleanses their soul. After this he goes to the greater goal.

v. 21-22

Lust, anger, and greed are the driving forces that lead one to darkness. Let go of these, and you are cleansed.

. . . .

23. One who gives up the wise teachings will be stuck in foolish actions born of lust. He will never attain power, never achieve happiness, never reach the greater goal.

24. Thus the teachings reveal to you the way to discriminate between right and wrong action. Being aware of the wisdom declared by the teachings, you should take action in the world.

v. 23-24

Remember the teachings of this chapter and you can see where your own anger, lust or greed are leading you into reaction. Free yourself from reaction, accept life on its terms and not yours, and you will be able to walk on the path of the Mystic.

Chapter 17
The Yoga of Threefold Love (shradhatraya)

1. *Arjuna said:*

Krishna, those who give up the wise teachings, but practice in their own way with full trust, in what element are they? Sattvas, Rajas or Tamas?

v. 1

Trust is a fundamental issue in the Mystic path. Mysticism does not base itself on faith or belief. On the contrary, it teaches that belief is a great barrier to progress on the path, because it is your beliefs – your preconceptions – that keep you from seeing reality as it is. But on the other hand, the mystic teaching emphasizes trust.

This is because Trust is not based on simply accepting what you read or what you are told. Trust has nothing to do with that, in fact. Trust has to do with a state of being, where you are open in your heart to the teacher and to God, and to life. When you trust, you do not trust a teaching or a dogma, you trust life.

Trust also requires hard work. Belief is easy; you just believe what you are told and you're done. Belief is a way to avoid hard work. But trust requires that you go on to practice and confirm your trust, it is not just a question of accepting some teaching (that is belief). It is about accepting and confiding in the teacher and in life enough to do what he asks you to DO, not just believe something you are asked to believe without doing anything about it.

So Arjuna in this verse is asking something very important: he is asking Krishna just how important is trust. Namely, he is asking whether someone who is full of trust, but imperfect or uninformed in his practice, could still get anywhere.

. . . .

2. *The Blessed One said:*

Trust is divided into three kinds among those with bodies, depending on their dominant element, whether they are in the element of Sattvas (truth), Rajas (passion) or Tamas (ignorance). Now hear what I have to say about this.

v. 2

Krishna's answer to him is that there are different levels of trust. Trust is not, in fact, an all or nothing affair.

. . . .

3. Scion of Bharata, a person's trust will vary according to each person's reality. One who lets himself trust will certainly become filled with trust.

v. 3

The more open you are to trusting, the more powerfully that trust will transform you. This is what Krishna means when he says that 'one who lets himself trust will be filled with trust.'

. . . .

4. Those who are in the element Sattvas will practice toward the divine spirits. Those who are in the element Rajas will practice toward the spirits of nature. Those people who are in the element Tamas will practice toward the ghosts, empty spirits.

v. 4

Krishna explains that the degree of trust one has is tied to the three spiritual elements, and where one is oriented in his balance of elements will determine the nature of his trust. Whether he will trust in the spirit (divine spirits), in the body and the senses (spirit of nature) or in false truths and empty beliefs (ghosts).

. . . .

5. Those people who undergo unwise abstinences that are harmful to themselves and others, they are bound by pride and arrogance. They are driven by lusts and attachments.

6. Torturing the natural impulses of the body because of a lack of true consciousness, understand that although I am within their individuality, they have also filled themselves with demons.

v. 5-6

There are some who will, through their beliefs in false truths, in dogmas, in what they would like life to be like, engage in unnecessarily unnatural behaviour. They will go against their natural selves, hate their bodies, and harm themselves. The demons they'll be filled with are the demons of their own devising, the demons of their own self-hate. But note: Krishna says that even then, he (as God) is within them. Even if you perform unnatural acts, there is no way to lose your divine nature; you only end up burying it under false nature.

. . . .

7. There are three different kinds of foods that will be appealing to each of the kinds of people; as well as three different kinds of ritual, disciplines, and charities. Now hear of the differences between these.

v. 7

When Krishna talks about 'food' here, he is not talking about physical food at all; he's talking about the food of the spirit, the kind of teachings that will appeal to a person based on the balance of their elements. The food is a metaphor.

. . . .

8. The food that is appealing to one who is in Sattvas is positive to one's health, strength and long life. It brings more satisfaction and pleasure. It is juicy, fatty, filling and fulfilling.

v. 8

Someone who is based in Truth will seek to trust in teachings that are positive, healthy and juicy. They will want something fulfilling and rich.

. . . .

9. The food that appeals to one in Rajas is bitter, sour, salty, spicy, pungent, dry, and hot. It causes sorrow, misery, and disease.

v. 9

When one is based in their Passions, they will seek teachings that are 'spicy' or 'bitter' or 'hot': that is to say, they will seek out teachings that are exciting. They will want teachings that are full of metaphysics, that have all kinds of complex systems and recipes and talk about 'secrets' and 'power.' They will want all the flash and lots of 'experiences,' thinking that this is the essence of real teaching.

Many who start out seeking this 'excitement' can come to grow and learn that it is not the flashy experiences that they really seek, but the solid fulfillment of simple meditative work. They will come to realize that they can leave the flash and pomp behind and simplify their teaching, and that the more simple they can keep their teaching the more natural and fulfilling and true it becomes.

But for those who don't grow in this way, the 'flash' becomes an addiction: they will turn from one experience to another, they will develop a disease of spiritual seeking, and they will find misery because all their flashy seeking will not fulfill them.

. . . .

10. The food that is the favourite of one in Tamas is old, tasteless, foul smelling, rotting and left over from the meals of others. It is untouchable.

v. 10

When someone is based in ignorance, they will seek out teachings that are old and rotting. They will be interested in institutional religion that will tell them what to think and to believe. They will seek religion. They will want to follow people who confirm that they are better than other people, and that God wants them to hate. They will want rules and control, to be controlled in their own life, and to have an excuse to control the lives of others.

. . . .

11. The rituals that are performed according to wise guidance and without lust of result could only be performed by someone who focuses their mind in the element of truth (Sattvas).

12. Best of the Bharatas, be informed that ritual performed for the sake of some goal is done in the element of passion (Rajas).

13. And ritual performed without wise guidance, for greedy purposes, without the vibrating of mantras, without sharing or service, and without trust is to be considered as being in the element of ignorance (Tamas).

v. 11-13

Krishna teaches also that regardless of what teaching one is exposed to, your motives will determine how you practice your ritual. How well you trust God will affect how you practice. In this way, someone who is in a true school can still end up practicing in an unnatural way, and someone who has never known anything besides institutional religion could still practice with sincerity. So do not think that this means Krishna is saying that his teaching is the only way to enlightenment, and the others will be 'bad rituals.' The 'ritual' he is talking about here is the motive with which you do your practices.

Someone who is true in their heart and has trust based on truth will perform their practices, whichever they may be, without any lust of result.

Someone who is governed by their passions will perform their practice for the sake of some goal; they will want to gain something from it in exchange. This is true whether they are practicing meditation or the rituals of some religion.

And someone who is guided by ignorance will perform their practices for purely greedy reasons, without any real caring for the Divine, without any real caring for others.

. . . .

14. Practicing service to the Divine, to the initiates, to the Guru, and to others worthy of service; cleanliness, simplicity, directing all desires to Brahma, and non-violence are said to be proper bodily disciplines.

15. Words that are not disturbing, truthful, appealing and helpful and which do not contradict the teaching of the Masters; these are said to be discipline of speech.

16. The gifted mind, without deceiving others, seriously focused on the soul, purifying one's being, is said to be practicing discipline of mind.

17. Having committed with greater trust these threefold disciplines, men who have no ulterior motives or lust of result are said to be practicing in the element of Sattvas (truth).

v. 14-17

Practice must be performed in a balanced way in the different dimensions; you must practice discipline, and develop trust, in the body, the mind and the heart. In these verses, Krishna emphasizes what proper discipline consists of on all these levels: he says that it is important to develop a discipline out of thinking of others besides yourself, always however in a good and balanced context. He emphasizes that you must be cautious with what you say, not trying to show off or speak about things you do not know, and without letting your own fears or resistance lead other people into confusion.

In other words, all of these things require sincerity. They require that you be sincere in your intention to practice, sincere in your concern to help the school and your fellow human beings, sincere in being honest about what you say, and sincere in your accepting of your experiences, without either trying to downplay them or blow them out of proportion, either in your own mind or toward other people. If you do this, you are in truth.

. . . .

18. Practicing worship for the sake of gaining honour or being respected by others, and practicing disciplines in this world out of pride are said to be done in the element Rajas (passion). Their results are wavering and temporary.

v. 18

If you are practicing to impress others or to get some kind of result, the energy of your effort is all taken up by that; and any results or experiences you gain will be temporary. They will happen, but if you are then absorbed in what you have gained, it will be lost again. This is Karma; it is a natural occurrence.

When you practice with goals, out of passions or lust, then you are stuck in a cycle of gaining and losing.

In fact, most students find themselves caught in these cycles, and it is not always easy to break out of them. It is here where trust makes the most difference. People who fail to trust will cling to whatever little things they have gained, because in their hearts they do not trust that they will continue to gain whatever they need from life. So they become attached, cling to and make a big deal out of their experiences, and will end up using those experiences up. From there, they will either move into the next big thing, or they will drop down into creating a false experience, recreating an illusion of what they once had for real, a simulacrum.

But if you cultivate trust in your heart, and do not cling to lust of result, then gradually the cycles can be decreased and sincere practice increased, until you are practicing for its own sake.

. . . .

19. Those who foolishly strive against their own souls, who perform disciplines of self-torture, or who wish to do harm to others, they are said to practice in the element Tamas (ignorance).

v. 19

If your 'practice' consists of fostering hate towards others or making yourself feel more important by making others feel less 'spiritual' than you, then you are in darkness. Your practices will be in the form of harming yourself in some way, and claiming that your self-denial is somehow a virtue that makes you better than others. This is practice based on utter false pride and self-hatred.

False pride and hatred of others are both actually forms of self-hatred. If you want to make yourself feel special by trying to put yourself above other people, you do so because you secretly hate who you are. If you use religion to condemn others, it is because you secretly hate what you are. You fear that if you do not do these things, then you will not be 'worth' anything.

This self-destructive behaviour can usually only be escaped through some extreme crisis, wherein you come to realize that this self-hatred can be overcome by opening your heart to divine love.

. . . .

20. Giving charity to those whom it is worth giving to, with no desire for return, in the right place and time and to the right person, is considered to be charity in the element Sattvas.

21. But charity done for some ulterior motive, lusting for a certain result, or given reluctantly, is considered to be charity in the element Rajas.

22. Charity done in a wrong place, at a wrong time, toward unworthy recipients, or without respect or proper attention, is said to be charity in the element Tamas.

v. 20-22

Charity is also determined by your level of trust, by where you are focused in the three elements. If you are charitable to others in the right place and time, without any desire for anything back, this is a sign of trust.

What is the 'right place and time'? It is where the person receiving it will benefit from it in a tangible way. When charity is given in a way that it will actually harm the person receiving it, where it will not help them to serve life, or to grow or better themselves; or when charity is given in a way that it will put down the one receiving it and make them feel small, or reinforce their negative patterns, addictions, or dependent behaviours, this is the wrong place and time to give the charity.

The way to give charity is to give charity to those who can do good work with it, or a kind of charity that will help raise a person up and improve himself.

This is what Jesus meant when he said that if you give a man a fish, he eats for a day; but if you teach him how to fish he eats for his entire life. The form of charity that you give is very important as well.

. . . .

23. Om, the real, symbolizes the threefold Brahma. The priests had used it in the past, in their scriptures and rituals.

v. 23

OM is nothing more and nothing less than 'the real." It is the basic fundamental vibration of the universe.

. . . .

24. Thus, Om symbolizes acts of ritual, charity and discipline. The practitioners of the way of Brahma always begin any of these acts with it, in accordance with the teachings.

25. Thus without lust of result, various acts of ritual, charity and discipline can be done by those who sincerely seek liberation.

26. The real beings, the initiates thus bring the real into their sincere acts, and the sound of the real is used, Scion of Partha.

v. 24-26

What this means is not that you must chant OM before doing charity or something like that. It means that your ritual, your discipline and your charity should all be grounded in the real. If these things are grounded on what is real around you, on reality rather than your fantasies, or your dreams or your hatreds, if you base it on the real, then it will bring real results.

. . . .

27. In ritual, in discipline, in charity the real is vibrated. That work is meant for the real, and so certainly the real is represented.

28. That which is given with no trust, whether in ritual or discipline, is said without the real. Scion of Partha, it has no purpose in this life or the next.

v. 27-28

In the end, Krishna is saying that trust and reality go hand in hand. If you trust in what is real before you, not in how you would wish things to be, then your trust will be able to lead you to perfect practice, no matter where you begin.

Chapter 18
The Yoga of Liberation (Moksha)

1. *Arjuna said:*

Mighty warrior, I want to understand the truth of Sannyas and how it is like and different from renunciation, Master of Sensing, Mighty Killer of Demons.

v. 1

Sannyas (initiation into a spiritual school) has traditionally been taken to mean "spiritual renunciation" in India. But here we see that Arjuna is asking Krishna to clarify whether Sannyas really means renunciation, and whether spiritual renunciation is the same as regular renunciation.

. . . .

2. *The Blessed One said:*

Renouncing the desire for activities is what the wise know as real Sannyas. The renunciation of all the results of activities is what the experienced call true renunciation.

3. Thus great thinkers will say that some types of work must be renounced as wrongdoing. But ritual, charity, discipline and other works should never be renounced.

v. 2-3

Note that Krishna says that Sannyas is the renunciation of the desire for activities. The keyword here is desire. It is the results of activities that must be renounced, not activities themselves. Certainly there is a place and time for all activities, and it is not action itself that is wrong, but doing the wrong thing at the wrong time for the wrong reasons. This is what Krishna is teaching. He says that real ritual, real charity, and real discipline should never be abandoned; that these things done the right way are never wrong.

. . . .

4. Hear from me definitely thus regarding renunciation, Best of the Bharatas. Tiger among men, I declare that there are three types of renunciation.

5. Acts of ritual, charity, and discipline must be done, they should never be renounced. And ritual, charity and discipline purify even the great beings.

6. But in all of these kinds of activities one should renounce one's attachment to results. Scion of Partha, it is my definite opinion that these acts are best done only as a duty.

v. 4-6

Krishna explains the context in which ritual, charity and discipline are real. They are real when they are done "as a duty"; that is when you are not doing them with any lust of result. You do them because it is right to do them, and for their own sake, the very act of practicing these things is its own reward, and seeking any other reward from them becomes wrongdoing.

. . . .

7. But the renunciation of natural activities is never correct. To declare that these activities should be given up is to be in the element of ignorance.

8. One who renounces such things out of fear will create misery for himself and problems in his body. Such renunciation is in the element of passion, and will not gain the results of true renunciation.

9. Thus, actions which are natural to you must be performed, Arjuna. Certainly, one should give up attachment to the results of these acts. To me, this is renunciation in the element of truth.

v. 7-9

Renouncing what is natural to you, because you are afraid of the body, or afraid of participating in the world, or because you have been taught to, is actually unhealthy. Some people have been convinced by others or want to convince themselves that by renouncing natural things, like eating properly, taking care of your body, sexuality, enjoyment, friendship or participation in the world, they are renouncing their passions. In fact, Krishna says that renouncing these things is being controlled by your passions! You don't renounce passion by running away from what is natural.

. . . .

10. A clever and true renunciate, free from doubts, will neither hate unfortunate work nor become attached to fortunate work.

11. It is impossible for anyone in a body to totally renounce all actions. But anyone who renounces the result of actions is said to be a renunciate.

v. 10-11

Krishna says that a real Sannyasin will not be concerned with avoiding actions, because it's utterly impossible to give up actions. No matter what you are doing, you are in action. Even sitting still and breathing is action. The only way you are not in action is if you are dead. And mysticism is the process of becoming truly alive, not becoming dead. Thus a real student will seek to give up his attachment to the results of actions, his desire to try to force life to go his way; he will not try to renounce things he dislikes and cling to what he likes.

. . . .

12. There are three kinds of action: action that moves one upwards, action that moves one downwards, and action that has mixed results. These results (Karma) will affect one who has not renounced them at the time of death. But they will never affect a true Sannyasin.

v. 12

It is the results of your action that are Karma. The actions themselves are not Karma. If you act without lust of result, you are thus free of Karma. Karma moves you out of harmony with existence. This is what Krishna really means by the "movement" of actions. By being a true Sannyasin, you will be free of disharmony.

. . . .

13. Mighty warrior, understand from me the five causes listed in the wisdom teachings, said there to lead to power in all actions.

14. They are: the place of action, the performer of action, the different kinds of instruments used for action, and the motivations of the person acting; and the influence of the Divine is the fifth.

15. It is these five factors that determine whether a person takes action with his body, words or thoughts; and whether the action is right or wrong.

v. 13-15

Every action is governed by these five things: where, who, what, why, and finally the influence of nature. There is nothing you can do that is inherently bad, or inherently good! No action is ALWAYS going to be good, or always evil. Instead, the right or wrongness of action is determined by the influence of nature, the place you are doing something, the way you do things, and the reasons you do things.

. . . .

16. One who believes it is his soul that takes action is being foolish and not enlightened.

17. One whose enlightenment is never blocked by his ego could do anything, even kill without truly killing. He will not become attached.

v. 16-17

"Believing your soul takes action" means thinking that the things you do are actually things that 'happen' to you, that you have no choice in what goes on, in what you do, or why you do it, or that you cannot change. These are all illusions.

It is also believing that you can only do certain things, and that doing certain things will make you 'right' or good or spiritual or enlightened, and doing other things will do the opposite. In reality, it is not a question of what you are doing, but of the interaction of all those factors listed before. In other words, if you take an action free of lust of result, without motivation, and because you are wholly natural, it doesn't matter what that action is. An awakened person watching television is more 'spiritual' than an ignorant person praying.

. . . .

18. Awareness, the subject of awareness, and the one who is aware are the factors that determine the three types of action. The senses, the action itself, and the performer of the action are the three ingredients that result in Karma.

19. Through the gunas, there are thus three kinds of awareness, actions, and performers of action. It is said that they can be in three different elements (gunas). Hear of these now.

20. One who sees that in all living beings there is an absolute oneness, indivisible yet infinitely divided, that one is aware in the wisdom of the real (Sattvas).

21. But one who, because of dividedness, is only aware of the various divisions, and sees all living beings as falling into different classifications, that one is aware in the wisdom of passion (Rajas).

22. And one who sees only their own attached actions as the be all and end all, with no deeper cause, is without true wisdom and very petty. That one is said to be in the element of ignorance (Tamas).

v. 18-22

Krishna creates a classification of three levels to awareness: understanding the unity and individuality of all things at once, seeing only differences, or seeing only one's self. An aware person will understand that the person next to him is as much a part of his being as his own body; a person with limited awareness will think of other people and things as individuals but won't understand the connections between themselves and others, and someone who is entirely ignorant will think only about themselves, and all other people or things will matter to them only in the context of how it relates to themselves.

. . . .

23. All action that is done with centeredness, without association, without desire or reluctance, and by one who has no lust of result, is called action that is real (Sattvas).

24. But action performed by one who has lust of result, or ego, or action that is done with great striving, is said to be action that is passionate (Rajas).

25. And that action which is born of illusion, self-motivated, without taking responsibility for the consequences, causing destruction or misery to others and which leads to further bondage is said to be action that is ignorant (Tamas).

v. 23-25

Likewise, someone who is aware will act without lust of result, completely naturally. Someone who has only limited awareness will make great concentration and effort in their actions, but because they have goals (maybe nice goals, or maybe selfish ones) in mind. And someone who is wholly ignorant will act without any consciousness, without concern for what their actions will do, or whether they will be harming others, and they will act even in ways that end up harming themselves.

. . . .

26. Performing action free of association, without ego, justified with drive and enthusiasm, trying equally though powerful or powerless, the performer of such actions is said to be real (Sattvas).

27. Doing action with great attachment to desired results, greedy, jealous and unclean, affected by joy and sorrow, the performer of such actions I declare to be passionate (Rajas).

28. Doing action that is unnatural, driven by material motives, stubborn, insincere, insulting to others, slothful, depressed, and hesitant, the performer of such actions is said to be ignorant (Tamas).

v. 26-28

Finally, the way one does things is also divided into three kinds: someone who is aware will act in a way that is whole, with all of their being, without concerns, and for the love of the action itself without caring if they succeed or fail. Someone who has some awareness will act in a way that they will be mostly concentrating on winning or losing, on their actual desires, not so concerned about what they're doing, but on what they might get for it, and will become encouraged or discouraged by whether it seems they will be getting their goals or not. Someone entirely ignorant will act without thinking much about either present or the future; they will only react to what is around them and to their conditionings, they will harm others, and will refuse to change what they are doing in light of what life is showing them.

. . . .

29. Now hear from me in detail about the different levels of centeredness in enlightenment that are determined by the three gunas, great champion.

30. Being wise about action and inaction, what should and should not be done, fear and fearlessness, attachment and liberation, this is enlightenment at the level of Sattvas.

31. Being informed by a teaching about what should or should not be done, this is imperfect enlightenment at the level of Rajas.

32. Being deluded and not knowing the difference between true and false teaching, and thinking always in the wrong direction, this is enlightenment covered by Tamas, Scion of Partha.

v. 29-32

The 'centeredness in enlightenment' that Krishna speaks of here is the level in which a personality relates to his or her enlightenment. Everyone is enlightened, but only those who are Awakened realize and identify themselves with their enlightened self, others will identify themselves with their personality or instincts or emotions.

Someone who is Aware of their enlightenment will know what to do or not to do without needing to hear it from any other source. They will be completely in tune with what is natural. Someone who is trying to reach awakening, who is practicing some awareness, will rely on outside teachings, on books or wise men to tell them what to do, and will be struggling to develop the ability to discern these things for themselves. But someone who is completely ignorant will not want to know for themselves, will cleave to ideas that they have become attached to, and will be unable to determine the difference between what is real and what is false.

. . . .

33. The will that focuses the mind, energy, senses, and actions, by the unwavering practice of Yoga, that will is in the element Sattvas, Scion of Partha.

34. But the will which focuses the way of lust and material effort, Arjuna, because of lust of result, that will is in the element Rajas, Scion of Partha.

35. And the will by which one never stops fantasizing, fearing, regretting, feeling sorry for one's self, and illusion, that foolish will is said to be in the element Tamas, Scion of Partha.

v. 33-35

Likewise, your Will, your ability to focus your energy, will vary according to which level of awareness you have.

. . . .

36. Best of the Bharatas, now hear from me of the three levels of joy one can enjoy by practice, through which one can also gain the end of misery.

37. That practice which can be compared at first to the taste of poison, but at the end is like the taste of nectar, is said to be joy in the element of the real. It is born out of the grace of the enlightenment of the soul.

v. 36-37

True practice will at first be hard, because it will not be glamorous; it will taste like poison. It won't entertain you; instead it will make your life a crisis. It's only by crisis that we can change. Only after one works through this crisis, and are able to let go of our false ideas about life and God and spirituality, and our desire to have fascinating experiences or entertainment from our practice, will this simple practice become like the taste of sweet nectar. It will be truly fulfilling.

. . . .

38. The joy that is born of the combination of the senses and sensation, which in the beginning is like nectar but later like poison, is said to be joy in the element of passion.

v. 38

Practicing in the state of passion is when you seek out 'spiritual entertainment.' If you are in this state you will be looking for lots of magical or metaphysical experiences, you will be hoping for lots of bells and whistles, or magic tricks and powers. You will be drawn to techniques that are complicated and really interesting to try, and will deal a lot with things like 'energy,' 'chakras,' and metaphysical systems (be it complicated texts, or descriptions of many universes and 'secret teachings' or 'hidden masters,' or 'powerful' healing techniques, or psychedelic trips, or complex divination systems). These things will appeal to you, and at first they will be really entertaining. But after a while, they will come to taste like poison, because you were only entertained by their novelty; when that novelty wears off, they will be boring to you.

Then, if you stay in the state of passion, you will rush off to try to find the next spiritual fad. It is only if you start valuing Truth more than Passion that you will be able to keep going with basic and essential practices that will actually fill you up, rather than only entertain you.

. . . .

39. And that which is in the beginning and end alike a joy that is due to the clouding of the soul, born of sleep, sloth, and illusion, is said to be in the element of ignorance.

v. 39

Krishna says that spiritual ignorance is "a joy like the clouding of the soul"; he doesn't say that it's a misery. What he is saying is that ignorance is its own kind of joy, the joy of being asleep, of being a slave, of giving up your responsibility, of just obeying what a priest tells you, of practicing without knowing what you are doing or why.

. . . .

40. There is no being in material existence, on this earth or in the heavens, even among the divine spirits, who is free of the influence of these three gunas.

v. 40

Every being in existence is influenced by all three of these gunas, these elements. But this means that everyone has the opportunity to achieve truth.

. . . .

41. Vanquisher of Enemies, the four types of men: godly (brahmanas), noble (ksatriyas), worldly (vaisyas), and unclean (sudras) are classified by their actions, born of their relation to the gunas.

42. Peacefulness, balance, discipline, purity, openness, sincerity, awareness, wisdom, and spirituality are the godly actions of a natural man.

43. Bravery, strength, will, cleverness, fearlessness when challenged, generosity, and a noble nature, are the actions of a noble being.

44. Stewardship of the earth and animals, as well as business, are the actions of a worldly man. And an unclean man should dedicate his soul to acting in service, for this is the natural role of the unclean.

v. 41-44

The Unclean, the Worldly, the Noble and the Godly are the four types of men that Krishna describes as being the product of the Gunas. These were mistakenly interpreted in Indian society as representing castes of birth. But the gunas are not a fixed status of birth, they are a fluid condition. And who your parents were has little to do with who you will be as a person. Being born of a rich man will not make you a better person, being the son of a priest will not make you holy. And Krishna never meant to imply this.

The Unclean are people who are trapped in their own ignorance and conditionings. The only way to even begin moving beyond this is to work in service.

A worldly man is one who is attached to his work, his business, his land or his possessions. Learning to care for these things in a wise way is a path to awareness for this kind of person.

A noble man is a person who shows the qualities of bravery and cleverness, and who lives up to their potential. Being total in living up to this potential leads to the culmination of one's nobility and to transcendence.

And finally, someone who is at peace, sincere, balanced in the gunas and wise is a natural man. This person has already balanced and transcended the gunas and is well on the path of the mystic.

. . . .

45. For each type of man, following his own type of actions will lead him to reach a higher power. Now hear how by acting in practices according to one's nature this power is achieved.

46. A man can achieve this power by serving, by dedicating his own natural actions, to that which is the source of all life, which is within all things.

47. It is better to follow one's own natural path, however imperfectly, than to follow the path of another, however perfectly. By performing actions correct to one's own nature, one will never commit wrongdoing.

48. Son of Kunti, one should never give up the actions that come of one's own nature. Certainly all actions will have their imperfections, just as smoke will cover a fire.

v. 45-48

Why is it important to detail the four types of man? Because Krishna says that the only way to reach real spirituality is to accept who you are, accept all of your nature, and work within what you are and what you have in this moment. It does no good for you to look at the practices of other times and places if they have no bearing on your current situation. It does no good for you to try to act like someone you are not. Being true to yourself is the only way to reach truth!

If you are true to yourself, even if you struggle in doing so, you will be getting closer to mystical truth than if you are false with yourself, if you try to deny your nature, no matter how good a job of denial you do.

. . . .

49. With an enlightened perspective to all things, focused on the soul, free of material wishes, through the greatest magical power, detachment, one attains Sannyas.

50. Achieving this power, one achieves Brahma. Try to understand me when I say this. Son of Kunti, it is essentially that state which is the highest.

51. Enlightened, fully practicing purification, with determination driving the soul, abandoning the senses and sounds, putting aside attachment and hate.

52. Living in a lonely place, eating only what is needed, controlling the speech of the body and mind, constantly united in the highest meditation, seeking comfort only in detachment.

53. Doing these things one will be freed from false ego, strength and pride, lust, anger and greed. One will be peaceful, knowing one owns nothing. Thus one will be ready for the nature of Brahma.

54. Within the nature of Brahma one has a joyful soul. One never regrets nor desires. Equally open to all living beings, one gains my greater devotion.

v. 49-54

If you free yourself of your attachments to what you think you have to be, you achieve real renunciation. If you do that, then you begin to see God. By acting naturally, by not being within lust of result, by practicing awareness, you will come to find that which you are really seeking. You become devoted to the real divine, and the real divine becomes devoted to you.

. . . .

55. One can know devotion to me in as much as I am true in this body. The part of me that is beyond truth can only be entered through awareness.

v. 55

Krishna is talking here about the teacher. The teacher is a representation of the Divine in a physical body, and you can automatically be devoted to the Divine by being devoted to the teacher within the limits of the teacher's physical existence. This is the easy part. It leads you to becoming more aware, and only through awareness do you eventually see beyond the physical question of the Guru and start to connect to the Divine itself. The teacher is only a gate to that, but a very useful gate because it facilitates the process of real devotion.

. . . .

56. Although constantly performing actions, through my care and by my grace one can achieve the eternal never ending abode.

57. Consciously renounce (Sannyas) all kinds of actions unto me, under my care, seeking comfort in union with enlightenment. Just be in my consciousness at all times.

58. In my consciousness you will be able to overcome all obstacles by my grace. But if, due to your ego, you do not hear, then you will be lost.

59. If you seek comfort in your ego, and thus think "I shall not fight", know this to be false. Your nature is to strive, with determination.

v. 56-59

The Guru encourages you to look beyond your own ideas, your own aspirations and lusts of result. You are able, with the teacher's encouragement, to let go of your own ideas. The Guru cannot take your ideas away for you, but you can find it easier to let go with his encouragement and remembrance. Even so, in the end only you can save yourself; if you choose not to listen, there will be nothing you can do.

The teacher is a force that confronts you; if like Arjuna did at the beginning, you refuse to accept this confrontation, it's like Arjuna declaring "I shall not fight", it is resisting the truth you see before you and choosing to remain in the stuckness of your ego.

. . . .

60. Son of Kunti, your natural self is being conditioned by your Karma. You are deluded to believe that you do not wish to follow your nature. But though you are reluctant, you must act.

61. The divine master of all that lives is found in everyone's heart, Arjuna. It is what leads all living beings to seek, behind these bodies of illusion.

62. Scion of Bharata, you must surrender unto him completely. By his grace, you will find great peace and the eternal home.

63. Thus have I shared with you this awareness, the secret of secrets. Consider this, do not take it lightly, and then do what thou wilt.

v. 60-63

The real Secret of Secrets is this: that you must save yourself, and that everyone has it within them to find that salvation. God exists in the heart, and everyone can connect to that: The heart is the ultimate Guru. The physical teacher, the Guru, is just pointing to your heart, and the heart is pointing to God.

Just as the Guru is reminding you to be aware, the heart has always been there, a voice inside you, pushing you toward the same thing.

. . . .

64. Hear from me again the greatest of secrets, the highest teaching. Because you are very dear to me, I will share it for your sake.

65. Take on the nature of my mind, become my devotee, my priest, offer your respects (namaste) unto me. Then you will come to me. This I promise to you, because you are dear to me.

66. Abandon all religious teachings, surrender unto me alone. I will free you from all wrongdoing, do not be worried.

67. This teaching must not be given to one who is not disciplined, nor to one who is not a devotee, ever. Nor also to one who is not practicing, or to anyone who is jealous of me.

v. 64-67

Surrendering, performing namaste (namaste means "I recognize the Divine") to the heart is the vital step. You may surrender to the Guru, but that surrender means nothing if you do not surrender to your own heart as well. This is why any religious teaching must be abandoned; what you have studied will not serve at all if you do not surrender in your heart.

It is important that this teaching be understood, because to one who is not 'disciplined,' to someone who has not already begun practicing, the teaching will always end up being misinterpreted. They will think it means that there's no need to practice, or that whatever they are already doing is right; they will misunderstand. Or if they are jealous, in the sense of wishing to be special, they will resent the idea of surrendering, because they will think of it as the Guru seeking power. They will not understand that the real surrender is to one's own heart, and the surrender to the Guru is only a step to that.

The real understanding only can be reached by the willingness to surrender.

. . . .

68. Anyone who explains this, the greatest of the secrets, to my devotees, will be performing the greatest devotion unto me and will certainly come to me, with no doubt.

69. There is no one among men who will be dearer to me than he, nor will there be any dearer than he in all existence.

v. 68-69

Anyone who is a sincere devotee, who has surrendered to their own heart, and seeks to help others find their true Guru and surrender to their heart as well is a blessed one, who is at that moment tied to God.

Likewise, anyone who seeks simply to teach in order to be listened to, or for their own purposes, without trying to lead people to their own hearts, is the worst kind of false student.

. . . .

70. Also, whoever studies this sacred conversation of ours is performing a sacred ritual of awareness. In this way I judge that he is showing service to me.

71. Any man who hears this conversation with trust, and without envy, will become free. He will be fortunate in the world, attaining to righteousness.

v. 70-71

The Bhagavad Gita itself is a secret key to all this wisdom. If you study this book with an open heart it will reveal truth and understanding to you. If you do not have an open heart, it will be just another book.

. . . .

72. Scion of Partha, have you heard all of this with total concentration of your consciousness? Has your deluded awareness been cleansed, Great Conqueror?

73. *Arjuna said:*

My illusion is washed away, my memory is restored by your grace, ideal one! I am free of doubts, and will follow your commands!

74. *Sanjaya said:*

Thus have I heard the debate between the greatest of spirits, Krishna, and Arjuna, also a great soul. Having heard such an awe-inspiring thing, my hairs stand on end!

75. By the mercy of the spirit, I have heard this greatest secret of Yoga, from the master of Yoga. Directly from Krishna, who spoke it himself.

76. My king, remember! Remember this awe-inspiring spiritual debate of Krishna and Arjuna. I am enthralled, again and again.

77. And also, remember! Remember the most awesome form of the Lord. My amazement is so great, my king, it enthrals me more and more!

78. Where Krishna the master of Yoga, and where the Scion of Partha, expert of the bow and arrow, are together, there is nobility, victory, strength, and righteousness. This is my feeling.

v. 72-78

This is the conclusion of the Bhagavad Gita. Its study leads to spiritual victory. Wherever a true Guru and a true Student are together and participate in real Satsang, sitting in truth, you gain the most sacred experience being in that presence.

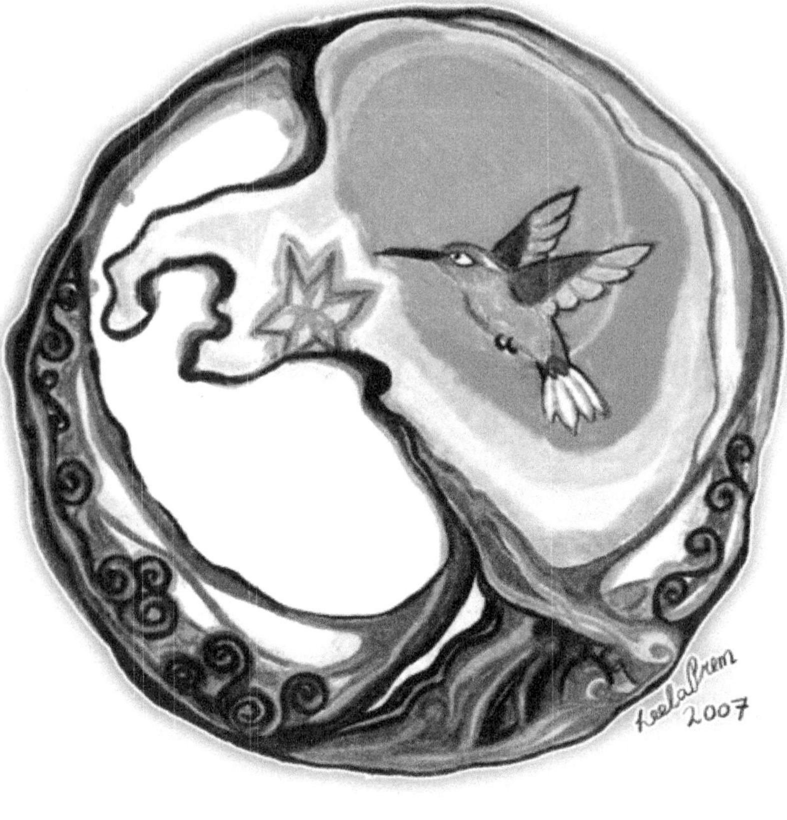

"Deva Peter"
Ma Leela Prem - 2007

The Godsong

Introduction

This book will not be easy to understand. In fact, you should assume NOT to understand it.

This is because the Godsong is a commentary. It is a commentary on the Divine itself. As such, if you read it in the course of an evening, and hope to understand it, you will fail.

Do not think of this as any other book, except for the scriptures.

The goal of this book is not the learning, but the experiencing of it.

Nevertheless, do not avoid paying attention to the words on purpose.

Whatever your mind is drawn to in these words to come, there you must let it go.

Where your heart is drawn, there you must follow.

And beyond is awareness.

This is a book to be read for the rest of your life.

Swami Anand Nisarg

Chapter 1

Spiritual Crisis

Why are you here?
What is this place, of all its beauty, and awe-full horror?
Is anyone listening?
Is there someone minding the cosmos?
What is killing us?
Why do we have to die?
Why do we have to change?
Why is there no justice in this world?
Who makes things happen?
Why do you feel powerless?
Why do you pretend not to?
Why are you ashamed?
Where is all this going?
Just to death?
Is there something else?
Why are you afraid of silence and the dark?
Can you really know anything that you can never be?
Can you even know yourself?
Are you anything at all?
What good are you?
Why are you so miserable?
And why do you hold on to staying where you are, if where you are is full of misery?
Who are you?

You are happy, but then forget.
There is wonder all around you that you ignore.
There is a music you can almost hear, but you close your ears.
You want to find a purpose, but waste your time on meaningless things.
You fear death so much you cannot live.
You would rather have longevity than fulfillment.
You feel like nothing ever happens, but you are terrified of having to grow.
You regret the world's suffering, but inflict harm on yourself.
You want adventure but are full of fear.
You want to feel in control but do not want to be responsible for yourself.
You are terrified of what others will think of you.
You think you are unworthy of love.
You want to know the future, but do not pay attention.
You cannot accept the end of things.
You cannot see the miraculous.
You cannot bear to be alone un-distracted with yourself.
You want to categorize everything and experience nothing.
You find it easier to accept an identity than to explore your true uniqueness.
You cloak yourself in what others have made you, so that you are yourself empty.
You want to force life to fit your agenda, but in reality can't change anything.
There is an emptiness in your heart, that you have tried to fill with everything you cling to.
Your pain has been there so long, you even fear the responsibility of living without it.
Live.

On the Master and Students

In life, there are many amateur catalysts.

But the master is in essence a professional catalyst.

What is a catalyst?
An agent of change.
And the important thing to remember is that all life is this, it is all a catalyst.
But then, why the need for a master?

First it must be understood: a master is not a master because of his own accomplishments.
It has nothing to do with his intelligence or dedication to spirituality.
It is only because of his experience, an experience that he was not responsible for bringing about.

There are those who insist a master would only be a teacher because he wants it.
The truth is that it has nothing to do with that.
Some people who become teachers may enjoy it.
Others may in fact be reluctant.
But they are teachers simply because it cannot be helped.
It is their nature.

The difference between a master and any other catalyst is that a teacher will be conscious of the catalytic space he is creating.
He will be directing it, and consistently enforcing it.

But understand that no one can be helped by a master.
People will come to you, and those who wish to be stuck, to be slaves, will remain slaves around you.
An element incapable of being catalyzed will not react.
And those who wish to be transformed, they will be transformed not because of you, but because of them.

Yes.
The master is the catalyst.
But anything could have been the catalyst.

Yet a student who is drawn to a master is not drawn to some other catalyst.
The master is not responsible for the student's transformation, but he has simply provided the service, the space, which the student was looking for.

It is important for students to understand: the master does not need his students.
But it is even more important to understand: the students do not need the master.
They will change or not due to themselves, not due to him.

There is no dependence; that is what makes the relationship with a master and student beautiful.
Yes, the master shares, and yes the student shares, but it is not based on any need, salvation, or instruction.

Most of all, remember that the master is not salvation; he is humanity.
He is human, and he can show you the way to being more human yourself.

It is purely natural.
Only love.

Chapter 2

Surrender

What is it to surrender to a master?
It is when you have come to a place where you know you cannot move further by yourself.
You may not wish to surrender, or you might, but it really has nothing to do with your want.
Instead, it is that you have come to such a place of distress in your heart, and such a sense in your heart that your distress is leading you to your teacher, that you can do nothing but surrender.

And surrender will mean different things at different levels.
It is not an action as much as it is a process.
You are a Sannyasin when you are in an ongoing state of surrender.
At each stage you will come to understand it in a deeper way.

Arjuna once said to Krishna, when he first surrendered to him, "tell me what can be known."
This is the first level of surrender.
You wish to have an answer.
But Arjuna puts it in a particularly good way; he does not say "tell me the answer", he simply asks to be told what can be known.
Most of what will be understood by surrender is not what can be 'known' or 'taught.'
It is an experiencing.

Krishna goes on to teach Arjuna first that there is no end to anything, and that for this reason all must be accepted equally.
This is in reality all that can truly be known.
It is a recipe, for experiencing.
If you take this as your thesis, you will be able to begin the process of actually experiencing surrender, to life.

To surrender is to surrender your ideas, that things have a beginning and end, and that there is a difference between one thing, one possession, one feeling, and any other.
Krishna compares joy and sorrow to winter and summer.
They are like the seasons – they will come and will go.
To surrender is to accept this coming and going, and realizing that there is a force that exists, behind these changing 'seasons,' that remains as it is, that does not depend on any subjective factors.

Your sense of attainments will rise and fall; sometimes you will feel that you are reaching great spiritual peaks, other times you will think you have fallen to deep valleys.
But they are both nonessential; whether you are in the peak or valley of your experience, you are still experiencing, still witnessing.

It is the same with your teacher.
You will sometimes feel very close to your master, sometimes very far away.
Do not let yourself be attached to these feelings.
The master is a constant, and only when you can look beyond these subjective sensations will you be able to see him as he truly is.
Then you will discover what it truly can mean to be human.

Become aware of this force, that which exists behind the rise and fall of sensations.
Then you can take any sensation, accept it and let it go as you would go into or out of a set of clothes.
This hidden force behind all things is the eternal – it is what I call the Mystery.

When you can understand this Mystery, you will come to know how to be natural.

Being natural is simply knowing the purpose of sensations.
Rather than clinging to them for their own sake, you will know that each sensation comes and goes, and has no inherent value.
The value is simply in accepting each in its proper time.
Thus the Zen masters say: "when you are hungry, eat; when you are tired, sleep."
This is naturalness, it is being in the sensation that has arisen, remembering the eternal force that is behind it, and thus living each sensation to its fullness without longing for its arrival or departure.

Then there is no more a need for analysis, there is simply a flowing in the experience.
No more doubt, you simply accept what is there at that moment.

Surrender is part of how this naturalness is achieved.
By surrendering, to a master, to the Divine, you will be able to slowly let go more and more of the attachment to sensations.
It is a reminder, to connect to that eternal force.

And surrender is the opposite of struggle.
At first, it may seem like the same.
One who begins on the mystical path will attempt to fight against attachment.
But to fight against attachment to sensations is a hopeless battle.
As soon as you have mastered one sensation another will appear.

They are like the endless waters flowing into a vast ocean.
This is how the Gita puts it; it is futile to fight the senses.
Instead, surrender is to simply release the association with the senses, and open one's self to the eternal force behind all senses.

This is the difference too, between religion and mysticism.

Religion will try to teach you to fight desires; it will call surrender obedience, and claim that to be obedient is to create rules for avoiding desires.
But this is an impossibility.

Mysticism says that surrender is a deep letting go, not fighting but accepting, and offering your sense desires to a higher force.

Thus, you allow yourself to become a vessel for the Divine.

Chapter 3

Awareness and Devotion

There are two general methods for the Divine illustrated in the Bhagavad Gita.
One is the path of awareness, of meditation.
The other is the path of devotion, of love.

Before you can understand what these are, you must first understand what they are not, and what is not a path.

First, it is not a path to attempt to renounce action.
Trying to be an ascetic, to create a false discipline in yourself, is not going to help.
Because the source of your misery is not in your actions but in the attachments that cause them.

You might be obsessed with making money, and so you take a vow of poverty.
Does this mean that your lust for money will go away?
On the contrary, you will be even more obsessed.
You will constantly be thinking about it, and you will be struggling and resenting yourself for denying yourself access to this money.
You will act out, in other ways.
You may create other, even more unhealthy lusts to replace your need for money.

Either that, or you will simply give up your vow eventually, and begin seeking money again.
They you will feel guilty and weak.

But the problem was never your pursuit in the first place.
It was your attachment, your desire.
Renouncing the actions will not help, only renouncing your attachment, coming to understand the fruitlessness of it will help.

You will always have to take actions of various sorts.
And inevitably, these actions will sometimes put you in situations of pursuing your desires.
Then, to try to resist or fight those situations is pointless.
Instead, you can only free yourself by awareness when you come to accept whatever comes.
Our friend with the money obsession will only be able to find peace when he can welcome an environment where he is making money, and be absolutely equally welcoming to a situation where he will not be able to make money.
When he can see that being rich or poor are equally valuable, then he will be free.

And remember, the way to do this is to be centred, 'united' the Gita calls it, no matter what situation you are in.
Regardless of what is going on around you, some kind of action will be demanded of you.
Even if the 'action' is to do nothing, that will still be a form of action.
The key is that in each action you must focus on that force that is behind the material world, that unchanging unity, the Mystery.
Then you can accept any situation equally, and perform any action with equal detachment.

This is what Krishna means by 'actions done for spiritual purposes.'
In some verses of the Gita, Krishna speaks of how 'in ancient times' the God Brahma taught that all manner of good things will come from these spiritual actions.

What is meant by this is that the more ancient Vedic cultures of India had taught this method of awareness, and knew that it led to well-being and a positive society.
But by Krishna's time already those old Vedic teachings had been corrupted into the dogmas of what Krishna called the 'false religionists.'
The real essence of the technique had been replaced with a dry, dead series of rules, and so Krishna had to once more restore the living essence to the dead teachings.

The other technique that Krishna wished to restore was the technique of devotion.
It too had degenerated into pointless ritual.
It is clear from what he says in the Gita that in Krishna's time there were rituals being performed, for food, for purification, for offerings to the 'spirits.'
But these rituals were being performed without any real essence.

The essence of devotion is to offer up your actions, to offer what you do and who you are, to the Divine.
When you can experience gratitude, the feeling of joy that comes from being alive, and in that way feel that whatever is happening you will accept, then you can be free of the suffering that comes from attachment to your personality and lusts.
Ritual done with this real purpose will let you connect to the Divine.

It is important to remember this: that all ritual is done with the ultimate purpose being devotion.
And a ritual done without this devotional attitude will lead to nothing.

On the other hand, when you capture that sense of devotion, then no ritual is truly needed.
Do not get hung up on particular forms. Understand the function.
Understand that devotion is the purpose, not the ritual itself.

Ultimately, one who has understood devotion will know this, and will then perform devotional acts not for some ulterior purpose, but simply out of gratitude.
Even when they achieve, they can still show devotion, because these rituals will then be transformed into acts of gratitude.
Then their real beauty will come through, they will be completely alive – so alive that even those who witness these rituals can be transformed.

This is what Krishna means when he tells Arjuna that even he practices devotion, and that if he didn't all the worlds would come into ruin.
It is because he can lead others, through his devotion, to achieving the unity he has.

But at the same time, Krishna warns Arjuna that there will be foolish or lazy people who will act out of their desires, who will not be devoted or grateful.
Of these he says "it is best not to disturb them."
What does this mean?
First he says that you must help others, then he says you must not disturb them.
But it is not a contradiction.

What Krishna means is that you cannot lead anyone to the Mystery.
You cannot save anyone or change anyone.
No one can.
You can only transform yourself.
Thus, the best thing to do is practice devotion, and to let that be your effort to change the world.
Let others see your devotion, let them see your gratitude, let them see your awareness, and let that be your evidence.
Let it be a torch.
Do not struggle to argue with them, or try to force them to see what you have seen, because that will only bring reactions to them.
Just by being, just by changing yourself, and by expressing yourself naturally, you can do the most good.

This is what Krishna means by 'human beings performing divine acts.'

When you can be human, it is a divine act.

Chapter 4

Re-Incarnation and the Avatar

There is a line from a song by Crosby Stills and Nash, "we have all been here before."

The song is called 'Deja Vu,' and is very good at capturing a sense of eeriness, of that moment when you realize that you're far more ancient than you believed.

Reincarnation is a reality.

There is no question of believing in it – do not try to simply believe in it.

Instead, there are three ways to directly experience it.

The first: become very open, and listen to yourself.

You will know, you will sense, that you are ancient.

You will see with absolute certainty that you have been doing much of what you are doing now for all your life.

Often, this certainty will be triggered best by an encounter with a person place or thing that you had previously encountered in a recent lifetime.

The second: There are meditations, especially Tantric ones from Tibetan Buddhism, that will allow you to experience direct recall of your past incarnations.

However, these meditations take a great deal of effort.

The meditations are detailed (but not completely) in my book, *Three Paths of Ecstasy*.

While there are many sources from which to learn the true technique for this, most of the 'past life' programs will not work.
Especially the idea that someone else can regress you with hypnosis or something like that.
It will only produce a psychological dream, but not a true memory.
Only you can remember yourself.

The third: this technique is the easiest, but also the least appealing to many people.
For it to work, you have to die first.
At the time of your death, you must remain conscious, meditative.
And for that to happen you must have been meditating for your entire life.
If you have been meditative, then with great effort you can be conscious and aware at the time of death, and from this you will remember, in your next lifetime, all of your previous lives.

But what is this that keeps us united to one form throughout many lives?
In reality, it is not us as we think of ourselves who are reincarnated.
It is not our personalities, but our individuality.

The individuality is the part of you that is a unique and individual facet of the Mystery.
It exists in the eternal, and will take a different form in each incarnation.
It will don and shed bodies like a body dons and sheds clothing.
But it always exists.
It is the eternal in you that you may seek out.

There is a term in Indian mysticism, Avatara, that has been misinterpreted by false religionists.
They will try to tell you that an Avatar is a god who has come down into a body, God in human form.
But in fact, an Avatar is a facet, this individuality when it is unmasked, uncovered by a persona.
The Avatar is the Divine incarnate in a man made manifest.

Proper Practice In Ritual and Meditation

Eat and delight in eating, and find the Avatar.
Love someone until it burns within you, and find the Avatar.
Have sex and share your body freely without restriction or shame, and find the Avatar.
Sit in a park, and find the Avatar.
Touch the bark of a tree, with your hand or your heart, and find the Avatar.
Bow before a painted stone, and find the Avatar.
Stand at the crossroads at midnight and find the gate between worlds, and find the Avatar.
Do something your mind says you'll regret, and find the Avatar.
Get into a fight you think you'll lose, and find the Avatar.
Dip your hands in a river, and find the Avatar.
Raise your arms to the sun, and find the Avatar.
Stay awake until you collapse, and find the Avatar.
Study the language of birds, and find the Avatar.
Raise a plant, and find the Avatar.
Go to a cafe on a rainy morning, and find the Avatar.
Build something out of wood, and find the Avatar.
Ride a horse, and find the Avatar.
Go to Brazil, or Paris, and find the Avatar.
Study the Tarot, and find the Avatar.
Watch a good movie, and find the Avatar.
Listen to Louis Armstrong and Ella Fitzgerald, and find the Avatar.
Suffer.
And live.

"Brahma is found in the sacrifice, and Brahma is found in the fire (where the sacrifice is performed). And Brahma is found in the one who makes the sacrifice." –Krishna

Chapter 5

The Golden Dawn

Once upon a time there was a Kingdom, and this Kingdom was named Vida. It was filled with cities, where all the people lived, and each of these cities had nine gates. Each city had one ruler (who was given the title of 'demiurge'), and the whole Kingdom was ruled by an Emperor, whose name was Om. The Emperor had a wife, who shared the love of the Emperor with the people, and her name was Shanti.

But one day, the Emperor was lost in the eyes of the people. No one knew where he had gone, and the Demiurges of the cities with nine gates were left to their own devices.

Immediately, the cities fell into chaos. Some made alliances with others, but most fell into distrust and warfare with themselves. All of the people wished to find the Emperor again, and some of the Demiurges claimed to wish it as well. But others wished to hold on to their own power, feeling it better to be absolute ruler of a single city than simply a governor as part of a great empire.

To this end, these Demiurges had to convince the people that the Emperor's disappearance was the fault of other cities, or their own fault. So in some cities, the people were tricked into paranoia and war with other cities, thinking that if only they could have power over these other cities they would be able to rediscover the Emperor. And in other cities, the people accepted harsh and repressive laws and taxes imposed by the Demiurges, being convinced that the Emperor had abandoned them because they were ungovernable, and that if they only proved their loyalty and obedience he would return.

Eventually, in some cities, the people were even convinced that there had never been an Emperor, and that the Demiurges were and had always been the proper ruler.

Now the Empire was in chaos. But what none of the Demiurges knew was that the Emperor had never left. He and his sons were still in the Empire, living in the cities, watching all that happened. The sons of the Emperor were all powerful magicians, and his daughters were priestesses. They spread out in secret to the cities, uniting the people where they could see that the people were still true and filled with a longing to rediscover the Emperor. To these cities they gradually revealed to the people that the Emperor was not dead, or lost, or a myth. He was right there among them, and all that was needed was to unite against the Demiurges, to unite in alliances with the people of other cities whose spirits were equally true. And so their eyes were opened.

Thus, these cities rose up, against the Demiurges; the sons of the Emperor rode in on mighty Chariots to vanquish the Demiurges, and the daughters (who were very mighty) vanquished all of the terrible beasts these Demiurges had summoned up to guard the gates. Then the sons and daughters of the Emperor kissed, and by this kiss called down lighting that shattered the Towers where the Demiurges hid, towers that had been built over the true temples the Emperor had constructed.

Thus a new Kingdom was born. And slowly, to this day, the Kingdom grows, as the sons and daughters of the Emperor reach out their influence to any people of any city with nine gates that is ready to hear the truth, and open their eyes.

The Yoga of Astral Travel

There are worlds to be discovered within you. Most people barely bother to discover the world beyond them, the outer world, and this is a shame.

There is so much in life to explore, to become connected to.

But beyond that outer world, there is the inner world.
Actually it is many worlds; it is an inner universe.

But how does one begin to explore this world?
The inner world was sometimes described by the ancient mystics as the Astral plane or dimension, a term which has since been badly abused and misunderstood by new-age practitioners.

It is an infinitely vast dimension, one that overlaps with the material, because in the inner world you are free, if you realize it, from attachment to the body.
In this freedom there is no difference between your 'inner world' and anyone else's.
It is not that you have yours and I have mine, there is only one inner world: the astral plane.

By what method do you reach it?
There is a technique, a Yoga.
First, you must be relaxed, in a quiet place.
Sit down, and relax your body.
Then close your eyes, and slowly focus all of your senses inwardly.
That is, first 'draw in' your vision, within yourself.
Focus your vision on the inside of your head, right in between the eyes.
Then, do the same with hearing; focus your ears, your hearing, into that same space right between the eyes.
Then the same with your sense of touch.
Let go of focusing your sense of touch on your outer skin, and instead try to feel the inside of your head, that space between the eyes.
And do the same with taste, and scent.

Now, totally drawn into yourself, hold your breathing in that space within your nose, again moving toward that space between the eyes.
By this, I do not mean to actually stop breathing or hold your breath.
Instead, breathe in and out in a normal relaxed way; but you must separate the actual air from the prana, the vital energy of the breath.

This you draw within yourself.

By this method, you will begin to experience certain things.
At first, what you will feel is that your attention, and this prana, this energy, will begin to accumulate in that space between the eyes.
Practice this technique slowly, gradually, and with patience over several days.
Over time, the accumulation of the energy will increase, until at some point, you will feel like something is opening up, flooding open, and you will have the sense of being in a very vast space.
Allow this to happen.
After this happens, entering into this state will become easy, and easier the more you do it.
You may begin to 'see' or 'hear' things, but not with your regular eyes or ears.
Allow this to happen.
You may experience a feeling of being able to move freely, within this vast inner space, to encounter and experience different things.

From here on, I will leave it to you to explore.
It is important, because it will be your own experience, do not burden it with expectations based on what I say or other things you have heard.
Let it be what it is.
And you will find that a whole vast inner universe will be yours.

Chapter 6

Balance

There is a Yoga of balance.
It consists of living a lifestyle balancing work, play, and eating.
Krishna has said, one who eats too much will not find their centre, nor one who eats too little.
One who lives in too much self-denial will be disturbed, not enlightened.
On the other hand, one who excessively indulges will not find their focus.

The Buddha has compared it to a musical instrument.
Draw the strings too tight and there will be no music, no vibration.
Keep the strings too loose, and again no vibration can occur.
Only in the middle can you create a symphony.

But how do you determine what is balanced?
How much food is too much, how much work is too much?
What kind of self-restraint is good, and what kind is negative?
You will not find the answer in a list of rules or a holy book.
This is because there are no absolute rules that can be made.

The only answer is to find balance in being natural.
They are synonymous: balance and nature.
Being natural is being in balance.

So how to be natural?
How do you find that balance?

There are two levels of naturalness.
In the first, you are practicing to be natural, because you must remember you are not natural now; you are operating unnaturally.
In the first level, you must develop naturalness through effort.
Here, you must pause when you take action, be a witness of yourself, and ask your heart to show you what is natural.
The heart is the temple of nature – it is what will guide you to flow.
You just pause, and watch your heart, and if what you are doing goes against your heart, you will find you are acting unnaturally, out of balance.

But in the more advanced form, to be natural is not to pause for consideration.
In time, you will listen more and more to the heart, and you will be able to be natural without making yourself witness.
You will always be witnessing, there will be no need to force it to happen.
Remember this, at first you make yourself witness, but do not think this is the goal, do not think this is it.
It is only the intermediate step.
The goal is always be in balance, to be able to act completely spontaneously, without consideration or examination.
Only then are you completely in the current, in the flow of the Divine.
Before that you are still trying to keep your head above water.
But do not try to do that, just dive in with all of yourself.
It is natural.

But what is the advantage of this?
It seems like a great risk: not considering, not planning, being spontaneous.
It is frightening.
What are its benefits?
Will it really mean an end to sorrow, to suffering, to pain?

No.

To be natural is not to find some means to escape pain; neither is it the dulling of happiness.
Rather, to be natural is to be balanced.
When there is happiness, be balanced.
When there is sorrow, be balanced.
This does not even mean to be artificially 'moderate.'
It simply means to keep acting natural.

Happiness draws people because it is active.
Then they wish to hold onto it, to stay in the excitement, the ecstasy of happiness.
But of course, when they do this, it generates sorrow, because inevitably you cannot keep holding on to happiness.
It is like trying to hold on to the daytime.
If you do not worry about it, daytime is lovely.
But if you wish for the daytime to last forever, then you will generate suffering, because of your attachment.

And there is nothing wrong with the nighttime, either.
Why fear it?
The night is like sadness; it is just passive.
What most people think of as sadness is not the same as suffering.
When sadness comes as a state of being, and not due to any cause, you should not be concerned about it.
It is just a time for being passive.
The feeling of happiness is like the daytime, and the feeling of sadness is like nighttime.
Just be in each for what they are.
Just be balanced in each, do not hold on, or reject.

Chapter 7

The Ninth Key

Mysticism teaches that there are a variety of methods, a technique, really, for every person.
These can be divided into general categories.
Silent meditation would be one of these.
Chanting another, and ecstatic motion still another.

What do these different techniques do?
They access different aspects of the Divine.
The divine is everywhere, in all things.
It exists in every phenomenon, and every energy.
When you practice a particular technique you are tapping into a certain energy.

The Bhagavad Gita teaches that there are eight such energies.
This is not to say that this is all there is, it is merely one way to consider the situation.
It is a metaphysic, one particular way of organizing reality, but is itself no more inherently real than any other filing system.

The first four energies are earth, air, water and fire.
These are the four elements.
Of these, the first three are accessible to absolutely everyone.
Earth is the energy of physical matter.

Science has today understood that even physical matter is itself energy, it is just energy that moves very slowly.
When you practice physical techniques you will access this energy, the energy of the body, of nature, of the earth.

The second is air, the energy of the mind.
This is an energy that most people have great amounts of, but it is out of control.
Whenever you practice a Yoga, a technique of mental discipline, you are redirecting this mental energy, toward transformation.

The third is water, the energy of the heart, of feeling.
When you connect to your emotion, to your feelings, you can tap into this energy.

Fire is the last of these four.
It is an energy that almost anyone can reach, but not all.
You must have developed some sense of longing, a spiritual desire.
There are many people in the world who are completely asleep – they have this not at all.
This key is then unavailable.
Even without being a mystic, you may have this longing and it can give you the energy to commit great acts.

Beyond the realm of the elements there is the energy of the ether, the mind, awareness, and ego.
They are accessible only to the mystics.
The ether is the first of these, it is the energy of the astral plane, through which one can gain a deeper vision of the real.
It is your deeper material senses.

The mind is the next level.
This is the pure mind, a state that eastern mystics often refer to.
When you have completely focused the energy of the mind, of air, you will suddenly tap into an entirely new source of knowing.
You will be aware of that which your conscious mind would never have believed itself capable of knowing.

You will gain the knowing that is beyond learning.

Awareness is the next of these.
It is the energy of the flow, of moving naturally.
With it you can develop empathy, the ability to truly see the hearts of others.

Finally, there is the ego.
It is the great barrier to consciousness, but when it is overcome, you can use its energy toward the Divine, rather than as an impediment of the Divine.
The ego is your mask, your false persona.
But when you have understood that you are beyond it, you may then don or drop it as you will.
You may assume all personae, and be the fullness of what it is to be human, you can put on any mask and be anything.

These are the eight energetic keys.
But there is a final one, a ninth key that lies beyond.
It is enlightenment.

It is the Divine itself.
It is life.
When you can reach this key, you become a Buddha.

Chapter 8

The Simple Core

At its essence, there is no complexity to meditation, nor is it hard. It is easy.

Too many people find ways to make it hard, and sometimes this complexity is appropriate as a way to draw people in, to keep your ego's attention long enough to trick it into awareness.

But the higher you go with meditation, the simpler it becomes.

Unlike other things, where the more advanced your studies become the more complex the issue becomes, with meditation the more advanced your practice becomes the simpler the practice is.

This is because meditation is truth.

Meditation is also freedom.

It is not restrictive because meditation, being truth, is natural.

And restriction is the opposite of being natural.

Don't think that meditation is creating rules for yourself, strictures.

Krishna used to joke about the people who did this, the ascetics.

Yes, sometimes a bit of discipline is necessary to get you into the knack of meditating.

But over time this discipline should be less and less necessary.

In meditation, if your master gives you a discipline you follow it; but do not add extra disciplines on top of that, which he has said nothing about.

Some students do this, thinking that they are being even better than what their master wanted; but in fact it is based on a

misunderstanding of why their master gave the discipline in the first place.
It was not because restriction is worthwhile in and of itself, it is because of very specific issues unique to that particular student.
And if a student follows by adding extra restrictions on his meditation he may then be adding extra and troublesome complications upon himself.
He is becoming less balanced, not more.

The ideal of meditation is that it should be very easy.
You should be able to do it easily, at any time.
If you can only do meditation when you are set apart, in a very quiet place, or at a certain time, then it is not as good.
It is ok if you're a beginner, but as you are becoming more advanced you should realize that this is also an un-needed discipline.
Real meditation can be done anywhere, at any time, and even while you are doing other things.
Because real meditation is simply mindfulness, being aware.

Krishna says that to practice Yoga you must simply make sure that the body and mind are focused, and centre your awareness at the top of your head.
This was a particular way of cultivating awareness that Krishna was advocating, because when you focus at this centre it becomes very easy to connect to the vibration of the mantra OM.
When you wish to vibrate the mantra OM, this is the way to do it.
At other times it may be better to simply focus awareness on the point between the eyebrows, or on the heart.
Or on no place whatsoever.
The last is the best, simpler still, but it is therefore the hardest to accomplish.

What will this do?
When you practice this, you develop awareness.
Whatever you are doing stops being a distraction and becomes meditation.

This is important to understand: there is no such thing as a distracting activity; it is YOU who makes things distracting.
Anything done while being aware is meditation.
And anything done while unaware, even a meditation technique, is nothing but distraction.

If you can cultivate this attention, then you can be attentive at the time of death.
If you are meditative then, if you are aware, chanting OM, you can reach enlightenment.
Or, even if not, if you can remain aware as much as possible, paying close attention at the moment of death, you will be able to achieve enlightenment in your next lifetime.

Through this practice you obtain a soul, and are saved from dissolution.
There is a deeper mystery to this, but it cannot be revealed like this.

Chapter 9

Namaste

What does this word mean, namaste?
It is one of two words, namaste and sammasati.
They go together.
Namaste means "I recognize the Divine in you," sammasati means "remember the Divine in yourself."
In India, the priests and mahatmas expect people to fold their hands when in their presence, to do namaste toward them.
Their disciples are to recognize and praise them for being so divine.

But my teacher, and other true teachers, did not do this.
Instead, they did namaste.
You perform namaste toward a false Guru, and he gives you a blessing.
He feels happy because you are saying he is like a god, and he blesses you with good luck, so you feel satisfied.
It is a false relationship.
No one can bless you.
Only you can bless yourself.
A master will do namaste to you, because he wants you to see that you are divine.
He will tell you to perform sammasati.
This is the essence of the Buddha's teaching, "remember that you are a Buddha."

Do not worship Gurus, but see in yourself what they have already seen in you.
When you are with a Guru, it is always good to practice devotion to them, if it comes from your heart.
Not because you want a blessing, but because it is sammasati.
Only do namaste to them, only offer devotion to them, only care for them or honour them as a way to remind yourself of who you are.
That you have seen in them a Buddha, and they have seen in you that you are a Buddha too.
So when you do devotion to them, you will remember you must also be a Buddha.

People recognize the Divine in various forms.
And any form that allows for sammasati is correct.
There is no difference, they are only outer forms; if they serve to unite you to the Divine, to remind you that you are a Buddha, then they are good.
For some, the Divine is seen as dual.
As a yin and yang.
This is acceptable, at an early stage of awareness.
If it will help you to think of certain things as 'aware' and others as not, if it will help you develop a discipline.
But do not let it keep you away from enlightenment.
Duality has often been used as a way to separate yourself from the Divine.
"The Guru is enlightened, and I cannot be," "the spiritual is good, and the material bad, and I am material so I can never reach enlightenment," all of these are barriers.
The non-dual is a higher understanding of the Divine.
To know that there is no difference, that the Divine is in everything, even if not everything is aware of that divinity.
It is not that you are not yet a Buddha; you are, you are only not yet aware.
Some will see the Divine as a oneness.
All is one, all comes down to one.
Others as an emptiness, all is nothingness.
Some will see it as an infinite diversity.

The divine as a multiplicity of forms, as many gods or many forces that can all be revered.

None of these are wrong views, all of them are correct all at once.
It is not a logical matter; it is not that, logically, only one can be correct.
How you view the Divine must only be as a vehicle for sammasati.
If you can remember your Buddhahood by thinking of the Divine as only one, or as none, or as all, or as infinite, or even as dual; then that is what you must do.
For the truest thing that can be said is that the Divine is entirely ineffable.
How you view it is not important, the Divine cannot be viewed, cannot be understood.
All of these understandings are true or false all at once.
The truth of the Divine is something beyond words.
All that matters for you, is to see the Divine, namaste, and to remember you are a part of it, sammasati.

The Celestial Realms

Often, people misunderstand what a master means when he talks of heaven.
In many cases, when a master speaks of a divine kingdom, the kingdom of God, or heaven, he isn't referring to a physical place at all, but to enlightenment.
But other times, he is referring to a state of being, of bliss.
These are two different things.
Often, people will confuse these two; bliss and enlightenment.
They think it is the same.
But in reality, they are not the same.
Bliss is a state, a state of consciousness.
Enlightenment is a higher path, it is beyond all definition, even bliss.

Thus, when Krishna or Buddha teach that there are certain methods by which you can reach heaven, they mean that you can perform techniques intended to reach bliss.
Bliss itself means more than happiness – it means a dissolving paradise, a joy beyond all conditions, where your individual consciousness seems to disappear.
Where you experience unity, becoming one, but not with awareness.

And you cannot reach enlightenment unless you have first experienced that bliss, unless you have first become dissolved in bliss.
The Alchemists taught that you must first be dissolved, then you will be restructured in a purer form, and only when you have done this, in some cases many times, will you be ready for the final purification into the alchemical gold of enlightenment.

So bliss is a necessary step, but it is not the last step.
It is worked toward, but it is not the final goal.
Heaven is described by mystics as a place where all your wishes are fulfilled, where there is no pain.
But it is also always emphasized that it is only a temporary state.
It is not the final state that is beyond change.
It may last for a long time, when you reach bliss you may float in it for what might seem like an eternity, but eventually that will cease.
In the Gita it is said that one who reaches the celestial realms will be able to enjoy them until the positive momentum, the good Karma that they have created, is exhausted.
And after that they will fall back to earth.

There are even methods, techniques, that have nothing to do with enlightenment; but are instead techniques specifically to reach that bliss.
These techniques are a waste of effort; they can seem to have very good results but in the end you go back to where you began with nothing to show for it, and much time lost.
It says in the Gita that some practitioners will drink soma juice, they will take certain drugs, and these will lead you to the heaven realms.

Drugs are one example of these methods that are not really methods.
It can lead to bliss, but never to enlightenment.
And remember, the bliss is not eternal, it is not permanent.
There are other methods too, disciplines of the body or mind, that can create certain reactions in your body or in your mind, and these produce bliss.
But the result is the same.
These are not worthwhile methods in the end.

But a mystic who does not use these methods will still experience bliss, inevitably.
It will happen even if they are not seeking it, that in time they will reach, as a result of their regular meditations, to a taste of bliss.
It is very pleasant, and necessary, because if understood and used properly, this bliss state will wipe away a great deal of what is false about you.
It will open you up, transform you and leave you ready to reach deeper awareness.
But in and of itself this state is not awareness, nor are you aware in it.
And if you mistake bliss for enlightenment you will find a great disappointment when it passes, as inevitably it will.
Instead, enjoy it, allow it, but do not cling to it.
When it passes, do not go back.
Some become addicted to bliss like a drug.
They will look for it again and again, thinking it is the way to enlightenment.
Then you will become stuck on that step.
Let it happen when it is there, when it is done, let yourself move on.
It will have served its purpose.

Instant Karma

Karma is not a process of 'crime and punishment,' nor is it an eventual process.
It is an immediate process of consequences.

What do I mean by this?
It is not crime and punishment; it does not mean that you will have good things happen because you try to be good, you try to be moral.
True morality is to be natural, and this is its own reward.
Any other kind of 'morality' is actually a conditioning; it is false.
Karma is not an individual process; it is not something that will 'catch up with you.'
False religionists have always used this as a method to oppress.
"Be a good boy or you won't go to heaven"; you must obey now or be punished later.
Also, you must suffer now, and will be rewarded later.
Neither of these is true.
In reality, Karma is an immediate process, what you see is what you get.
The consequences of natural action are immediate; the consequences of unnatural action are likewise immediate.
You might be so repressed that you will ignore those consequences, but they will be there, and they will be internal.

Krishna says, "those who worship the gods will go to the gods, those who worship ancestors will go to ancestors. Those who worship ghosts will go to ghosts, and my devotees will go to me".
What does this mean?
It is the most direct explanation of Karma.

If you worship gods, if you are devoted to an archetype, whether it is money, or knowledge, or sex, or nationalism, or politics or religion, then this is what you will get.
When Krishna says "go to" he does not mean eventually, it is immediate.
Worship money, and money will be your entire life.
It will be your consummation.
In some cases it will bring you temporary pleasure, other times temporary suffering, but this will be all that has meaning to you.

Worship the ancestors, your family lines, and that will be your reward.

You live for your family, its past and its future.
You may find some joy in family, or some suffering.
But that will be all there is.

Worship ghosts, live in the past; and that will be all there is.
You will not taste of the here and now, you will only have the past.
It will torment you.
The Buddha added to this term, he called them 'hungry ghosts,' because the ghosts, the spirits of the past, are always of longing.
You will give up the nourishment of what you can have now, in exchange for longing over what was.
And that will be all there is.

But become a devotee, and that will be all there is.
If you are a devotee, then you seek union with the Divine, with Krishna, with the Guru, with God.
Then you are not worshiping; please notice that there is a great difference.
You are not worshiping, you are uniting.
And then everything can open to become union.
You will see the Divine in everything, you will be in the moment, and no matter what you have or do it will be for the Divine.
Krishna says that a leaf, flower, fruit or even water is a good enough offering.
In his time there were religionists saying that if you 'gave' great sums of money, or built great temples, or sponsored the priests, you will gain good Karma and go to heaven.
Krishna was saying that what you give doesn't matter.
Just give what you are, give what you have, in the sense that by seeking devotion you will live your life seeing this union.
Seek and you shall find was what Jesus said.
If you centre yourself in devotion, then that which you seek will immediately be found all around you.
Whatever you give, whatever you did, it will fulfill.

Chapter 10

Grace

Love.
Know that all feelings, virtues, or states of being do not come from you.
Happiness, sadness, anger, excitement, laziness, clarity, uncertainty, fear, passion, even enlightenment itself; these do not belong to you.
They are from the Divine.
What is your duty, then?
It is to accept these for what they are, and to take responsibility for yourself by remaining aware.
Awareness, witnessing is yours.
Anything else, you can take neither pride nor regret for.
To fight these other things, or to let yourself be consumed by them, both of these paths are foolish.
Simply know that they are.
Be watchful, and be transformed.

Love.

Chapter 11

Opening The Celestial Eye

The divine exists everywhere, in all places and holds all forms at once.
But regular human consciousness is unable to recognize this.
Our minds work by the principle of duality.
We see things, inherently, as a division of opposites.

Our senses, left as they are, serve the mind in this.
You will experience a sensory perception, seeing or hearing or touching, and this perception will then be sent to your mind.
The mind will interpret this perception through the structure of duality.
You see an apple, and the mind will divide the perception into criteria.
Criteria means 'classification': you would classify the apple as 'not an orange,' or on a deeper level as 'fruit,' which you'd define as 'not a vegetable,' or 'not an animal.'
This is duality; it is a process of 'nots,' so that in reality your definitions or anything at all are only negative, your mind can only understand something as being 'not something else.'

This is entirely normal, and in mysticism at first you will have to classify things spiritually in the same way.
All metaphysics are actually systems of classification.

The Tarot, the Kabbalah, Astrology, religious metaphysics of heavens and hells, good and bad, are all systems of creating criteria. Problems arise in this area when people do not comprehend this, and instead mistake metaphysics for being real truths.
People who literally believe in astrology, or in Kabbalah, or heaven and hells of a specific religious system, will miss the point entirely.
The useful purpose of any metaphysic, as taught in a mystery school, is to give you a new set of criteria, to re-wire your mind and your senses in preparation for a jump, a jump into something totally new.
Remember, metaphysics themselves are not new, they are not different from how your mind worked before.
It is still criteria, still a filing system.
Before, you filed things one way in your mind, now you file them a different way.
But it is inherently no better; there is nothing inherently superior in classifying an apple as some kind of Kabbalistic symbol rather than as 'not an orange.'
If that is where you stop, you will have in fact gained nothing.
In fact, you may be worse off than before, because now you will believe that you are experiencing wisdom or the spiritual.
You'll have gained a spiritual ego instead of a normal one.
And a spiritual ego is much worse, because it can be much harder to get over.

Metaphysics prepare you for the deeper experience of non-dual perception.
This is what mystics have sometimes called 'spiritual vision,' or the 'celestial eye.'
You cannot go straight to this form of perception without first developing a metaphysic; sometimes it will happen by accident, but this is very dangerous.

Someone who directly experiences the Divine without going through preparatory stages will be unprepared for the experience.
Often, they will seem to go mad.

It is an ego-shattering experience, it can separate you completely from being able to operate in the regular world.
For people who have reached this accidentally, the result can be terrifying.
If you go straight from the regular set of criteria to dropping criteria completely, it will shatter the ego.
At best, it may force you backwards, out of fear, into a total denial of the experience.
Otherwise, if that cannot be achieved, it can leave you incapable of operating in the world.
There are many people in mental asylums who have had this experience of true perception.
Sometimes you can become catatonic, unable to communicate at all in any normal way.
Or you will be so divorced from dualism that what you say will be meaningless to a 'normal' person.

So the process has to be gradual.
Even then, early experiences of this perception, of the celestial eye, will be awe-inspiring and sometimes terrifying.
A master will gradually prepare his students to handle these experiences.
A system of metaphysics serves to slowly open your perceptions, to allow you to understand that there are ways to understand reality outside of dualism.

When you perceive though the celestial eye, it allows you to see the inherent reality of any individual object.
To understand that there is a positive definition for things, that there is an essential reality to all things that are all their own, not only by comparison to other phenomena.
An apple is an apple.
You cannot 'know' this experience, it is beyond the mind.
You can never know what an apple is, only what it isn't.
But you can see what an apple is, when you open the senses that go beyond the mind.

At the same time, with this perception you will also 'see' how this thing you once called 'apple' is not separate from the whole of existence.
Duality, your normal perceptions, creates an illusion of separateness.
Metaphysics, the perception you are trained with in a mystery school, creates an illusion of unity.
In metaphysics you are taught to see that everything is connected.
This is no different from dualism, it is not real, but it is a new way of perception in the sense that you are encouraged to think of the apparently invisible connection between all phenomena.
That an 'apple' is not just an apple, but also a symbol that connects to all other symbols in some form, and all these connections ultimately become a single united symbol, often described as God.

But when you develop the celestial vision, you will see that this is not true either.
That an apple or any other phenomenon (including your 'self') is both inherently its own uniqueness and also a wholeness.
That is why the closest way to describe reality is not as 'dualism,' nor as 'oneness,' nor as 'nothingness,' but as 'not-twoness.'
In Sanskrit there is a word for this, Advaita.
It means literally 'not two.'
Individual and at the same time not divided.

This is a concept that cannot in fact be understood by the mind.
The celestial eye is not your normal eye; your celestial vision is not normal seeing.
It is a whole other sense.
We only call it an eye, we only call it seeing, because there is no other way to describe it in language.
It can only be experienced.

Fear of the Non-Dual

Most forms of mysticism emphasize this point: that the first encounter with the non-dual perception, the celestial eye, creates a sense of terror in the beholder.
That terror is the sound of your ego cracking apart.

The ego is a structure completely dependent upon duality, on dividing into two.
If the ego doesn't have an 'other' to define itself in comparison to, it cannot exist.
It is revealed for an illusion.

God cannot be defined as anything but the non-dual.
God is love, the mystics have said. And love is union.
When you unite opposites and, step by step, eliminate dualities, you approach closer and closer to the Divine.

It is said that God seeks you out.
This is true.
God is nature.
Duality is not a natural state, it is an illusory state.
Ultimately, the natural will triumph over the illusory.
This is what Buddha means when he says that ultimately all beings will reach enlightenment.
It is also what Krishna means when he says "I am Time, the destroyer of worlds."

God can be very aptly described as time.
As the inevitable, as a force that brings death.
Anyone who cannot achieve non-duality in life, will certainly see their dualities dissolve in death.
This is why the Sufis say you must 'die before you die.'

Thus there is a twofold reason for the fear that will sometimes strike meditators when they reach a level of non-duality.

First, because the closest thing their mind can relate the experience to is death.
Second, because in fact it is death, as far as the ego is concerned.

But God is also love.
If you accept that non-dual experience, if you welcome it rather than struggle, you will find union.

Know that the fear is your ego.
Know that it is not you.
Accept your experience.
Be very open.
Transform.

The Longing for God

The other side of awe from the experience of the Divine is the longing for union.
Just as we fear the non-dual experience, all human beings also desire it.
In fact, it is the only true desire.
It is the only true satisfaction.
Lusts for power, sex, possessions, knowledge and even love are only reflections of this true desire, to be united.

This is what mystics call longing.
It is a knowledge deep within you that there is a hole, an emptiness that must be filled.
And some of the most powerful meditation can come from this.

In reality, the non-dual state cannot be attained through austerities, techniques, knowledge or any other form.
Only through devotion, which is how we express this longing.
The great mystical poets write of this longing for God, also as a longing for the Beloved.
It is also the longing of the Beloved for you.

Life wants to unite with you, God wants you to unite with him.

Allow yourself to experience your longing, your devotion to God, the Guru, and life.
Let it be a positive expression, and it has the power to transform you.

Chapter 12

The Steps

The greatest work that you can do in this life is to practice devotional awareness.
Awareness can come in two forms, devotional or non-devotional.
Non-devotional awareness is simple meditation.
Meditation of this sort can be quite difficult – it is a path of struggle.
Practicing meditation, you will take many steps forward and many steps back.
For some, this is the only way.
Simply keeping focus, continue to practice despite any setbacks.
Remain confident even when it seems you are not making any progress, and don't put any expectations into your practice.

But for many, there is an easier way.
Devotional meditation can be a quick way, with fewer pitfalls.
Focus on the Divine, in an aspect or as a whole.
Or focus on the Guru, and dedicate your meditation to him.
In this way, you will find more confidence in what you are doing.
But this system too has its pitfalls.
First, one can mistake worship for meditation.
It is not enough to simply adore the Guru or God.
If you are not practicing, and you do not take responsibility for your practice, it will lead to nowhere.
There are some who cannot make this distinction, and there are others who cannot yet open themselves to devotional practice.

Usually, if you have a master it is easy to feel devotion for him, to become aware that he is always there when you are in meditation. But some will try to practice without a master, and others will not be able to feel this connection at first.

If you can feel devotion but cannot be meditative at the same time, this can create problems.
Do not mistake worship for meditation.
If you cannot begin with devotional meditation, instead you should begin with devotional work.
Dedicate what you are doing to the Divine; know that when you are working, when you are doing your job, or studying, or learning, or helping others, if you are a student of mysticism then you are also practicing devotion to the Divine, and your work will help the world.
All it takes is for you to be aware as you are doing this.

But for some, this is also too difficult.
It is hard to concentrate at all times on the work you are doing as sacred work.
It is difficult to practice devotion, but also it is even difficult to remember devotion.
For those people, for whom it is not possible to even do this, the answer is only in the 'Yoga of Refuge.'
If you cannot devote your work to the Divine, do your work while devoting the result of your work to the Divine.
Go about your work as you will, but be certain that whatever you make of it, you are offering as your gift to God, to life, to the Guru.
You will find that over time even if you cannot begin by practicing awareness in your work, dedicating the product of your work to the Divine will allow you to take 'refuge' in awareness, and you will find your awareness.
In time this would allow you to grow into being aware in what you do. So if you cannot start as aware in what you are doing, at least start by offering up the results of what you are doing as a sacrifice to God.
It is not yours, it is his.

There are many levels to meditation.
At the beginning, formal practice may be the most useful, the only thing you can do.
Performing set ritual of meditation or prayer in certain ways, at certain times, and for certain durations.
But the next step, higher than this, is to simply practice being aware.
Being able to watch your actions, to witness.
Better still is the next step, true meditation, where you can understand that your actions are not your own.
And the best is when you can practice true detachment.
Knowing that who you are and what you do is not due to you, but to the product of life's flow, you can let go of being attached to the results of who you are or what you do.
You can understand that these things are all dependent on God, and belong to God.
They are his to give or take.
This is the road to peace.

Boldness

D.
Y.
U.'.
P.
Know you are going to die.
Choose how you will stand when you do.

Humility or Awareness

There is a misunderstanding of what it means to be human.
Foolish seekers have often thought that to be surrendered to the Divine is to be humble.
Humility, as they understand it is to make yourself small, to put yourself down in the idea that this makes room for the Divine.
It does not.

There is no room if you fill yourself with 'small self' anymore than with 'large self'; they are the same size, only with different labels.

People who try to escape their ego by claiming they are stupid, by admitting their self-interest, by crying and shedding false tears of humility, gratefulness, or anguish at their own 'stuckness' are in reality doing nothing to aid their progress.
This is in fact a trap that you can become stuck in.
It is a never-ending spiral of self-abasement without ever finding a centre outside the self.

So how do you become a true human being?
Do not be desiring what you are not or do not have.
Be giving.
Do not worry about holding on to what you have or what you are.
Do not get swept away in feelings of happiness or sorrow, just let them be.

Do not let your past trap you.
Too often, the great barrier to becoming really human is that you are stuck with all the hurts, wants or concerns over what you were.
Let it go.

Do not be concerned about what other practitioners will think of you.
Do not seek any praise from your Master, either for your self-proclaimed humility, or awareness.
Do not claim to be a poor student or a good one.
This is not your concern.

Do not be concerned about being silent or speaking.
Accept what comes.

Do not get attached to the idea that your spiritual work must go a certain way, or that the Master must act a certain way toward you.

If you can be like this, and practice simply, and be solid in yourself, you will have found your humanity and achieve love with the Guru and God.

Chapter 13

The Power of Unknowing

Real spirituality is not found in speaking about spirituality.
The spiritual man is the one who can admit that he does not know.
To say "I don't know" is the most powerful, most liberating statement you can make.
It frees you, it liberates you of the walls you have made, of pretending.
Your pretensions of knowing the truth are a source of misery.
They are meant to protect you from your fears, but they only reinforce them.
Your fears cannot go away by pretending you know the truth about God, heaven, death.
They will be there, under the surface, devouring you.

God is found in admitting your truth.
In surrendering to the reality that only God is the knower, he is unknowable, ineffable to you.

Spirituality is not making claims about God.
Spirituality is in saying that you do not know, and accepting this.
It is found after that in trusting what you experience.
Be grateful for what can be known; be grateful for life.
Let yourself show up to live life, rather than hiding from it in your pretensions.
Be happy, or angry, do not justify yourself.

Involve yourself fully in what is before you.
Love.

Chapter 14

On the Mysteries of the Gunas

The Gunas are a simple metaphysic.
That is, they were a symbolic set of classifications used by Krishna to help explain human states of awareness.
An interesting thing has happened in many modern Hindu interpretations of the Bhagavad Gita; in many of these interpretations the Gunas have been seen as a ladder, a set of steps to be taken.

This is not so. In reality, the Gunas are an alchemical formula.
Just as you could say a chemical compound is made of several ingredients, no one of which is 'better' or 'worse' than the other, in Alchemy (the chemistry of the soul) you can say that the human spirit is made up of a number of ingredients.
And just as in chemistry, it is not that one ingredient is better and another worse.

Mankind is described as a bridge between the animal and the divine. We are neither gods nor beasts, but have both within us, and on top of this have a complex set of frustrations and desires born of our intermediate state.

In the alchemy of the Gunas this is expressed through the interaction of the three Gunas, or elements.
The Guna Tamas is the element of our animal nature.

It is the bestial, the deluded, within us.
The Guna Rajas is the intermediate.
It is our passion and frustration, our lusts that make us human.
The Guna Sattvas is the godlike element.
It is what makes us nobler, and able to conceive of a reality beyond our senses.
A human being is not simply one of the three; modern would-be Hindu alchemists have tried to say "this type of person is a Rajas person, or this one is a Tamas person."
And they see the goal as that of becoming a Sattvas person, thinking that this state of 'holiness' is enlightenment, when you are only thinking of good and kind things and of God.

In fact, they are wrong.
No one is ever only one of the three.
Someone who is enlightened will still be Rajas, Tamas and Sattvas; in fact they will be all three to the fullest.
And all people, enlightened or not, have all three components in them, just as all people have blood and water and air inside of them.
It is not an either/or choice; it is impossible to avoid having all three if you are human.

Different people will have different balances of these elements.
For some, Tamas will be the most prominent.
These people will be little more than animals.
They will care about nothing more than sex, violence, and gross physical pleasures.
They will often fight, often get drunk or high on drugs, they will have no sense of the Divine and a very limited understanding of death.
A person who is mainly Rajas will have a very acute awareness of death, they will know fear, they will know uncertainty far better than a Tamas person.
The Tamas person will be very simple compared to someone who is mostly Rajas.
The 'Rajas person' will live for causes, with goals, with passion, always desiring for themselves or for the world.

They will try to put their agenda on life.
Someone who is mostly Sattvas will know death also, but they will have an understanding, an acceptance.
They will be less likely to try to force life to fit their desires.
They will be conscious of God, they will be devoted, and will try to be caring for the world without trying to 'save' it.

For this reason many religionists think it would be best to be all Sattvas, that this is spirituality.
But it is not so.
It cannot be.
Krishna says that spirituality is when you can see that there is a presence beyond all elements.
When you understand that all three elements are within you, and no longer struggle against them, you will find something greater.
A Sattvas person may try very hard to resist his human and animal side.
They may try to always behave as what they consider to be godlike.
But only when you can accept that you are all three, when you can be at peace with all of yourself, all elements, only then will you start to see God.
Do not deny yourself.
Do not fixate on any element – let them all be.
Find the force that is beyond all the elements, you will see that humanity and life itself is greater than the sum of its parts.
Then you can discover yourself, and then you can begin to discover God.

Chapter 15

A Prayer for Peace.

So long as there are those in the world who are aware, there will one day be peace.

So long as there are those who seek to break free of what they have been told is the truth, there will one day be peace.

So long as there are those who are not tricked into foolish anger by their pride, there will one day be peace.

So long as there are those who question all assumptions, there will one day be peace.

So long as there are those who understand that the well-being of their own soul depends on the souls of others, there will one day be peace.

So long as there are those who can put aside their own greed and desires for comfort, there will one day be peace.

So long as there are those who know that all sorrows and all joys will be healed by time, there will one day be peace.

So long as there are those who know the preciousness of each sunrise, there will one day be peace.

So long as there are those who remember what is truly good in life, there will one day be peace.

So long as there are those who never forget that we are brothers with all that lives, there will one day be peace.

So long as there are those who dare to live their lives without fear, there will one day be peace.

So long as there are those who remember that death, any person's death, impoverishes all of humanity, there will one day be peace.

May the day come to pass, in the name of the most high.

Chapter 16

Darkness

What is evil?
When is it right to combat it?
There are those who think that to be peaceful is to avoid all conflict, all struggle.
Then there are those who feel that you must struggle, crusade, jihad, against the forces of the world that are evil, or unjust.
Both of these views are mistaken.

To avoid conflict is impossible, unless you are dead.
There are particular conflicts that are falsely created, that can be avoided or let go.
But there is one battle at least that everyone must fight, and this fight is real because its origins are within yourself.
Likewise to struggle against the evil you envision in the outside world is meaningless.
If you triumph in the struggle within you, then you will be able to vanquish darkness everywhere.
If you do not do this, then you cannot even comprehend what is dark or not.

If you are blind, then darkness and light have no meaning – they would only be make-believe.

On the other hand, when you have light within yourself, the darkness can do nothing against it.
You can enter a room filled with darkness, the darkness could be ancient, it may have been dark there since the dawn of time, but the moment you turn on a light, the darkness is gone.
There is not even a question of struggle – the dark can do nothing against the light.

What are the forces of darkness?
I have said before that the three essential qualities of life are truth, love, and being.
These are all functions of awareness.

Likewise, all the features of darkness are born of ignorance, of an absence of awareness.
The darkness cannot fight against light because darkness is not a real force at all.
It is not that the world is divided by two forces, 'good' and 'evil.'
There is no such thing; there is only awareness, and the absence of awareness.
And as soon as even a little bit of awareness is created, ignorance is lost.

The qualities that are born of ignorance are lust, anger and greed.
These qualities lead to the suffering of the world.
Lust for possessions, for sex, for rightness, for fulfillment, is born out of an ignorance of the fullness of life.
As soon as you become aware that everything that you need is already present, then lust is no longer real.

Anger is born of a wish to impose your lusts upon the world.
It may be a lust for power, or for revenge; anger is always born of a desire to change the way things are or have been for you.
When you can see that there is nothing that can be demanded of life, dictated, or certain, in either past or present, then anger is no longer real.

Greed is the desire to hold on to what you have and to accumulate more.
It is the desire to possess.
It is born of a belief that the world is limited, that you can only have if others do not, that you can only enjoy if you hold on to what you believe is yours.
As soon as you can see that life is unlimited, and that all is connected, then you will know that sharing is the only reality.

The time to engage in conflict is when you witness these dark qualities around you.
To stand against them.
To oppose people, nations, or groups that wish to cause suffering due to their lust, greed, or anger.
But lust cannot defeat lust, greed cannot defeat greed, and anger cannot defeat anger.
Darkness opposing darkness will only breed more suffering.
The moment you can demonstrate awareness, love, sharing, then you defeat darkness.
Even if in the world you must struggle for the sake of it, the victory is already yours.
But fight it with darkness, and you have already lost.

Chapter 17

Trust and Reality

The Bhagavad Gita teaches that the pursuit of mysticism is the pursuit of the real.
The real is symbolized by the word OM, the divine sound of creation.
Any ritual, charity or discipline conducted within the realm of the real is said to be the vibration of the sound OM.
But any discipline, charity or ritual conducted outside of the real is said to serve no purpose in this life or the next.

It is further said that the difference between performing these things in the real or outside of the real is found in trust.
If you perform these things with trust, then you will be real and obtain real results.
If you perform outside of trust, you will obtain nothing.

Krishna says that anyone who opens himself to trust, will be filled with trust.
He also speaks about the differences in the three elements of being (Tamas, Rajas, and Sattvas), and the varieties of 'food' that are appealing to each.
These are all great mysteries.

Most important to all of this is the question of trust.
What is trust?

Although Krishna does not seem to address this question, in reality he does when he is speaking of the types of food appealing to each element.
He says that someone in the element of Sattvas (truth) will desire juicy and wholesome food, someone in Rajas (passion) will desire spicy and hot food, and someone in Tamas (ignorance) will desire dead and rotting food.

What this means is that people at different levels will approach the spiritual, and thus spiritual work, in different ways.
Someone who is operating sincerely will commit the work not for a reward of purpose but because the work is good in and of itself, and because they seek to experience the real (nourishing food).
Someone who is operating out of passions will want excitement, entertainment and ecstasy.
They will do spiritual work because they crave recognition or some form of emotional reward (spicy food).
And someone who is in ignorance will only conduct these acts out of rote mechanical reasons, because they have been taught or told to by tradition (dead or rotting food).

The last of these three will almost never be found in a mystery school, but may be very common in organized religious institutions.
However, the second kind, Rajas, is very commonly found among 'seekers' of the mystical.
You will find many people within a school who are working in the school because they want excitement, or emotional support, or attention.
These students will want to be paid attention to by the master and the other students; they will want to be recognized.
Or they will crave a dependence on the master, they will want to be present near the master, to have the master provide them with emotional support or a sense of purpose or 'love' and will mistake this for devotion.
Or they will want their practice of mysticism to act as justification for their own 'persecution complexes,' to give them something that

makes them special or different from anyone else and therefore more worthy of attention and excused from being 'normal.'

In each of these cases this attitude must be overcome before any real work can proceed.

This is all a function of the definition of trust.

To trust the Divine or to trust a master is to be able to let go of one's own limitations; to acknowledge that these 'diseases' that cause the behaviours above are real and cannot go away, but that a mystery school is not meant to serve to fuel these behaviours.

Instead, a mystery school has a higher purpose.

By trusting that ritual, charity, and disciplines will lead to the experience of the real if performed for that purpose rather than some other purpose, one will quickly discover the real benefits of these actions, which are a spiritual benefit totally unrelated to any kind of emotional need, ecstatic experiences or attention.

Once you begin to perform these activities for their own sakes, instead of for ulterior motives, you will be able to place things in their proper context, and realize that those lesser desires are irrelevant to spirituality.

If you recognize you have a need for emotional support, entertainment or attention; understand that these are not necessarily a barrier to spiritual work.

They are only a barrier if you try to force these needs into the work of the Mystery School.

If, alternatively, you find ways to address these needs outside of the school, you will then be able to continue your spiritual work in a focused way.

Attempt to satisfy these needs as required through everyday work, relationships and activities where they are appropriate.

Do not look for the school to serve this purpose.

Trust that what you really need spiritually is not what you believe it to be but something you cannot yet understand, that will nevertheless become comprehensible to you over time if you do not create barriers to it with your own assumptions and expectations.

You may be wondering how one can recognize if a student is operating out of these undesirable behaviours.
The answer is this: if a student, when in the presence of a master or other students, acts in such a way that an everyday person (a stranger) who is not from the school would feel uncomfortable around this student, then the student is operating from these undesirable behaviours.
In that case, changes must be made.

A Further Note on 'Entertainment'

It is a common 'disease' in a Mystery School that students will seek to be 'entertained' by the work they are doing or their interactions with their teacher.
By this I mean that they will have the expectations that their work will constantly produce in them a state of ecstasy or whatever they consider to be 'advancement,' and the absence of this will be interpreted as failures on their part or on the part of the teacher.
This will result in several undesirable activities.
Students will expect to be constantly trying new techniques as opposed to experiencing one technique with depth or time.
If their master will not humour them in this regard they will blame themselves, assume they are not doing well, or blame their master and assume that he is not giving them enough attention because he is not doing things the way they want.
They will either drop the work he has suggested for them or they will add extra work for themselves that he had not advised, on the assumption that more work will somehow mean better results.

This need to be 'entertained' will cause terrible problems and is based on faulty demands.
One does not expect, or should not expect, constant entertainment or 'results' when they go to a doctor or a lawyer, nor will they go to a regular school and expect that the teacher will constantly entertain them or present them with only the information that they want.

That would be fine if they were only seeking trivia, but not if they wanted a thorough educational experience.
The same understanding must be prevalent in a Mystery School.
Often students will look for diversion in mystical practices that they should be receiving in other pastimes and pursuits.
Seek out entertainment in hobbies or pastimes, rather than warping the nature of the work that your teacher has offered.
If you are not being given additional work by a teacher it is not because you are a failure, but rather because you must continue to go deeper in your current work.
Often students who, of their own accord, drop work given to them or take on additional work that is not given to them will end up missing the entire real purpose of an exercise rather than 'enrich' their studies; and this is all too often because they have assumed they know the 'purpose' of a technique when in fact they do not.
So they will assume they've understood what they were supposed to, when in reality they are barely skimming the surface.
To take on additional work that was unassigned in these cases is much like the Sufi story of the man who tries to dig fifty 1-foot wells instead of going to the 'trouble' of digging one 25-foot well.
He will not get anywhere.

Just as bad as the assumption that you've already 'got' a task is the assumption that you are 'not getting anywhere' in your current task, either on the premise that your master hasn't assigned anything new for you or on the premise that you aren't 'experiencing' anything from the task.

This is as before based on the assumption, often faulty, that you already understand the reason why a teacher gives you a task to do, or that you know what is supposed to happen.
You may be placing the expectation on your work that it should result in emotional breakthroughs, bliss, visions or any number of other things, all of which might be completely beside the point of what you'd been told to do.
If anything, this reaction is even more serious than the false idea that you've 'gotten it,' because a student that assumes that 'nothing

is happening' will fall into a pattern of stagnation that will keep them stuck and often disrupt the whole working of the school.

The remedy to all of this is quite straightforward.
All that is required is for the student to return to where they began, drop any additional work, and drop not only the attitude of defeatism about not getting the experiences you expect, but also the twin ideas that you already know what is 'supposed to happen' from doing a particular task and the expectation that work will not be tedious or must constantly provide you with emotional or 'spiritual' stimulus.
In some cases it is this very stimulus that is supposed to be avoided at your present stage.
Many students will claim that these expectations are actually their desire to learn or their desire to experience the Divine.
But in reality, to have these expectations is the opposite of trust; and it is the opposite of a 'desire to learn' or 'desire to experience.'
They are the desire to have your pre-existing expectations fulfilled, rather than a sincere openness toward the work, master, or school.

Chapter 18

The End

It seems that even after all this there are still those who misunderstand what it is to be a mystic, what it was that Krishna spoke of.

When Krishna said that you must renounce attachment not activities, many have interpreted this 'attachment' to mean their emotions, or other things that are in fact activities.
Anything you have no choice about is activity.
And you have no choice about the fact that emotions exist.
You cannot prevent yourself from feeling emotions.
Attachment is not the fact that you have them.
Neither is it a particular way to react to them.
You are equally attached to an emotion if you accept it, as if you reject it.
And neither of these are 'spiritual acts.'
There are some that think that embracing their joy and feeling it deeply is a spiritual act.
No.
It may be a useful thing to do under certain circumstances, under others it may be very hindering.
Getting swept away by joy is almost always counterproductive to meditative work.
Likewise it is not spiritual to reject or repress your joy.
Nor is it spiritual to let yourself get swept away by sorrow.

Again it may be useful, as catharsis, but if done too much or for too long or in the wrong time or place, it will make you useless for the purposes of meditation work.

Real detachment is not the acceptance or rejection of emotion.

It is the third way: the ability to transcend emotion without rejecting it.

If you feel joy, know it is there.

Do not fight it, but do not feed it either; and be willing to drop it as an issue so that you can go on to do your work.

Too often I have found students become unteachable, often for weeks or months at a time, because they operate under the delusion that they must (and worse, that I must) address and somehow 'resolve' their joy or their sorrow.

They actually believe that getting stuck on these emotions is proof that the Mystery School is 'working' because they are feeling something (a common mistake), or 'not working' because they are feeling something they dislike (an even more common mistake).

This is the way to stuckness.

Many people have misunderstood Krishna in thinking that he suggests that renouncing activities is unimportant, or undesirable.

In fact, it is neither of these.

It is simply impossible.

You cannot renounce activity.

At all times, in every circumstance there are at least three activities taking place.

Physical activity, mental activity, and emotional activity.

There is not a single second where your body is not active, breathing and moving.

Your mind is also always thinking or operating, at least at a low level.

And you are always in some form of emotional state, even if it is only indifference.

These are the absolutes of being alive.

You cannot renounce the body, mind or heart.

You could no more renounce thinking or emotion than you could 'renounce breathing.'

It could not happen, unless you were dead.
Thus, anyone who wastes their time with trying to regulate or alter the physical, mental or emotional selves for the purpose of 'stopping' them is not engaged in any spiritual activity.
To renounce, you must renounce your 'lust of result,' your attachment to what is happening in these three areas.

Also, in the context of the spiritual, this is not the end; rather it is the beginning.
No real spiritual work can happen until you have begun to develop detachment.
By becoming detached from your physical, emotional and mental issues you remove them as blocks.
To be detached from them means that you accept they exist and let go of your interest in what they yield.
It is by this transcendence that you can focus on spiritual unity (Yoga).

When you succeed in doing this, you will be able to develop real trust.
So long as you are attached to these issues, and under the idea that the only way to 'solve' the problems of these issues is to dwell on them, you will fail to be able to trust your teacher.
Rather than accepting your work, you will consider all work only in the context of your perceived issues.
You will be more interested in the work that you think relates to these issues, and will be uninterested in others.
Work that, done by itself, would help alleviate these issues, you will instead modify by your undue attention and alterations into work that will actually enhance your stuckness.
In short, you become unteachable.
Krishna describes the nature of a 'clever renunciate' as one who 'will not hate unfortunate work' and 'will not become overly attached to fortunate work.'

"Messed up"

Krishna is clear when he speaks about how to focus one's self to spiritual work.
He says that someone who is focused unwaveringly in Yoga is in the state of truth (Sattvas).
Someone who is focused in lusts, desiring a result, is in a state of passion (Rajas), and they will inevitably create new problems for themselves.

I have seen students who seek out constant realizations, constant revelations, new ideas that they think will explain how everything is supposed to work, how their practice is supposed to work, how their relationships are supposed to work.
And they are constantly doing this; it is always something new that they 'realize.'
This is because they are simply creating these realizations for themselves by first creating assumptions about what the problem is and then making assumptions about the solution.
Both are assumptions; not only is their solution an illusion, so is their 'problem.'
So their very 'realizations' will keep them frustrated, because even though they will feel great pleasure and bliss about having these realizations, they will know underneath that their answers are not fulfilling.
So they will have to assume a new problem, and go looking again...

But there is a third state as well, the state of someone who "never stops fantasizing, fearing, regretting, feeling sorry for themselves, and deluded."
Krishna calls this the 'foolish will,' and says it is in the state of ignorance (Tamas).
I have spoken about this above, when I spoke about transcending the emotional level.
There are some students who will be deeply mired in this, in particular at the level of 'feeling sorry for themselves.'

In fact, this is an attempt to make yourself special, to separate yourself from the rest of humanity.
If you can't be the most fortunate, the richest, the most famous, then at least you get to be the most unfortunate, and have terrible problems that you couldn't do anything about.
Tamas is also sometimes called 'heaviness,' it is a level of sloth.
And this 'feeling sorry for yourself' is also a way to be lazy, to avoid having to do any work because, after all, your problems are 'obviously' impossible to overcome.
Someone operating at this level will be unteachable if they do not change first.

But there are also people who are otherwise doing well, who suddenly come to a realization of their own scars, and then fall into a state of feeling sorry for themselves.
They realize more intensely than they ever did before that they are critically flawed, 'messed up' as one student put it.
This realization can come as a powerful shock, as it is something that most people struggle intensely to avoid having to confront.

I have had students admit to me that they were 'messed up.'
Some were actually filled with pride at admitting this, at demonstrating their own humility in being able to say what a coward they are, or what a jerk they are, or what a fool they are, or how uncertain they are.
There were others who admitted this to me with great trepidation, sure that they couldn't possibly become mystics.

In reality it is important to admit that you are 'messed up,' but it is also no great accomplishment.
Everyone, everywhere is 'messed up.'
Remember this, there is no one who is any less or more messed up than you are!
It is true!
You are in no way special for being this way.

Have you ever looked at patients in a mental hospital?

They can scream, shout, swear, spit, act like animals, let out all their rage.
It is because society has decided that they are 'messed up.'
Of course, society has only done this to try to convince itself that everyone else isn't just as 'messed up.'
But these people in the mental hospital, society has decided that they can be completely messed up, that they are allowed.
There is no more hiding it for them, not like the rest of the world that tries very hard to avoid admitting it.
So they can scream, they can shout, then can writhe on the floor.
They can beat the walls.
Whatever they want.
And there is no difference from these people and yourself, only that they are allowed to do this.
You would all do the same if you had permission.

That is why in a mystical practice a bit of catharsis is necessary at the beginning.
When you want to become a meditator, first you have to do meditations that let you release your hidden nature.
You do Kundalini meditation, and let out your issues.
But to linger too much on this is pointless; it is actually counter-productive.
You could keep doing catharsis for fifty years, you could keep shaking and dancing in Kundalini meditation for fifty years, you will never get rid of these issues.
You cannot 'stop' being messed up, you cannot be 'fixed.'
All you can do is know it is there, let yourself experience it a little bit so as to remove some of the immediate tension, and then let yourself move on to do the spiritual work.
This work will not 'fix' you, it will make the problem irrelevant.

The Greatest Magickal Power

It is for this reason that Krishna has called detachment the 'greatest of magickal powers.'

If you achieve real detachment, you can move past all those barriers of your ego.
They do not need to be resolved.
So in essence, detachment allows you to solve the unsolvable problem.
You can accept that you are a flawed entity, and nevertheless move forward to do the practice of union.
This is why Krishna had said never to give up an action that comes out of your nature, even though all actions will have imperfections, just like smoke obscuring a fire.
In other words, this is natural too.
It is not natural to become obsessed, or disgusted with these actions.
It is not natural to revel or to be trapped and linger in these actions.
But to simply accept them, and then move past them, is highly natural.

Why then do most people get trapped at this level of mental/ emotional stuckness?
Why don't more people understand this key of moving past?
The answer is simple: most do not want to move past.
Most people wish to be attached.
More than anything that is their desire, because the attachment gives them the sense that something is theirs, something belongs to them; that they have something to hold on to that will keep them alive.
If you realize that you can simply move past your 'issues,' you end up with the realization that you own nothing, have nothing that is your own.
This realization many equate with death, and it causes great terror.
If you have nothing to hold onto, you will have to confront that you are just a very small and passing phenomenon, that you will soon be gone from this world.
The world does not revolve around you, nor will you any longer have your own little world of issues to mask your inherent emptiness.
To transcend your issues you must truly be ready to confront the reality of death.

You must be ready to accept and discover death, and to confront your fears about both the termination of your existence and your lack of importance in the 'big picture' of things.

These are very difficult tasks.
They are addressed in part by devoting yourself to the practice of union, of meditation.
To come to realize that there is no difference between you and the rest of life.
As you develop in meditation, and if you are willing to confront this truth, you will see that there is no difference between life and death.
The two are one and the same.
IF you can find that which is essential within you, that essential will exist eternally beyond death, even if you do not.
There is nothing that needs to be held on to.

In the End

This is all I have to say on these matters.
There is nothing more that needs to be added.
So do not add, and do not miss anything.
Simply practice, and simply remember.
Sammasati.

Made in United States
North Haven, CT
07 August 2022

22409205R00196